The longing for a greater under. and for a closer relationship with him is as strong now as it has been throughout time.

Today we can draw on the wisdom and experiences of the spiritual masters of the past. This selection of extracts is from seventeenth-century writers whose love for God and their fellow human beings has been an inspiration and help to thousands. Many of the extracts have been slightly reworded using present-day English, but without losing the original beauty of expression. The truth which they convey is timeless and will prove as enlightening and stimulating now as when it was first expounded.

Exploring the Spiritual Life

SHERWOOD ELIOT WIRT
Editor

A LION PAPERBACK
Tring · Belleville · Sydney

Copyright © 1983 Sherwood Eliot Wirt

Published by
Lion Publishing plc
Icknield Way, Tring, Herts, England
ISBN 0 85648 884 4
Albatross Books
PO Box 320, Sutherland, NSW 2232, Australia
ISBN 0 86760 631 2

First edition 1983 Crossway Books
Published by arrangement with Good News Publishers
First UK edition 1985

British Library Cataloguing in Publication Data

Exploring the spiritual life.
  1. Christian life—Sources
  I. Wirt, Sherwood Eliot
  248.4'09'032   BV4501
  ISBN 0 85648 884 4

Printed in Great Britain by
Cox and Wyman, Reading

Contents

Blaise Pascal (1623–1662) ranks among the great minds of Western intellectual history. A physicist by profession, he discovered "Pascal's law," which laid the foundation of modern hydraulics. In addition, he invented the barometer and the calculator, the latter becoming the forerunner of today's computer. It has also been claimed that Pascal wrote the finest prose ever written by a Frenchman. Certainly he developed a style of polite controversial irony that permanently influenced the nation's literature.

Pascal's appeal for Christians, however, lies in his spiritual biography, for a tremendous change of direction occurred in his life following a remarkable vision he experienced in 1654, when he was thirty-one years old. Never enjoying robust health, Pascal devoted most of the remaining eight years of his life to studying the Scriptures and making notes for a work that was to be a literary and personal vindication of the truth of Christianity.

Retiring from Paris to Port Royal, France, Pascal became a friend of the Jansenists, a conservative Roman Catholic reform movement that urged a return to the Augustinian emphasis upon grace alone as the basis of salvation. While he never left the Roman Church, his searing attacks on the Jesuits, which he published under an assumed name as "The Provincial Letters," made him a target of the Inquisition. He was never caught.

The masterwork Pascal had hoped to write was never completed. His notes for it were edited after his death, however, and published as Pensées (thoughts). Some were brief, some several pages in length. In the section we have chosen, we have tried to group scattered Pensées around five different themes, in order to make them more appealing to the reader.

Toward the end we have added some isolated Pensées and finally a translation of the notes concerning his 1654 vision. Pascal's valet found these in the lining of his coat shortly after his death.

The Pensées present some of the most magnificent statements about God, man and Jesus Christ to be found in any literature outside the Holy Scripture.

1

From Pensées
by Blaise Pascal

All men seek happiness. This is without exception. Whatever means they employ, everyone tends toward this end. Some go to war, others don't; but all have the same desire in view. The human will never takes the least step but toward this object. It is the motive of every action of every human being, even of those who hang themselves.

Yet without faith no one ever reaches the goal of happiness toward which we all aspire, even after years of trying. Everybody complains: princes and subjects, noblemen and commoners, old and young, strong and weak, learned and ignorant, healthy and sick; people of all countries, of all times and ages, and of all conditions. Surely such a mass of evidence, gathered over so long a time, should convince us of our inability to reach the good life by our own efforts. Yet example seems to teach us little, and experience dupes us and leads us from one misfortune to another and finally to death.

What then do this desire and this inability proclaim to us? That there was once in man a true happiness, of which there now remains to him only an empty trace which he vainly tries to fill out of his environment. He seeks from things absent the help he cannot obtain from things present. Yet all these efforts are inadequate, because the infinite abyss can only be filled by an infinite and immutable object, that is, by God himself.

He alone is our true good, and since we have forsaken him, it is a strange fact that there is nothing in nature that has been able to take his place, whether it be the stars, the heavens, the earth, the elements, plants, cabbages, leeks, animals, insects, calves, snakes, fever, pestilence, war, famine, vices, adultery or incest. Since man has lost the true good, everything can now appear equally good to him, even his own destruction, which is contrary to God, to reason and to the whole course of nature. Some seek good in authority, others in scientific research, still others in pleasure (425). But when the true nature is lost to creation, everything becomes its own nature; and when the true good is lost, everything becomes its own good (426).

Man is but a reed, the most feeble thing in nature; but he is a thinking reed. The entire universe does not need to arm itself to crush him. A vapor, a drop of water is enough to kill him. But if the universe were to crush him, man would still be more noble than that which killed him, because he knows that he dies; the universe knows nothing of this (347).

The greatness of man is that he knows himself to be miserable. A tree does not know itself to be miserable (397). The miseries themselves prove man's greatness. They are the miseries of a great lord, of a deposed king (398). The greatness of man is proved even by his wretchedness; for what is natural in animals, we call in man wretchedness. We sense that when man behaves like an animal, he has fallen from a better nature which was once his (409).

What a chimera then is man! What a novelty! What a monster, what a chaos, what a contradiction, what a prodigy! Judge of all things, but an imbecile worm of the earth. Depositary of truth, yet a cesspool of uncertainty and error. The glory and rubbish of the universe!

Who will unravel this tangle? Nature confounds the skeptics, and reason confutes the dogmatists. What then will you become, O man who seeks to find out by your natural reason what your true condition is? You cannot avoid one of these groupings, and yet you cannot live with either one.

Know then, superb one, what a paradox you are to yourself. Humble yourself, weak reason. Be silent, imbecilic nature. Learn that man infinitely transcends man, and learn from your Master your true condition which you ignore. Hear God (434).

Man does not know in what rank to place himself. He has plainly gone astray and fallen from his true place without being able to find it again (427). Man is not worthy of God, but he is not incapable of being made worthy. It would be unworthy of God to unite himself to wretched man as he is; but it is not unworthy of God to pull man out of his misery (510).

The man who knows God but does not know his own misery, becomes proud. The man who knows his own misery but does not know God, ends in despair (526). That is what is strange about Christianity.

It bids a person recognize that he is vile, even abominable, and yet it bids him desire to be like God. Knowledge of the one without the counterpoise of the other could make a person either horribly vain or horribly abject (383). The Incarnation shows man the greatness of his misery by the greatness of the remedy which he required (525). The knowledge of Jesus Christ constitutes the middle course because in him we find both God and our own misery (526). Jesus Christ is therefore a God whom we approach without pride, and before whom we humble ourselves without despair (527).

* * *

Men blaspheme what they do not know. The Christian religion consists in two points: that there is a God whom men can know, and that there is a corruption in their nature which renders them unworthy of him. It is equally important to know both these points; and it is equally dangerous to know God without knowing one's own wretchedness, and to know one's own wretchedness without knowing the Redeemer who can free us from it. The knowledge of only one of these points gives rise either to the pride of philosophers, who have known God and not their own misery, or to the despair of atheists, who know their own misery but not the Redeemer.

We can have an excellent knowledge of God without that of our own wretchedness, and of our own wretchedness without that of God. But we cannot know Jesus Christ without knowing at the same time both God and our own misery.

The God of Christians is not a God who is simply the author of geometrical truths, or of the order of the elements; that is the view of pagans and Epicureans. He is not merely a God who exercises his providence over the lives and fortunes of men, to bestow on those who worship him a long and happy life.

The God of Abraham, the God of Isaac, the God of Jacob, the God of Christians is a God of love and comfort, a God who fills the soul and heart of those whom he possesses, a God who makes them conscious of their inward wretchedness, and his infinite mercy; who unites himself to their inmost soul, who fills it with humility and joy, with confidence and love, who renders them incapable of any other end than himself (555).

Let them at least learn what is the religion they attack, before attacking it. If this religion boasted openly of having a clear view of God, it would be attacking it properly to say that we see nothing in the world that provides such open evidence. But on the contrary it says that men are in darkness and estranged from God; that God has hidden himself from their knowledge, and that this is in fact the name which he gives himself in the Scriptures, *Deus absconditus* (Isaiah 45:15).

Christianity endeavors to establish these two things: that God has set up in the church visible signs to make himself known to those who seek him sincerely; and that he has nevertheless so disguised them that he will be perceived only by those who seek him with all their heart.

In order to attack it they should have protested that they had made every effort to seek him everywhere, but without satisfaction. If they talked in this manner, they would in truth be attacking one of the church's pretensions. But I hope to show that no reasonable person can speak thus, and I venture even to say that no one has ever done so.

We know well enough how those who are of this mind behave. They believe they have made great effort for their instruction, when they have spent a few hours reading some book of Scripture, and have questioned some priest on the truths of their faith. After that, they boast of having searched without success in books and among men. But this negligence is unsupportable.

The immortality of the soul is a matter of such great consequence to us, and touches us so profoundly, that we would have to have lost all feeling to be indifferent toward it. All our actions and thoughts must take different courses, according as there are or are not eternal joys to hope for. Thus our first interest and duty is to enlighten ourselves on this subject, upon which depends all our conduct.

I make a vast distinction between those who strive with all their power to instruct themselves, and those who live without troubling or thinking about it. I can have only compassion for those who sincerely bewail their doubt and who, sparing no effort to escape it, make this search their principal and most serious occupation. But as for those who pass their lives without thinking of this ultimate end of life, I look upon them in a manner quite different.

This negligence in a matter which concerns themselves, their eternity, their all, moves me more to irritation than pity; it astonishes and shocks me. It is to me monstrous. I do not say this out of the pious zeal of spiritual devotion. On the contrary, I expect we ought to have this feeling from principles of human interest and self-love.

How can people hold such opinions? What joy can we find in the expectation of nothing but hopeless misery? What reason for boasting that we are in impenetrable obscurity? And how can it happen that the following argument occurs to a reasonable man:

"I do not know who sent me into the world, or what the world is, or what I myself am. I am in terrible ignorance of everything. I do not know what my body is, or my senses, or my soul. I see the frightful spaces of the universe which surround me, and I find myself tied to one corner of this vast expanse, without knowing why I am put in this place rather than in another, or why the short time which is given me to live is assigned to me at this point rather than at another of the whole eternity which was before me or which shall come after me. I see nothing but infinity on all sides, which surrounds me as an atom, and as a shadow which endures only for an instant and returns no more. All I know is that I must soon die, but what I ignore the most is this very death which I cannot escape.

"As I do not know where I came from, so I do not know where I am going. I only know that in leaving this world, I fall forever either into annihilation or into the hands of an irritable God; but to which I shall be forever assigned, I remain ignorant. Such is my state, full of weakness and uncertainty.

"From all this I conclude that I ought to spend all the days of my life without caring to inquire into what must happen to me. Perhaps I might be able to find some clarification of my doubts, but I will not take the trouble, nor will I make one step toward seeking it. After I have scorned those people who are working at this matter, I wish to go without foresight and without fear to prove this great event, and so let myself be led carelessly to death, uncertain of the eternity of my future state."

Who would wish to have for a friend a man who talks in this fashion? Who would choose him out of others to tell of one's affairs? Who would resort to him in affliction? Indeed, what use is he in life to others?

Nothing is so important to man as his own state. Nothing is so formidable to him as eternity. Thus it is not natural that men should be so indifferent to the loss of their existence, and to the perils of an eternity of misery. They are quite different with regard to all other things. They are afraid of mere trifles: they foresee them, they feel them. And the same man who spends so many days and nights in rage and despair over the loss of a position, or over some imaginary insult to his honor, is the very one who goes to his death completely lost, without anxiety and without emotion.

It is a monstrous thing to see in the same heart, at the same time, this sensibility to trifles and this strange insensibility to the greatest objects. It is an incomprehensible enchantment, a supernatural slumber.

There must be a strange confusion in the nature of man, that he should boast of being in such a state. What do we gain by hearing it said of a man that he has now thrown off the yoke, that he does not believe there is a God who watches our actions, that he considers himself the sole master of his conduct, and thinks he is accountable for it only to himself? Does he think he has brought us to have complete confidence in him, and to look to him for consolation, advice and help in every need of life?

Do such persons profess to delight us by telling us that they hold our soul to be only a little wind and smoke, especially by saying it to us in a haughty and self-satisfied tone of voice? Is this a thing to say gaily? Is it not, on the contrary, the saddest thing in the world?

If they thought of it seriously, they would see that this is so bad a mistake, so contrary to good sense, so opposed to honesty, and so remote in every respect from that good breeding which they seek, that they would be more likely to correct than to corrupt those who were inclined to follow them. If you ask them to give an account of their sentiments and the reasons they have for doubting religion, they will tell you things so feeble and so petty that they will convince you otherwise. Thus one person made the remark, "If you continue to talk this way, you will truly convert me!" And he was right.

Nothing is more dastardly than to act with bravado before God. If they cannot be Christians, let them at least be honest men. Let them recognize that there are two kinds of people whom one can call reasonable: those who serve God with all their heart because they know him, and those who seek him with all their heart because they do not know him (194).

*　　*　　*

The God of Christians is a God who makes the soul feel that he is its unique good, that all its repose is in him, that there is no other joy than in loving him. He makes the soul abhor the obstacles that hold it back, and at the same time prevent it from loving God with all its strength. God makes self-love and lust, which hinder the soul, unbearable; and causes it to realize that he alone can cure the root of self-love which would destroy it (543).

M. de Roannez once said, "Reasons come to me afterward, but at first a thing pleases or shocks me without my knowing the reason, and yet it shocks me for that reason which I only discover afterward." But I believe not that it shocked him for the reasons which were found afterward, but that these reasons were only found because it shocked him (276).

The heart has its reasons which reason does not know. We feel it in a thousand things. I say that the heart naturally loves the Universal

Being, and also loves itself by nature; and it gives itself to one or the other, and hardens itself against one or the other, as it chooses (277).

It is the heart that feels God, not the reason: this is faith (278). Faith is a gift of God; do not believe that we said it was a gift of reasoning. Other religions do not say this of their faith. They only offer reasoning in order to arrive at it, and yet it does not bring them to it. The knowledge of God is very far from the love of him (279).

* * *

We know God only by Jesus Christ. Without this Mediator all communication with God is taken away; through Jesus Christ we know God. All those who have pretended to know God and to prove him without Jesus Christ have only impotent proofs. But to prove Jesus Christ we have the prophecies, which are solid and palpable proofs. These prophecies have been fulfilled and proved by the event. They mark the certainty of these truths and therefore prove the divinity of Jesus Christ.

In him then and through him we know God. Apart from him and without Scripture, without original sin, without a necessary Mediator promised and come, we cannot prove God absolutely, nor teach right doctrine nor proper morality. But by Jesus Christ and in Jesus Christ one can prove God and one can teach morality and doctrine. Jesus Christ is therefore the true God of mankind.

But at the same time we know our misery, for this God is none other than the Redeemer of our misery. Thus we can only know God well when we know our own sin. And those who have known God without knowing their wretchedness have not glorified him, but have glorified themselves (546).

Not only do we know God by Jesus Christ alone, but we know ourselves only by Jesus Christ. We do not know life or death except by Jesus Christ. Apart from Jesus Christ we do not know what is our life, or our death, or God, or ourselves. Thus without the Scripture, which has Jesus Christ alone for its object, we can know nothing, and see only obscurity and confusion in the nature of God and in our own nature (547).

I love poverty because he loved it. I love wealth because it gives me the means to help the poor and wretched. I keep faith with the whole world. I do not render evil to those who wrong me, but I could wish them a condition like mine, in which I receive neither evil nor good from men. I try to be just, true, sincere and faithful to all men. I have a tender heart for those to whom God has bound me tight.

Whether I am alone, or seen of men, I do all my actions in the sight of God, who must judge them and to whom I have consecrated them all.

These are my sentiments, and every day of my life I bless my Redeemer who has given them to me. Out of a man full of weakness, of wretchedness, of lust, or pride and ambition, he has made a man exempt from all these evils by the power of his Grace, to which all the glory is due, since of myself I have only misery and error (549).

*   *   *

What do the prophets say of Jesus Christ? That he will evidence God? No. They say that he is a God truly hidden; that he will be unrecognized, that no one will think it is he; that he will be a stone of stumbling upon which many will bruise themselves, and so on. Let people reproach us no longer for lack of clarity, then, since we make no profession of it (750).

Jesus Christ came to blind those who see clearly, and to give sight to the blind; to heal the sick, and to leave the healthy to die; to call to repentance, and to justify sinners, and to leave the righteous in their sins; to fill the needy and to leave the rich empty (770).

I find Jesus Christ in all persons and in ourselves: Jesus Christ as a father in his Father, Jesus Christ as a brother in his brothers. Jesus Christ as a poor man among the poor, Jesus Christ as a rich man among the rich. Jesus Christ as a doctor and priest among the priests. Jesus Christ as Sovereign among the princes. For it is by his glory that he is all that is great, being God; and it is by his mortality that he is all that is puny and abject. He has taken this unhappy condition so that he could be in all persons, and model all conditions (784).

Jesus Christ is an obscurity (according to what the world calls obscurity), such that historians, writing only of important matters of state, have hardly noticed him (785). So far is this from telling against Christianity, that on the contrary it tells for it. For it is a certainty that Jesus Christ existed; that his religion made a great commotion; and that these persons were not ignorant of it. It is plain that they purposely concealed it; or if they did speak of it, their account has either been suppressed or altered (786).

What man ever had more renown? The whole Jewish people foretell him before his coming. The Gentile people worship him after his coming. Yet what man enjoys his renown less? Of thirty-three years, he lives thirty without appearing. For three years he passes as an imposter; the priests and the chief people reject him. His friends and his nearest relatives despise him. Finally he dies, betrayed by one of his own disciples, denied by another, and abandoned by all.

What part, then, has he had in this renown? Never had man so much renown; never had man so much ignominy. All that renown has served only for us, to render us capable of recognizing him; he had none of it for himself (791).

Great geniuses have their power, their glory, their grandeur, their victory, their luster, and have no need of worldly greatness. They are seen not by the eye, but by the mind; that is enough. Archimedes, apart from any renown, would have the same veneration. He fought no battles for the eyes to feast upon; but he has given his discoveries to all humankind. Oh! How brilliant he was to the mind!

Jesus Christ, without riches and without any external exhibition of knowledge, is in his order of holiness. He did not make inventions. He did not reign. But he was humble, patient, holy, holy, holy to God, terrible to demons, without any sin. Oh! in what grand pomp and magnificent splendor he comes to the eyes of the heart which perceive wisdom!

It would have been useless for Archimedes to act like a prince in his books on geometry, even though he was one. It would have been useless for our Lord Jesus Christ to make a show of his reign of holiness, and come on like a king. But he came appropriately in the glory of his own order.

It is ridiculous to take offense at the lowliness of Jesus Christ, as if his lowliness was of the same order as the grandeur he came to manifest. If we consider the greatness in his life, in his passion, in his obscurity, in his death, in the choice of his friends, in their desertion, in his secret resurrection, and all the rest, we shall see it to be so grand that we shall have no reason to be offended at a lowliness which is not of that order.

But there are some who can admire only carnal greatness, as though they had no intellectual qualities; and others admire only intellectual qualities, as if there were not infinitely higher qualities of wisdom. All bodies, the firmament, the stars, the earth and its kingdoms, are not equal to the lowest human spirit. For the human spirit knows all these and itself; and the bodies know nothing. All bodies together, and all minds together, and all their products are not equal to the least motion of love. That is of an order infinitely higher. From all the bodies together one cannot obtain a single little thought; it is impossible, for it is of another order. In the same way from all bodies and minds one is not able to draw a single gesture of true love, for it also is impossible, being of another and supernatural order (792).

Why did Jesus Christ not come in a visible manner instead of drawing proofs from prophecies that preceded him? Why did he cause himself to be foretold in types? (793). If Jesus Christ had come only to make people holy, all Scripture and everything else would have tended to that end, and it would be quite easy to convince unbelievers. If Jesus Christ had come only to blind people to the truth, all his conduct would have been confused and we would have no means of convincing unbelievers. But he came, as Isaiah 8:14 says, *in sanctificationem et in scandalum* (as the Holy One and as a stumbling-block) (794). Jesus Christ said great things so simply that it appeared as if he had not thought them through, and yet he spoke so distinctly that we easily see that he had indeed thought them through. This clarity, joined to his simplicity, is most admirable (796).

The style of the Gospel is also admirable in so many ways: among others, in never hurling invectives against the persecutors and enemies of Jesus Christ. If this moderation of the Gospel historians had been affected, and if they only assumed it to attract notice, they would not have failed to procure friends who would have made remarks to their advantage. But they acted without affectation, from totally disinterested motives, and did not trade on them. I believe that many of these things have not been noticed until now, which is testimony to the impartiality with which they were done (797).

Who taught the evangelists [the Gospel writers] the qualities of a perfectly heroic soul, that they were able to paint it so perfectly in Jesus Christ? Why do they make him weak in his agony? Don't they know how to paint a resolute death? Yes. For Luke paints the death of Saint Stephen as being braver than that of Jesus Christ. They make Jesus Christ capable of fear before the necessity of dying arrived; after that he was totally brave. But when they make him so troubled, that is when he troubled himself. When men trouble him he is altogether strong (799).

The supposition that the apostles were imposters is absurd. Let us think it through. Let us imagine those twelve men, assembled after the death of Jesus Christ, plotting to say that he had risen from the grave. By this they attack all the powers. The heart of man is strangely inclined to fickleness, to change, to promises, to gain. If any of the disciples might in any way have been led astray by such attractions, or even more, by imprisonment, torture, or death, they would have been lost (800).

[It is said that] the apostles were either deceived or deceivers. Either supposition has difficulties; for it is not possible to mistake a man raised from the dead. While Jesus Christ was with them, he could sustain them. But after that, if he did not appear to them, who inspired them to act? (801).

*   *   *

There is an important difference between tempting and leading into error. God tempts, but he does not lead into error. To tempt is to provide occasions which impose no necessity; if a person does not love God, he will do a certain thing. To lead into error is to put a man into the necessity of concluding and following a falsehood (820).

*   *   *

Here is not the country of truth. She wanders unknown among men. God has covered her with a veil, which leaves her unrecognized by those who do not hear her voice (842).

*   *   *

Truth is so obscured in these times, and falsehood so established, that unless one loves the truth, he cannot know it (863).

*   *   *

It is such an evident thing that we ought to love one God only, that miracles are not needed to prove it (836).

*   *   *

Man is neither angel nor beast, and the unfortunate part of it is that the one who would act the angel acts the beast (358).

*   *   *

The virtue of a man should not be measured by his efforts, but by his ordinary life (352).

*   *   *

One never does evil so thoroughly and gaily as when he does it from conscience (894).

*   *   *

He who wishes to give the meaning of the Scripture and does not take it from the Scripture is the enemy of the Scripture (Augustine) (809).

*   *   *

The law required what it could not give. Grace gives that which it requires (521).

*   *   *

Experience makes us see an enormous difference between devotion and goodness (496).

*   *   *

Instead of complaining that God has hidden himself, you should render thanks to him that he has revealed so much of himself (288).

*   *   *

If man is not made for God, why is he only happy in God? If man is made for God, why is he so against God? (438).

*   *   *

[Jesus says:] "Do not compare yourself with others, but with me. If you do not find me in those with whom you compare yourself, you are comparing yourself to one who is abominable. If you would find me in them, compare yourself to me. But whom will you compare? Yourself, or me in you? If it be I, you are comparing me to myself. So now I am God in all" (554).

*   *   *

[Jesus says:] "You would not seek me if you did not possess me. Therefore you need not be disquieted" (554).

*   *   *

THE MEMORIAL OF BLAISE PASCAL
(Found at his death in 1662, sewn into the lining of his
coat, written by hand, describing his experience
of spiritual illumination in 1654)

In the Year of Grace, 1654, on Monday, 23rd of November, Feast of St. Clement, Pope and Martyr, and of others in the Martyrology. Vigil of Saint Chrysogonus, Martyr, and others. From about half past ten in the evening until about half past twelve.

FIRE
God of Abraham, God of Isaac, God of Jacob, not of the philosophers and scholars.
Certitude. Certitude. Feeling, Joy, Peace.
God of Jesus Christ. My God and your God.
Your God shall be my God.
Forget the world and everything but God.

He is to be found only in the ways taught in the Gospel.

Greatness of the human soul.

"Righteous Father, the world hath not known thee, but I have known thee."

Joy, Joy, Joy, tears of joy.

I have departed from him.

"They have forsaken me, the fountain of living water."

My God, will you forsake me?

May I not be separated from him eternally.

"This is life eternal, that they might know thee, the only true God, and Jesus Christ whom thou hast sent."

Jesus Christ.

Jesus Christ.

I have departed from him. I have fled from him, renounced him, crucified him.

May I never be separated from him!

He is preserved only by the ways taught in the Gospel.

Renunciation total and sweet.

Notes

Excerpts from Pascal's *Pensées* taken from the translation by W. F. Trotter, Modern Library edition © 1941, used by permission of Random House, New York.

"Thomas Fuller (1608–1661) was incomparably the most sensible, the least prejudiced, great man of an age that boasted a galaxy of great men." So wrote Samuel Taylor Coleridge in 1836, reflecting the esteem in which the Reverend Thomas Fuller, D.D., was once held in England. Although called "one of the wittiest and wisest divines who have ever ascended the pulpit," Fuller, as well as his writings, passed into oblivion with the coming of the twentieth century. Today he is known only to literary historians who usually describe him as "quaint." But Fuller's literary works reveal an originality and fertile imagination that go far beyond quaintness.

So popular was Fuller in his day that he managed to survive the hazards of civil war even while taking the royalist side. Despite his support of the monarchy, he was considered a fair man who "held the rights of the people in sacred respect." That may explain why "he was not disturbed at Waltham in 1655, when the Protector's edict prohibited the adherents of the late king from preaching."

After the Restoration, Fuller was appointed chaplain in extraordinary to Charles II. His preaching in London on the Strand at the Chapel of St. Mary Savoy drew crowds that filled even the chapel yard and the windows and sextonry.

A graduate of Queen's College, Cambridge, Thomas Fuller in 1634 became rector of Broadwindsor, Dorsetshire. In 1640 he was elected proctor for Bristol. During the civil war he served for a time as chaplain to a royalist regiment and then in 1658 became rector of Cranford parish. Before a scheduled appointment as bishop could be realized, he died at Cranford in 1661.

Fuller's best-known writings are The History of the Holy War *(the Crusades),* The Holy and Profane State, The Church History of Britain, The History of the Worthies of England, *and a volume of prayers and meditations called* Good Thoughts in Bad Times, *from which we have chosen several excerpts. Printed in Exeter in 1645, during England's bloodiest era, this collection of sage and witty observations is still highly relevant, and a new edition of this devotional landmark is overdue.*

2

From Good Thoughts in Bad Times
by Thomas Fuller

Lord, this morning my unseasonable visiting of a friend disturbed him in the midst of his devotions: unhappy to hinder another man's goodness. If I myself build not, shall I snatch the axe and hammer from him that doth? Yet I could willingly have wished that, rather than he should have cut off the cable of his prayers, I had twisted my cord to it, and had joined with him in his devotions. However, to make him the best amends I may, I now request of thee for him whatsoever he would have requested for himself. Thus he shall be no loser, if thou be pleased to hear my prayer for him, and to hearken to our Savior's intercession for us both.[1]

* * *

Lord, since these woeful wars began, one, formerly mine intimate acquaintance, is now turned a stranger, yea, an enemy. Teach me how to behave myself towards him. Must the new foe quite justle out the old friend? May I not with him continue some commerce of kindness? Though the amity be broken on his side, may I not preserve my counterpart entire? Yet how can I be kind to him without being cruel to myself and thy cause? O guide my shaking hand, to draw so small a line straight; or rather, because I know not how to carry myself towards him in this controversy, even be pleased to take away the subject of the question, and speedily to reconcile these unnatural differences.[2]

* * *

Lord, my voice by nature is harsh and untunable, and it is vain to lavish any art to better it. Can my singing of psalms be pleasing to thy ears, which is unpleasant to my own? Yet though I cannot chant with the nightingale, or chirp with the blackbird, I had rather chatter with the swallow, yea, rather croak with the raven, than be altogether silent. Hadst thou given me a better voice, I would have praised thee with a better voice. Now what my music wants in sweetness, let it have in sense, singing praises with understanding. Yea, Lord, create in me a new heart (therein to make melody), and I will be contented with my old voice, until in thy due time, being admitted into the choir of heaven, I have another more harmonious bestowed upon me.[3]

*　　*　　*

Lord, I do discover a fallacy, whereby I have long deceived myself. Which is this: I have desired to begin my amendment from my birthday, or from the first day of the year, or from some eminent festival, that so my repentance might bear some remarkable date. But when those days were come, I have adjourned my amendment to some other time. Thus, whilst I could not agree with myself when to start, I have almost lost the running of the race. I am resolved thus to befool myself no longer. I see no day like today; the instant time is always the fittest time. Grant, therefore, that today I may hear thy voice. And if this day be obscure in the calendar, and remarkable in itself for nothing else, give me to make it memorable in my soul thereupon, by thy assistance, beginning the reformation of my life.[4]

*　　*　　*

Lord, thy servants are now praying in the church, and I am here staying at home, detained by necessary occasions, such as are not of my seeking, but of thy sending; my care could not prevent them, my power could not remove them. Wherefore, though I cannot go to church, there to sit down at table with the rest of thy guests, be pleased, Lord, to send me a dish of their meat hither, and feed my soul with holy thoughts. Eldad and Medad, though staying still in the camp (no doubt on just cause), yet prophesied as well as the other elders. Though they went not out to the Spirit, the Spirit came home to them. Thus never any dutiful child lost his legacy for being absent at the making of his father's will, if at the same time he were employed about his father's business. I fear too many at church have their bodies there, and minds at home. Behold, in exchange, my body here and heart there. Though I cannot pray with them, I pray for them. Yea, this comforts me. I am with thy congregation because I would be with it.[5]

*　　*　　*

Lord, when in any writing I have occasion to insert these passages, "God willing," "God lending me life," etc., I observe, Lord, that
I can scarce hold my hand from encircling these words in a parenthesis,
as if they were not essential to the sentence, but may as well be left out
as put in. Whereas, indeed, they are not only of the commission at large,
but so of the quorum, that without them all the rest is nothing; wherefore hereafter I will write those words fully and fairly, without any en-
closure about them. Let critics censure it for bad grammar, I am sure it
is good divinity.[6]

* * *

Lord, this day I disputed with myself, whether or no I had said
my prayers this morning, and I could not call to mind any remarkable
passage whence I could certainly conclude that I had offered my prayers
unto thee. Frozen affections, which left no spark of remembrance behind them! Yet at last I barely recovered one token, whence I was assured that I had said my prayers. It seems I had said them, and only said
them, rather by heart than with my heart. Can I hope that thou wouldst
remember my prayers, when I had almost forgotten that I had prayed?
Or rather have I not cause to fear that thou rememberest my prayers too
well, to punish the coldness and badness of them? Alas! are not devotions thus done in effect left undone? Jacob advised his sons at their second going into Egypt, Take double money in your hand; peradventure
it was an oversight. So, Lord, I come with my second morning sacrifice:
be pleased to accept it, which I desire, and endeavor to present with a
little better devotion than I did the former.[7]

* * *

Lord, the motions of thy Holy Spirit were formerly frequent in
my heart; but alas! of late they have been great strangers. It seems they
did not like their last entertainment, they are so loath to come again. I
fear they were grieved that either I heard them not attentively, or believed them not faithfully, or practiced them not conscionably. If they
be pleased to come again, this is all I dare promise that they do deserve,
and I do desire they should be well used. Let thy Holy Spirit be pleased
not only to stand before the door and knock, but also to come in. If I do
not open the door, it were too unreasonable to request such a miracle to
come in when the doors were shut, as thou didst to the apostles. Yet let
me humbly beg of thee that thou wouldst make the iron gate of my heart
open of its own accord. Then let thy Spirit be pleased to sup in my
heart. I have given him room. But O thou that sendest the Guest, send

the meat also. And if I be so unmannerly as not to make the Holy Spirit welcome, O let thy effectual grace make me to make him welcome.[8]

* * *

Lord, I confess this morning I remembered my breakfast, but forgot my prayers. And as I have returned no praise, so thou mightst justly have afforded me no protection. Yet thou hast carefully kept me to the middle of this day, intrusting me with a new debt before I have paid the old score. It is now noon, too late for a morning, too soon for an evening sacrifice. My corrupt heart prompts me to put off my prayers till night; but I know it too well, or rather too ill, to trust it. I fear if I defer them till night, at night I shall forget them. Be pleased, therefore, now to accept them. Lord, let not a few hours the later make a breach, especially seeing (be it spoken not to excuse my negligence, but to implore thy pardon) a thousand years in thy sight are but as yesterday. I promise hereafter, by thy assistance, to bring forth fruit in due season. See how I am ashamed the sun should shine on me, who now newly start in the race of my devotions, when he like a giant hath run more than half his course in the heavens.[9]

* * *

Lord, this day casually I am fallen into a bad company, and know not how I came hither, or how to get hence. Sure I am, not my improvidence hath run me, but thy providence hath led me into this danger. I was not wandering in any base bypath, but walking in the highway of my vocation; wherefore, Lord, thou that calledst me hither, keep me here. Stop their mouths, that they speak no blasphemy, or stop my ears, that I hear none; or open my mouth soberly to reprove what I hear. Give me to guard myself; but, Lord, guard my guarding of myself. Let not the smoke of their badness put out mine eyes, but the shining of my innocency lighten theirs. Let me give physic to them, and not take infection from them. Yea, make me the better for their badness. Then shall their bad company be to me like the dirt of oysters, whose mud hath soap in it, and doth scour rather than defile.[10]

* * *

Lord, the preacher this day came home to my heart. A left-handed Gibeonite with his sling hit not the mark more sure than he my darling sins. I could find no fault with his sermon, save only that it had too much truth. But this I quarrelled at, that he went far from his text to come close to me, and so was faulty himself in telling me of my faults. Thus they will creep out at small crannies who have a mind to escape;

and yet I cannot deny that what he spoke (though nothing to that portion of Scripture which he had for his text) was according to the proportion of Scripture. And is not thy word in general the text at large of every preacher? Yea, rather I should have concluded that if he went from his text, thy goodness sent him to meet me; for without thy guidance it would have been impossible for him so truly to have traced the intricate turnings of my deceitful heart.[11]

*　　*　　*

Lord, the Apostle saith to the Corinthians, God will not suffer you to be tempted above what you are able. But how comes he to contradict himself, by his own confession in his next epistle? where, speaking of his own sickness, he saith, We were pressed out of measure above strength. Perchance this will be expounded by propounding another riddle of the same Apostle's: who, praising Abraham, saith that against hope he believed in hope. That is, against carnal hope he believed in spiritual hope. So the same wedge will serve to cleave the former difficulty. Paul was pressed above his human, not above his heavenly strength. Grant, Lord, that I may not mangle and dismember thy Word, but study it entirely, comparing one place with another. For diamonds can only cut diamonds, and I find no such comments on the Scripture as the Scripture itself.[12]

*　　*　　*

Lord, I find the genealogy of my Savior strangely checkered with four remarkable changes in four immediate generations.
1. Rehoboam begat Abia; that is, a bad father begat a bad son.
2. Abia begat Asa; that is, a bad father a good son.
3. Asa begat Jehoshaphat; that is, a good father a good son.
4. Jehoshaphat begat Joram; that is, a good father a bad son.
I see, Lord, from hence, that my father's piety cannot be handed on; that is bad news for me. But I see also that actual impiety is not always hereditary; that is good news for my son.[13]

*　　*　　*

Lord, when in my daily service I read David's Psalms, give me to alter the accent of my soul according to their several subjects. In such psalms, wherein he confesseth his sins, or requesteth thy pardon, or praiseth for former, or prayeth for future favors, in all these give me to raise my soul to as high a pitch as may be. But when I come to such psalms wherein he curseth his enemies, O there let me bring my soul down to a lower note. For those words were made only to fit David's mouth. I have the like breath, but not the same spirit to pronounce them. Nor let me flatter myself, that it is lawful for me, with David, to curse thine enemies, lest my deceitful heart entitle all mine enemies to be thine, and so what was religion in David prove malice in me, whilst I act revenge under the pretense of piety.[14]

*   *   *

Lord, I read of my Savior, that when he was in the wilderness, then the devil leaveth him, and behold angels came and ministered unto him. A great change in a little time. No twilight betwixt night and day. No purgatory condition betwixt Hell and Heaven, but instantly, when out devil, in angel. Such is the case of every solitary soul. It will make company for itself. A musing mind will not stand neuter a minute, but presently will side with legions of good or bad thoughts. Grant therefore that my soul, which ever will have some, may never have bad company.[15]

*   *   *

Lord, this morning I read a chapter in the Bible, and therein observed a memorable passage whereof I never took notice before. Why now, and no sooner, did I see it? Formerly my eyes were as open, and the letters as legible. Is there not a thin veil laid over thy word, which is more rarefied by reading, and at last wholly worn away? Or was it because I came with more appetite than before? The milk was always there in the breast, but the child till now was not hungry enough to find out the teat. I see the oil of thy word will never leave increasing whilst any bring an empty barrel. The Old Testament will still be a New Testament to him who comes with a fresh desire of information.[16]

*   *   *

Lord, I read how Paul, writing from Rome, spake to Philemon to prepare him a lodging, hoping to make use thereof; yet we find not that he ever did use it, being martyred not long after. However, he was no loser whom thou didst lodge in a higher mansion in Heaven. Let me always be thus deceived to my advantage. I shall have no cause to complain, though I never wear the new clothes fitted for me if, before I put them on, death clothe me with glorious immortality.[17]

*   *   *

Lord, I discover an arrant laziness in my soul. For when I am to read a chapter in the Bible, before I begin it, I look where it endeth. And if it endeth not on the same side, I cannot keep my hands from turning over the leaf, to measure the length thereof on the other side. If it swells to many verses, I begin to grudge. Surely my heart is not rightly affected. Were I truly hungry after heavenly food, I would not complain of meat. Scourge, Lord, this laziness out of my soul; make the reading of thy word not a penance, but a pleasure unto me. Teach me that as amongst many heaps of gold, all being equally pure, that is the best which is the biggest, so I may esteem that chapter in thy Word the best that is the longest.[18]

* * *

The Roman senators conspired against Julius Caesar to kill him. That very next morning Artemidorus, Caesar's friend, delivered him a paper (desiring him to peruse it) wherein the whole plot was discovered. But Caesar complimented his life away, being so taken up to return the salutations of such people as met him in the way, that he pocketed the paper, among other petitions, as unconcerned therein; and so, going to the senate-house, was slain. The world, flesh and devil have a design for the destruction of men. We ministers bring our people a letter, God's Word, wherein all the conspiracy is revealed. But who hath believed our report? Most men are so busy about worldly delights, they are not at leisure to listen to us, or read the letter; but thus, alas! run headlong to their own ruin and destruction.[19]

* * *

The Sidonian servants agreed amongst themselves to choose him to be their king who, that morning, should first see the sun. Whilst all others were gazing on the east, one alone looked on the west. Some admired, more mocked him, as if he looked on the feet, there to find the eye of the face. But he first of all discovered the light of the sun shining on the tops of houses. God is seen sooner, easier, clearer in his operations than in his essence, best beheld by reflection in his creatures. For the invisible things of him, from the creation of the world, are clearly seen, being understood by things that are made.[20]

* * *

The poets fable that this was one of the labors imposed on Hercules, to make clean the Augean stable. For therein, they said, were kept 3,000 kine, and it had not been cleansed for thirty years. But Hercules, by letting the river Alpheus into it, did that with ease which before was conceived impossible. This stable is the pure emblem of my impure soul, which hath been defiled with millions of sins for more than thirty years together. O that I might by a lively faith and unfeigned repentance let the stream of that fountain into my soul, which is opened for Judah and Jerusalem. It is impossible by all my pains to purge out my uncleanness, which is quickly done by the rivulet of the blood of my Savior.[21]

* * *

Almost twenty years since I heard a profane jest, and still remember it. How many pious passages of far later date have I forgotten. It seems my soul is like a filthy pond, wherein fish die soon, and frogs live long. Lord, raze this profane jest out of my memory. Leave not a letter thereof behind, lest my corruption (an apt scholar) guess it out again; and be pleased to write some pious meditation in the place thereof. And grant, Lord, for the time to come (because such bad guests are easier kept out), that I may be careful not to admit what I find so difficult to expel.[22]

* * *

When in my private prayers I have been prepared to confess my bosom sins unto God, I have been loath to speak them aloud; fearing (though no man could, yet) that the devil would overhear me, and make use of my words against me. It being probable that, when I have uncovered the weakest part of my soul, he would assault me there. Yet since I have considered that I shall tell Satan no news which he knew not before. Surely I have not managed my secret sins with such privacy but that he, from some circumstances, collected what they were. Though the fire was within, he saw some smoke without. Wherefore for the future I am resolved to acknowledge my darling faults, though alone, yet aloud; that the devil, who rejoiced in partly knowing of my sins, may be grieved more by hearing the expression of my sorrow. As for any advantage he may make from my confession, this comforts me: God's goodness in assisting me will be above Satan's malice in assaulting me.[23]

* * *

How easy is pen and paper piety for one to write religiously! I will not say it costeth nothing, but it is far cheaper to work one's head than one's heart to goodness. Some, perchance, may guess me to be good by my writings, and so I shall deceive my reader. But if I do not desire to be good, I most of all deceive myself. I can make a hundred meditations sooner than subdue the least sin in my soul. Yea, I was once in the mind never to write more; for fear lest my writings at the last day prove records against me. And yet why should I not write? that by reading my own book, the disproportion betwixt my lines and my life may make me blush myself (if not into goodness) into less badness than I would do otherwise. That so my writings may condemn me, and make me to condemn myself, that so God may be moved to acquit me.[24]

*   *   *

A person of great quality was pleased to lodge a night in my house. I durst not invite him to my family prayer; and therefore for that time omitted it: thereby making a breach in a good custom, and giving Satan advantage to assault it. Yea, the loosening of such a link might have endangered the scattering of the chain. Bold bashfulness, which durst offend God whilst it did fear man. Especially considering that, though my guest was never so high, yet by the laws of hospitality I was above him whilst he was under my roof. Hereafter, whomsoever cometh within the doors shall be requested to come within the discipline of my house. If accepting my homely diet, he will not refuse my home devotion. Sitting at my table, he will be entreated to kneel down by it.[25]

*   *   *

Shameful my sloth, that have deferred my night prayer till I am in bed. This lying along is an improper posture for piety. Indeed, there is no contrivance of our body but some good man in Scripture hath made use of it with prayer. The publican standing, Job sitting, Hezekiah lying on his bed, Elijah with his face between his legs. But of all gestures give me St. Paul's: For this cause I bow my knees to the God and Father of my Lord Jesus Christ. Knees, when they may, then they must be bended.[26]

*   *   *

Lord, how come wicked thoughts to perplex me in my prayers, when I desire and endeavor only to attend thy service? Now I perceive the cause thereof; at other times I have willingly entertained them, and now they entertain themselves against my will. I acknowledge thy justice, that what formerly I have invited, now I cannot expel. Give me hereafter always to bolt out such ill guests. The best way to be rid of such bad thoughts in my prayers is not to receive them out of my prayers.[27]

*   *   *

Pope Boniface the Ninth, at the end of each hundred years, appointed a jubilee at Rome wherein people, bringing themselves and money thither, had pardon for their sins. But centenary years returned but seldom; popes were old. Few had the happiness to fill their coffers with jubilee-coin. Hereupon Clement the Sixth reduced it to every thirty-three years, Paul the Second and Sixtus the Fourth to every twenty-fifth year. Yea, an agitation is reported in the conclave to bring down jubilees to fifteen, twelve or ten years, had not some cardinals opposed it. I serve my prayers as they their jubilees. Perchance they may extend to a quarter of an hour, when poured out at large. But some days I begrudge this time as too much, and omit the preface of my prayer, with some passages conceived less material, and run two or three petitions into one, so contracting them to half a quarter of an hour. Not long after, this also seems too long. I decontract and abridge the abridgement of my prayers, yea (be it confessed to my shame and sorrow, that hereafter I may amend it) too often I shrink my prayers to a minute, to a moment, to a Lord have mercy upon me![28]

* * *

There was, not long since, a devout but ignorant Papist dwelling in Spain. He perceived a necessity of his own private prayers to God, besides the Pater Nosters, Ave Marias, etc., used of course in the Romish church. But so simple was he, that how to pray he knew not. Only every morning humbly bending his knees and lifting up his eyes and hands to heaven, he would deliberately repeat the alphabet. And now, said he, O good God, put these letters together to spell syllables, to spell words, to make such sense as may be most to thy glory and my good. In these distracted times I know what generalities to pray for: God's glory, truth, and peace, his Majesty's honor, the privileges of Parliament, liberty of subjects, etc. But when I descend to particulars, when, how, by whom I should desire these things to be effected, I may fall to that poor man's A,B,C,D,E, etc.[29]

* * *

Strange was the behavior of our Savior toward his beloved Lazarus. Informed by a messenger of his sickness, he abode two days still in the place where he was. Why so slow? The cause was, because Lazarus was not bad enough for Christ to cure. He intended not to recover him from sickness, but revive him from death, to make the glory of the miracle greater.

England doth lie desperately sick of a violent disease in the bowels. Many messengers we dispatch (monthly fasts, weekly sermons, daily prayers) to inform God of our sad condition. He still stays in the same place, yea, which is worse, seems to go backward, for every day brings less likelihood and less hope of help. May not this be the reason, that our land must yet be reduced to more extremity, that God may have the higher honor of our deliverance?[30]

* * *

In the year of our Lord 1606 there happened a sad overflowing of the Severn Sea on both sides thereof, which some alive do remember. An account hereof was written to John Stow, the chronicler, by Dr. Still, then bishop of Bath and Wells, with three other gentlemen, to insert it in his history. One passage of the account I cannot omit. It is found on page 889 of Stow's Chronicle: "Among other things of note, it happened that upon the tops of some hills, divers beasts of contrary nature had got up for their safety, as dogs, cats, foxes, hares, conies, moles, mice and rats, who remained together very peaceably, without any manner or sign of fear of violence one toward another." How much of man was there then in brute creatures? How much of brutishness is there now in men? Is this a time for those who are sinking for the same cause to quarrel and fall out? In the words of the Apostle, consider what I say; and the Lord give you understanding in all things.[31]

* * *

I looked upon the wrong or back side of a piece of arras; it seemed to me as a continued nonsense. There was neither head nor foot therein. Confusion itself had as much method in it: a company of thrums and threads, with many pieces and patches of several sorts, sizes, and colors, all which signified nothing to my understanding. But then looking on the reverse or right side thereof, all put together did spell excellent proportions and figures of men and cities. So that indeed it was a history, not wrote with a pen, but wrought with a needle. If men look upon our late times with a mere eye of reason, they will hardly find any sense therein, such is their huddle and disorder. But alas! the wrong side is objected to our eyes, whilst the right side is presented to the high God of Heaven, who knoweth that an admirable order doth result out of this confusion, and what is presented to him at present may hereafter be so showed to us as to convince our judgments in the truth thereof.[32]

* * *

Considering with myself the causes of the growth and increase of impiety and profaneness in our land, amongst others this seemeth to me not the least, viz., the late many false and erroneous impressions of the Bible. Now know, what is but carelessness in other books is impiety in setting forth of the Bible. As Noah in all unclean creatures preserved but two of a kind, so among some hundreds in several editions we will cite only two instances. In the Bible printed at London, 1653, we read in 1 Corinthians 6:9, "Know ye not that the unrighteous shall inherit the kingdom of God?" (instead of "shall not inherit"). Now when a reverend doctor in divinity did mildly reprove some libertines for their licentious life, they did produce this text from the authority of this corrupt edition, in justification of their vicious and inordinate conversations. The next instance shall be in the Bible printed in London in quarto in the singing Psalms, Psalm 67:2: "That all the earth may know the way to worldly wealth" (instead of "godly wealth"). It is too probable that too many have perused and practiced this erroneous impression, namely, such who by plundering, oppression, cozening, force, and fraud, have in our age suddenly advanced vast estates.[33]

*   *   *

God in his providence fixed my nativity in a remarkable place. I was born at Aldwinkle, in Northamptonshire, where my father was the painstaking preacher of St. Peter's. This village was distanced one good mile west from Achurch, where Mr. Browne, founder of the Brownists (Congregationalists) did dwell; whom out of curiosity when a youth I often visited. It was likewise a mile and a half distant east from Lavenden, where Francis Tresham, Esquire, so active in the (Catholic) Gunpowder Treason, had a large and ancient habitation. My nativity may mind me of moderation, whose cradle was rocked betwixt two rocks. Now, seeing I was never such a churl as to desire to eat my morsel alone, let such who like my prayer join with me therein. God grant we may hit the golden mean and endeavor to avoid all extremes: the fanatic Anabaptist on the one side and the fiery zeal of the Jesuit on the other, that so we may be true Protestants, or, which is a far better name, real Christians indeed.[34]

*   *   *

A minister of these times sharply chided one of his parish for having a base [illegitimate] child, and told him that he must take order for the keeping thereof. "Why, sir," answered the man, "I conceive it more reasonable that you should maintain it. For I am not book-learned, and ken not a letter in the Bible; yea, I have been your parishioner this seven years, present every Lord's day at the church. Yet did I never there hear you read the ten commandments; I never heard that precept read, 'Thou shalt not commit adultery.' Probably, had you told me my duty, I had not committed this folly."[35]

*   *   *

King James was desirous of discovering such who falsely pretended themselves possessed with a devil. A maid dissembled such a possession, and for the better color thereof, when the first verses of the Gospel of St. John were read in her hearing, she would fall into strange fits of fuming and foaming, to the amazement of the beholders. But when the king caused one of his chaplains to read the same in the original, the same maid (possessed it seems with an English devil, who understood not a word of Greek) was tame and quiet, without any impression upon her. I know a factious parish wherein, if the minister in his pulpit had but named the word "kingdom" the people would have been ready to have petitioned against him for a malignant. But as for "realm," the same word in French, he might safely use it in his sermons as oft as he pleased. Ignorance, which generally inflameth, sometimes by good hap abateth men's malice.[36]

*   *   *

A careless maid which attended a gentleman's child fell asleep whilst the rest of the family were at church. An ape, taking the child out of the cradle, carried it to the roof of the house and there (according to his rude manner) fell a-dancing and dandling thereof, down head, up heels, as it happened.

The father of the child, returning with his family from the church, commented with his own eyes on his child's sad condition. Bemoan he might, help it he could not. Dangerous to shoot the ape where the bullet might hit the babe. All fall to their prayers as their last and best refuge, that the innocent child might be preserved. But when the ape was well wearied with its own activity he fairly went down, and formally laid the child where he found it, in the cradle.

Fanatics have pleased their fancies these late years with turning and tossing and tumbling of Christianity, upward and downward and backward and forward. They have cast and contrived it into a hundred antic postures of their own imagining. It is now to be hoped that after they have tired themselves out with doing of nothing, but only trying and tampering to no purpose, they may at last return and leave Christianity in the same condition wherein they found it.[37]

*   *   *

I could both sigh and smile at the simplicity of a native American [Indian] who was sent by a Spaniard, his master, with a basket of figs and a letter (wherein the figs were mentioned) to carry them to one of his master's friends. On the way this messenger ate up the figs but delivered the letter, whereby his deed was discovered and he punished.

Being sent a second time on the like message, he first took the letter and hid it in the ground, sitting himself on the place where he put it; and then fell to feed on his figs, presuming that that paper which saw nothing could tell nothing. Then taking it again out of the ground, he delivered it to his master's friend, whereby his fault was perceived and he worse beaten than before. Men conceive they can manage their sins with secrecy; but they carry about them a letter, or book rather, written by God's finger, their conscience bearing witness to all their actions. But sinners being often detected and accused, grow wary at last. To prevent this "speaking paper" from telling any tales, they do smother, stifle and suppress it, when they go about the committing of any wickedness. Yet conscience (though buried for a time in silence) hath afterward a resurrection and discovers all, to their greater shame and heavier punishment.[38]

* * *

I saw a mother threatening to punish her little child for not rightly pronouncing that petition in the Lord's prayer: "And forgive us our trespasses, as we forgive them that trespass against us." The child essayed and offered as well as it could to utter it, adventuring at "tepasses," "trepasses," but could not pronounce the word aright. Alas! It is a shibboleth to a child's tongue, wherein there is a confluence of hard consonants together. Therefore if the mother had punished defect in the infant for default, she deserved to have been punished herself; the more so because what the child could not pronounce the parents do not practice. Oh, how lispingly and imperfectly do we perform the close of this petition: "As we forgive them that trespass against us." It is well if, with the child, we endeavor our best, though falling short in the exact observance thereof.[39]

* * *

Lord, be pleased to shake my clay cottage before thou throwest it down. May it totter awhile before it doth tumble. Let me be summoned before I am surprised. Deliver me from sudden death—not from sudden death in respect of itself, for I care not how short my passage be, so it be safe. Never any weary traveler complained that he came too soon to his journey's end. But let it not be sudden in respect of me. Make me always ready to receive death. Thus no guest comes unawares to him who keeps a constant table.[40]

Notes

1. *Good Thoughts in Bad Times*, Personal Meditations, 3, p. 6.
2. *Ibid.*, 4, p. 7.
3. *Ibid.*, 5, p. 8. Cf. Isaiah 38:14, Ps. 47:7.
4. *Ibid.*, 8, p. 10. Cf. Ps. 95:7.
5. *Ibid.*, 10, p. 12. Cf. Numbers 11:26.
6. *Ibid.*, 17, p. 17.
7. *Ibid.*, 19, p. 18. Cf. Genesis 43:12.
8. *Ibid.*, 20, p. 19. Cf. Revelation 3:20, John 20:19, Acts 12:10.
9. *Ibid.*, 21, p. 20.
10. *Ibid.*, 22, p. 21.
11. *Ibid.*, 24, p. 23. Cf. Judges 20:16.
12. *Good Thoughts in Bad Times*, Scripture Observations, 6, p. 28. Cf. 1 Corinthians 10:13, 2 Corinthians 1:8.
13. *Ibid.*, 8, p. 30. Cf. Matthew 1:7, 8.
14. *Ibid.*, 9, p. 30.
15. *Ibid.*, 13, p. 33. Cf. Matthew 4:11.
16. *Ibid.*, 15, p. 34.
17. *Ibid.*, 19, p. 37. Cf. Philemon 22.
18. *Ibid.*, 21, p. 38.
19. *Good Thoughts in Bad Times*, Historical Applications, 6, p. 46.
20. *Ibid.*, 22, p. 58. Cf. Romans 1:20.
21. *Ibid.*, 20, p. 57.
22. *Good Thoughts in Bad Times*, Mixt Contemplations, 12, p. 69.
23. *Ibid.*, 17, p. 72.
24. *Ibid.*, 25, p. 78.
25. *Good Thoughts in Worse Times*, Personal Meditations, 5, p. 89.
26. *Ibid.*, 6, p. 89. Cf. Job 2:8, 2 Kings 20:1-3, 1 Kings 18:42, Ephesians 3:14.
27. *Ibid.*, 19, p. 101.
28. *Ibid.*, 20, p. 102.
29. *Good Thoughts in Worse Times*, Meditations on the Times, 11, p. 132.
30. *Ibid.*, 14, p. 135. Cf. John 11:6.
31. *Mixt Contemplations in Better Times*, 36, p. 223.
32. *Ibid.*, 43, p. 230.
33. *Ibid.*, 8, p. 246.
34. *Ibid.*, 43, p. 282.
35. *Ibid.*, 45, p. 284.
36. *Ibid.*, 49, p. 288.
37. *Ibid.*, 46, p. 284.
38. *Good Thoughts in Bad Times*, Historical Applications, 13, p. 51.
39. *Mixt Contemplations in Better Times*, 38, p. 225.
40. *Good Thoughts in Bad Times*, Personal Meditations, 25, p. 23.

Excerpts taken from the 1863 edition of *Good Thoughts in Bad Times* published in Boston by Ticknor and Fields. It includes *Good Thoughts in Bad Times; Good Thoughts in Worse Times*, published some time after 1645; *Mixt Contemplations in Better Times*, which appeared at the time of the Restoration in May 1660.

To omit John Milton (1608–1674) from a discussion of the seventeenth century is like omitting the Taj Mahal from a description of India. One of England's two greatest poets (with Shakespeare), he is still a lively subject of research and study. His poem Paradise Lost *is considered one of the epochal literary works of the world. Among British statesmen, Milton was the most articulate of his day. When England wished to put something into writing, it asked Milton to write it. He left little to be desired.*

The English-speaking world today owes much of its political freedom to the courageous writings of John Milton. At the time he issued his tracts, he did so at the risk of death or confinement in the Tower of London. He spoke to his time; yet his incredible breadth of learning and his writing skill made him a timeless man.

John Milton submitted to the authority of the Bible and revered it as no other book. He was called "the very genius of English Puritanism." For all that, Milton rejected the orthodox doctrine of the Trinity, considering both Jesus Christ and the Holy Spirit to be subordinate to God the Father. He further scandalized the Christians of his day by approving divorce on grounds of what we call today incompatibility.

John Milton was born in London and educated at Christ's College, Cambridge. Although his poetry won him early fame, he chose the life of a scholarly recluse. At age thirty-five he married. Nine years later his eyesight completely failed. His middle years were spent as Latin secretary to Oliver Cromwell. After the Restoration he was imprisoned briefly, but spent his final years at liberty, writing his poetic masterpieces.

In the nineteenth century the manuscript of Milton's Christian Doctrine, *a piece that shocked his contemporaries, was discovered in a London archive. We have chosen most of the Milton excerpts in the present volume from this source. Other selections are identified in the footnotes. We have also included two of his sonnets; one of them,* On the Late Massacre in Piedmont, *has been called "the most powerful sonnet ever written." A passage from* Paradise Lost *rounds out our Milton selections.*

3

From Christian Doctrine
by John Milton

How to Think of God
When we speak of knowing God, it must be understood with reference to man's limited powers of comprehension. God, as he really is, is far beyond man's imagination, let alone his understanding. God has revealed only so much of himself as our minds can conceive and the weakness of our nature can bear.

Our safest way is to form an image of God in our minds which corresponds to his representation and description of himself in the sacred writings. For granting that, both in the literal and figurative descriptions of God, he is exhibited not as he really is, but in such a manner as may be within the scope of our comprehensions; yet we ought to entertain such a conception of him as he, in condescending to accommodate himself to our capacities, wishes us to conceive.

Indeed he has brought himself down to our level expressly to prevent our being carried beyond the reach of human comprehension, and outside the written authority of Scripture, into vague subtleties of speculation.

In my opinion, then, theologians do not need to employ anthropomorphisms, or the ascription of human feelings to God. This is a rhetorical device thought up by grammarians to explain the nonsense poets write about Jove. Sufficient care has been taken, without any doubt, to ensure that the Holy Scriptures contain nothing unfitting to God or unworthy of him. This applies equally to those passages in Scripture where God speaks about his own nature.

So it is better not to think about God or form an image of him in anthropomorphic terms, for to do so would be to follow the example of men who are always inventing more and more subtle theories about him. Rather we should form our ideas with Scripture as a model, for that is the way he has offered himself to our contemplation. We ought not to imagine that God would have said anything or caused anything to be written about himself unless he intended that it should be a part of our conception of him. On the question of what is or what is not suitable for God, let us ask for no more dependable authority than God himself.

If Jehovah repented that he had created man (Genesis 6:6) and repented because of their groanings (Judges 2:18), let us believe that he did repent. But let us not imagine that God's repentance arises from lack of foresight, as man's does, for he has warned us not to think about him in this way.

If God grieved in his heart (Genesis 6:6), and if similarly his soul was grieved (Judges 10:16), let us believe that he did feel grief. For those states of mind which are good in a good man, and count as virtues, are holy in God. If it is said that God, after working six days, rested and was refreshed, let us believe that it is not beneath God to feel what grief he does feel, and to be refreshed by what refreshes him.

However you may try to tone down these and similar texts about God by an elaborate show of interpretative glosses, it comes to the same thing in the end. After all, if God is said to have created man in his own image, and if God attributes to himself again and again a human shape and form, why should we be afraid of assigning to him something that he assigns to himself, provided we believe that what is imperfect and weak in us is, when ascribed to God, utterly perfect and utterly beautiful?

We may be certain that God's majesty and glory were so dear to him that he could never say anything about himself which was lower or meaner than his real nature, nor would he ever ascribe to himself any property if he did not wish us to ascribe it to him.

In short, God either is or is not really like he says he is. If he really is like this, why should we think otherwise? If he is not really like this, on what authority do we contradict God? If, at any rate, he wants us to imagine him in this way, why does our imagination go off on some other tack? Why does our imagination shy away from a notion of God which he himself does not hesitate to promulgate in unambiguous terms? For God in his goodness has revealed to us in ample quantity those things which we need to understand about him for our salvation.

We do not imply by this argument that God, in all his parts and members, is of human form, but that so far as it concerns us to know, he has that form which he attributes to himself in Holy Writ. God, then, has disclosed just such an idea of himself to our understanding as he wishes us to possess. If we form some other idea of him, we are not acting according to his will, but are frustrating him of his purpose, as if, indeed, we wished to show that our concept of God was not too debased, but that his concept of us was.[1]

*   *   *

The One Basis of Authority

If I were to say that I had devoted myself to the study of Christian doctrine because nothing else can so effectually rescue the lives and minds of men from those two detestable curses, slavery and superstition, I would show that I had been acting not from a concern for religion, but from a motive of human interests.

But in fact I decided not to depend upon the belief or judgment of others in religious questions for this reason: God has revealed the way of eternal salvation only to the individual faith of each man, and demands of us that any man who wishes to be saved should have a personal belief of his own. So I thought fit to scrutinize and ascertain for myself the several points of my religious belief, and accordingly I read and pondered the Holy Scriptures themselves with all possible diligence, never sparing myself in any way. The only authority I accepted was God's self-revelation.

I began by devoting myself when I was a youth to an earnest study of the Old and New Testaments in their original languages, and then went carefully through some of the shorter systems of theologians. I began listing under general headings all passages from the Scriptures which suggested themselves for quotation, to make use of them as occasion might require.

Later, gaining confidence, I transferred my attention to more diffuse volumes of divinity, and to the conflicting arguments in disputed points of faith. But to be frank, I was sorry to find in these works that the authors frequently evaded an opponent's point in a thoroughly dishonest way, or countered it by an affected display of logical ingenuity or linguistic quibbles. So they sometimes attacked the truth as error and heresy, while calling error and heresy truth, and upheld their views not upon the authority of the Bible but from deference to custom and party spirit.

I considered that I could not properly entrust either my creed or my hope of salvation to such guides. The Christian doctrine is that divine revelation disclosed in various ages by Christ (though he was not known under that name in the beginning) concerning the nature and worship of the Deity, for the promotion of the glory of God and the salvation of mankind. This doctrine is to be obtained not from the schools of the philosophers nor from the laws of man, but from the Holy Scripture alone, under the guidance of the Holy Spirit.

I do not urge or enforce anything upon my own authority. But I intend to make people understand how much it is in the interests of the Christian religion that men should be free not only to sift and winnow any doctrine, but also openly to give their opinions of it and even to write about it, according to what each believes.

It is disgraceful and disgusting that the Christian religion should be supported by violence. Without this freedom we are still enslaved: not as once by the law of God, but what is vilest of all, by human law, or rather, to be more exact, by an inhuman tyranny.

There are some irrational bigots who, by a perversion of justice, condemn anything they consider inconsistent with conventional beliefs and give it an invidious title—"heretic" or "heresy"—without consulting the evidence of the Bible upon the point. To their way of thinking, by branding anyone out of hand with this hateful name, they silence him with one word and need take no further trouble. They imagine that they have struck their opponent to the ground, as with a single blow, by the impact of the name heretic alone.

To these bigots I retort that in apostolic times, before the New Testament was written, the word *heresy,* whenever it was used as an accusation, was applied only to something which contradicted the teaching of the apostles as it passed from mouth to mouth. On the same grounds I hold that, since the compilation of the New Testament, nothing can correctly be called heresy unless it contradicts that.

For my own part I devote my attention to the Holy Scriptures alone. I follow no other heresy or sect. I had not even studied any of the so-called heretical writers. In common with the whole Protestant Church I refuse to recognize any other arbiters of or any other supreme authorities for Christian belief, or any faith not independently arrived at but "implicit," as it is termed.

For the rest, brethren, cherish the truth with love for your fellowmen. Assess this work as God's Spirit shall direct you. Do not accept or reject what I say unless you are absolutely convinced by the clear evidence of the Bible; and live in the Spirit of our Lord and Savior Jesus Christ.[2]

*   *   *

Hirelings in the Church

How can it be but ever unhappy to the Church of England, while she shall think to entice men to the pure service of God by the same means that were used to tempt our Savior to the service of the devil—by laying before him honor and preferment? Fit professors indeed are they like to be, to teach others that godliness with content is great gain, whenas their godliness of teaching had not been but for worldly gain.

The heathen philosophers thought that virtue was inestimable for its own sake, and the greatest gain of a teacher was to make a soul virtuous. So Xenophon writes of Socrates, who never bargained with any for teaching them. He feared not lest those who had received so high a benefit from him would not of their own free will return him all possible thanks.

Was moral virtue so lovely and so alluring, and heathen men so enamored of her, as to teach and study her with greatest neglect and contempt of worldly profit and advancement? And is Christian piety so homely and so unpleasant, and Christian men so cloyed with her, as that none will study and teach her but for lucre and preferment?

But they will grant, perhaps, piety may thrive, but learning will decay. I would ask these men at whose hands they seek inferior things, such as wealth, honor, their dainty fare, their lofty houses? No doubt they will soon answer that all these things they seek at God's hands. Do they think, then, that all these meaner and superfluous things come from God, and the divine gift of learning from the den of Plutus, or the cave of Mammon?

Certainly never any clear spirit, nursed up from brighter influences, with a soul enlarged to the dimensions of spacious art and high knowledge, ever entered there but with scorn, and thought it ever foul disdain to make pelf or ambition the reward of his studies—it being the greatest honor, the greatest fruit and proficiency, of learned studies to despise these things. Not liberal science, but illiberal, must that needs be that mounts in contemplation merely for money.

And what would it avail us to have a hireling clergy, though never so learned? For such can have neither true wisdom nor grace, and then in vain do men trust in learning where these be wanting. If, in less noble and almost mechanic arts, according to the definitions of those authors, he is not esteemed to deserve the name of a complete architect, an excellent painter, or the like, that bears not a generous mind above the peasantly regard of wages and hire; much more must we think him a most imperfect and incomplete divine who is so far from being a contemner of filthy lucre that his whole divinity is moulded and bred up in the beggarly and brutish hopes of a fat prebendary, deanery, or bishopric; which poor and low-pitched desires, if they do but mix with those other heavenly intentions that draw a man to this study, it is justly expected that they should bring forth a base-born issue of divinity.

In matters of religion, there is not anything more intolerable than a learned fool or a learned hypocrite. The one is ever cooped up at his empty speculations—a sot, an idiot, for any use that mankind can make of him. Or else he is sowing the world with idle questions, and with much toil and difficulty wading up to the eyebrows in deep shallows that wet not the instep. The plain unlearned man that lives well by that light which he has is better and wiser, and edifies others more toward a godly and happy life, than he.

The hypocrite is still using his sophisticated arts, and bending all his studies, how to make his insatiate avarice and ambition seem pious and orthodox by painting his lewd and deceitful principles with a smooth and glossy varnish in a doctrinal way, to bring about his wickedest purposes. But a true pastor of Christ's sending has this special mark, that for greatest labors and greatest merits in the church he requires either nothing, if he could so subsist, or a very common and reasonable supply of human necessaries.

We cannot therefore do better than to leave this care of ours to God. He can easily send laborers into his harvest that shall not cry, "Give, give," but be contented with a moderate and beseeming allowance. Nor will he suffer true learning to be wanting where true grace and our obedience to him abounds. For if he gives us to know him right, and to practice our knowledge in right-established discipline, how much more will he replenish us with all abilities in tongues and arts that may conduce to his glory and our good!

He can stir up rich fathers to bestow exquisite education upon their children, and so dedicate them to the service of the Gospel; for certainly there is no employment more honorable, more worthy to take up a great spirit, more requiring a generous and free nurture, than to be the messenger and herald of heavenly truth from God to man. There is no employment more worthy than by the faithful work of holy doctrine, to procreate a number of faithful men, making a kind of creation like to God's by infusing his Spirit and likeness into them to their salvation, as God did into him; arising to whatsoever climate he turn him, like that Sun of Righteousness that sent him, with healing in his wings.

Such a messenger causes new light to break in upon the chill and gloomy hearts of his hearers, raising out of darksome barrenness a delicious and fragrant spring of saving knowledge and good works.

Can a man thus employed find himself discontented or be discouraged though men call him not "lord"? Would he tug for a barony to sit and vote in Parliament, knowing that no man can take from him the gift of wisdom and sound doctrine, which leaves him free, though not to be a member, yet to be a teacher and persuader of the Parliament?

In all wise apprehensions the persuasive power in man to win others to goodness by instruction is greater, and more divine, than the compulsive power to restrain men from being evil by terror of the law. That is why Christ left Moses to be the lawgiver, but himself came down among us to be a teacher, with which office his heavenly wisdom was so well pleased that he was angry with those that would have put a piece of temporal judicature into his hands, disclaiming that he had any commission from above for such matters.

To speak freely, it were much better that they who intended to be ministers were trained up in the church only by the Scripture, and in the original languages thereof at school, without fetching the compass of other arts and sciences more than what they can well learn at secondary leisure, and at home. I do not speak this in contempt of learning or the ministry, but hating the common cheats of both; hating that they who have preached out bishops, prelates and canonists should, in what serves their own ends, retain their false opinions, their pharisaical leaven, their avarice, their ambition, their pluralities, their nonresidences, and their odious fees.

Doubtless, if God only be he who gives ministers to his church till the world's end; and if God, though the whole Gospel, never told us to send our ministers to the schools of philosophy, but rather bids us beware of such "vain deceit"; then there will not want ministers elected out of all sorts and orders of men. For the Gospel makes no difference, from the magistrate himself to the meanest artificer, if God chooses to favor him with spiritual gifts, as he can easily, and oft has done; while those bachelor divines and doctors of the tippet [a black clerical scarf signifying nongraduate status] have been passed by.[3]

* * *

The New Life in Christ

The calling of man is that natural mode of renovation whereby God the Father, according to his purpose in Christ, invites fallen man to a knowledge of the way in which he is to be propitiated and worshiped.

The change which takes in plan by reason of his calling, is that whereby the natural mind and will of man, being partially renewed by a divine impulse, are led to seek the knowledge of God, and, for the time being at least, undergo an alteration for the better.

The intent of supernatural renovation is not only to restore man more completely than before to the use of his natural faculties as regards his power to form right judgment, and to exercise free will; but to create afresh, as it were, the inward man, and infuse from above new and supernatural faculties into the minds of the renovated.

Regeneration is that change operated by the Word and the Spirit, whereby, the old man being destroyed, the inward man is regenerated by God after his own image, in all the faculties of his mind, insomuch that he becomes as it were a new creature, and the whole man is sanctified both in body and soul for the service of God and the performance of good works.

The primary functions of the new life are comprehension of spiritual things and love of holiness. And, as the power of exercising these functions was weakened, and in a manner destroyed, by the spiritual death, so is the understanding restored in great part to its primitive clearness, and the will to its primitive liberty, by the new spiritual life in Christ.

The comprehension of spiritual things is a habit or condition of mind produced by God, whereby the natural ignorance of those who believe and are ingrafted in Christ is removed, and their understandings enlightened for the perception of heavenly things, so that by the teaching of God, they know all that is necessary for eternal salvation and the true happiness of life. In the present life, however, we can only attain to an imperfect comprehension of spiritual things.[4]

*   *   *

How to Interpret Scripture

True religion is the true worship and service of God, learned and believed from the Word of God only. No man or angel can know how God would be worshiped and served unless God reveal it. He has revealed and taught it to us in the Holy Scriptures by inspired ministers, and in the Gospel by his own Son and his apostles, with strictest command to reject all other traditions or additions whatsoever.

The Mosaic law was a written code consisting of many precepts, intended for the Israelites alone, with a promise of life to such as should keep them, and a curse on such as should be disobedient. It was designed to the end that they, being led thereby to an acknowledgement of the depravity of mankind, and consequently of their own, might have recourse to the righteousness of the promised Savior. It was also intended that they, and in the process of time all other nations, might be led under the Gospel from the weak and servile rudiments of this elementary institution to the full strength of the new creature, and a manly liberty worthy of the sons of God.

The Gospel is the new dispensation of the covenant of grace, far more excellent and perfect than the law. It was announced first obscurely by Moses and the prophets, and afterwards in the clearest terms by Christ himself, and his apostles and evangelists. It has been written since by the Holy Spirit in the hearts of believers, and ordained to continue even to the end of the world. It contains a promise of eternal life to all in every nation who shall believe in Christ when revealed to them, and a threat of eternal death to such as shall not believe.

The Scriptures, partly by reason of their own simplicity and partly through the divine illumination, are plain and perspicuous in all things necessary to salvation, and adapted to the instruction of even the most unlearned, through the medium of diligent and constant reading.

If, then, the Scriptures be in themselves so perspicuous, and sufficient of themselves "to make men wise unto salvation through faith" that "the man of God may be perfect, throughly furnished unto all good works," through what infatuation is it that even Protestant divines persist in darkening the most momentous truths of religion by intricate metaphysical comments, on the plea that such explanation is necessary?

They string together all the useless technicalities and empty distinctions of scholastic barbarism, for the purpose of elucidating those Scriptures which they are continually extolling as models of plainness. As if Scripture, which possesses in itself the clearest light, and is sufficient for its own explanation, especially in matters of faith and holiness, required to have the simplicity of its divine truths more fully developed, and placed in a more distinct view, by illustrations drawn from the abstrusest of human sciences.

The requisites for the public interpretation of Scripture have been laid down by divines with much attention to usefulness, although they have not been observed with equal fidelity. They consist in knowledge of languages; inspection of the originals; examination of the context; care in distinguishing between literal and figurative expressions; consideration of cause and circumstance, of antecedents and consequents; mutual comparison of texts; and regard to the analogy of faith. Attention must also be paid to the frequent anomalies of syntax.

Lastly, no inferences from the text are to be admitted but such as follow necessarily and plainly from the words themselves, lest we should be constrained to receive what is not written for what is written, the shadow for the substance, the fallacies of human reasoning for the doctrines of God. For it is by the declarations of Scripture, and not by the conclusions of the schools, that our consciences are bound.[5]

*   *   *

Milton as a Young Man

I will now mention who and whence I am. I was born at London of an honest family. My father was distinguished by the undeviating integrity of his life, and my mother by the esteem in which she was held and the alms which she bestowed.

My father destined me from a child to the pursuits of literature; and my appetite for knowledge was so voracious that from twelve years of age I hardly ever left my studies or went to bed before midnight. This primarily led to my loss of sight. My eyes were naturally weak, and I was subject to frequent headaches; which however could not chill the ardor of my curiosity or retard the progress of my improvement.[6]

*   *   *

Though Christianity had been but slightly taught me, yet a certain reservedness of natural disposition, and moral discipline learned out of the noblest philosophy, was enough to keep me in disdain of far less incontinences than the bordello. I had the doctrine of Holy Scripture unfolding those chaste and high mysteries, with timeliest care infused, that "the body is for the Lord, and the Lord for the body."

Thus I argued to myself that if unchastity in a woman, whom St. Paul terms the glory of man, be such a scandal and dishonor, then certainly in a man, who is both the image and glory of God, it must, though commonly not so thought, be much more deflowering and dishonorable. For the man sins both against his own body and his own glory, and against the image and glory of God which is in himself.[7]

*   *   *

Authority Human and Divine

If indeed I were a member of the church of Rome, which requires implicit obedience to its creed on all points of faith, I should have acquiesced from education or habit in its simple decree and authority. But since I enroll myself among the number of those who freely acknowledge the Word of God alone as the rule of faith, and freely advance what appears to me much more clearly deducible from the Holy Scriptures than the commonly received opinion, I see no reason why anyone who belongs to the same Protestant, or reformed, church, and professes to acknowledge the same rule of faith as myself, should take offence at my freedom.

Particularly is this so as I impose my own authority on no one, but merely propose what I think more worthy of belief than the creed in general acceptation. I only entreat that my readers will ponder and examine my statements in a spirit which desires to discover nothing but the truth, and with a mind free from prejudice. For, without intending to oppose the authority of Scripture, which I consider inviolably sacred, I only take upon myself to refute human interpretations, as often as the occasion requires, conformably to my right, or rather to my duty, as a man.

If, indeed, those with whom I have to contend were able to produce direct attestation from Heaven to the truth of the doctrine which they espouse, it would be nothing less than impiety to venture to raise, I do not say a clamor, but so much as a murmur, against it. But inasmuch as they can lay claim to nothing more than human powers, assisted by that spiritual illumination which is common to all, it is not unreasonable that they should on their part allow the privileges of diligent research and free discussion to another inquirer, who is seeking truth through the same means and in the same way as themselves, and whose desire of benefiting mankind is equal to their own.[8]

ON HIS BLINDNESS

When I consider how my light is spent
   Ere half my days, in this dark world and wide,
   And that one talent which is death to hide
   Lodged with me useless, though my soul more bent
To serve therewith my Maker, and present
   My true account, lest he returning chide;
   "Doth God exact day-labor, light denied?"
   I fondly ask. But Patience, to prevent
That murmur, soon replies: "God doth not need
   Either man's work or his own gifts. Who best
   Bear his mild yoke, they serve him best. His state
Is kingly: thousands at his bidding speed,
   And post o'er land and ocean without rest;
   They also serve who only stand and wait."

ON THE LATE MASSACRE IN PIEDMONT

Avenge, O Lord, thy slaughtered saints, whose bonds
   Lie scattered on the Alpine mountains cold;
   Ev'n them who kept thy truth so pure of old,
   When all our fathers worshipped stocks and stones.
Forget not: in thy book record their groans
   Who were thy sheep and in their ancient fold
   Slain by the bloody Piedmontese that rolled
   Mother with infant down the rocks. Their moans
The vales redoubled to the hills, and they
   To Heaven. Their martyred blood and ashes sow
   O'er all the Italian fields where still doth sway
The triple tyrant: that from these may grow
   A hundredfold, who having learned thy way
   Early may fly the Babylonian woe.

FROM PARADISE LOST

"Be sure they will," said the angel; "but from Heaven
He to his own a Comforter will send,
The promise of the Father, who shall dwell
His Spirit within them, and the law of faith
Working through love upon their hearts shall write,
To guide them in all truth, and also arm
With spiritual armor, able to resist
Satan's assaults, and quench his fiery darts,
What man can do against them, not afraid
Though to the death, against such cruelties
With inward consolations recompensed,
And oft supported so as shall amaze
Their proudest persecutors. For the Spirit
Poured first on his apostles, whom he sends
To evangelize the nations, then on all
Baptized, shall them with wondrous gifts endue
To speak all tongues, and do all miracles,
As did their Lord before them. Thus they win
Great numbers of each nation to receive
With joy the tidings brought from Heaven: at length
Their ministry performed, and race well run,
Their doctrine and their story written left,
They die; but in their room, as they forewarn,
Wolves shall succeed for teachers, grievous wolves,
Who all the sacred mysteries of Heaven
To their own vile advantages shall turn
Of lucre and ambition, and the truth
With superstitions and traditions taint,
Left only in those written records pure,
Though not but by the Spirit understood."

Notes

1. From *Christian Doctrine*, Book I, Chapter II.
2. From the opening epistle of *Christian Doctrine*, entitled "John Milton, Englishman, to All the Churches of Christ, etc."
3. From two essays, "Animadversions upon the Remonstrant's Defence Against Smectymnuus," and "Considerations Touching the Likeliest Means to Remove Hirelings out of the Church."
4. From *Christian Doctrine*, Book I, Chapters XVII, XVIII and XXV.
5. From *Christian Doctrine*, Book I, Chapter XXVI, and from the essay, "Of True Religion."
6. From "The Second Defence of the People of England."
7. From the essay "Animadversions upon the Remonstrant's Defence Against Smectymnuus."
8. From *Christian Doctrine*, preface to Book I, Chapter V.

Excerpts taken by permission from *The Complete Prose Works of John Milton*, Yale, 1973, volume 6 (Maurice Kelly, editor); *Milton on Education, with Supplementary Extracts from Other Writings of Milton* (O. M. Ainsworth, editor), Yale, 1928; and *Complete Poetical Works of John Milton* (H. F. Fletcher, editor), Cambridge, Houghton Mifflin, 1941.

*Perhaps the most astonishing fact about Henry Scougal (1650–1678), in
light of his accomplishment, was the brevity of his life. Born in Fife,
Scotland, the son of the bishop of Aberdeen, he lived only twenty-seven
years; yet he left as his legacy one of the spiritual classics of the English
language.*

*While he wrote a number of other pieces, it would seem from the
perspective of three centuries that Scougal's life finds its main signifi-
cance in the production of this one book,* The Life of God in the Soul
of Man. *Written when he was twenty-six, and published a year before
his death, it was originally prepared "for the private use of a noble
friend of the author's, without the least design of making it more
public."*

*Scougal entered King's College, Aberdeen, at the age of fifteen and
became a tutor upon graduation four years later. He was ordained an
Anglican priest in 1672 and after a year in a country pastorate,
returned to King's College as professor of divinity. Tuberculosis overtook
him in 1677 and he died a year later.*

The Life of God in the Soul of Man *proved enormously popular
immediately upon publication. It seemed to strike a happy balance
between Puritan strictness and Anglican tolerance by emphasizing the
inner values of Christian faith, particularly the cultivation of holiness
and loving interpersonal relationships.*

*At Scougal's funeral service the Reverend George Gairden praised
the book for its "clear representation of the life and spirit of true
religion, and its graces, the great excellency and advantages of it, the
proposal of the most effectual means for attaining to it by the grace of
God; the piety and seasonableness of the devotions, together with the
natural and affectionate eloquence of the style" which could not help but
"inspire us and warm our hearts. . . ."*

4

From The Life of God in the Soul of Man *by Henry Scougal*

I cannot speak of religion, but I must lament that among so many pretenders to it, so few understand what it means. Some place it in the understanding of orthodox notions and opinions. All the account they can give of their religion is that they are of this or the other persuasion, and have joined themselves to one of those many sects into which Christendom is most unhappily divided.

Others place it in the outward man, in a constant course of external duties and a model of performances. If they live peaceably with their neighbors, keep a temperate diet, observe the returns of worship, frequenting the church and their closet, and sometimes extend their hands to the relief of the poor, they think they have sufficiently acquitted themselves.

Others again put all religion in the affections, in rapturous heats and ecstatic devotion. All they aim at is to pray with passion, and think of Heaven with pleasure, and to be affected with those kind and melting expressions wherewith they court their Savior, till they persuade themselves that they are mightily in love with him. From this they assume a great confidence of their salvation, which they esteem the chief of Christian graces.

There are too many Christians who would consecrate their vices, and hallow their corrupt affections; whose rugged humor and sullen pride must pass for Christian severity; whose fierce wrath and bitter rage against their enemies must be called holy zeal; whose petulancy toward their superiors, or rebellion against their governors, must have the name of Christian courage and resolution.

But certainly religion is quite another thing. True religion is a union of the soul with God, a real participation of the divine nature, the very image of God drawn upon the soul; or in the Apostle's phrase, it is Christ formed within us.[1] I know not how it can be more fully expressed than by calling it a divine life.

Religion may be defined by the name of life, because it is an inward, free and self-moving principle. Those who have made progress in it are not actuated only by external motives, driven merely by threatenings, nor bribed by promises, nor constrained by laws; but are powerfully inclined to that which is good and delight in the performance of it. The love which a pious man bears to God and goodness is not so much by virtue of a command enjoining him so to do, as by a new nature instructing and prompting him to it.

Nor does he pay his devotions as an unavoidable tribute to appease the divine justice, or quiet his clamorous conscience. Those exercises are the proper emanations of the divine life, the natural employments of the newborn soul. He prays, and gives thanks, and repents, not only because these things are commanded, but rather because he is sensible of his wants, and of the divine goodness, and of the folly and misery of a sinful life.

His charity is not forced, nor are his alms extorted from him. His love makes him willing to give, and though there were no outward obligation, his "heart would devise liberal things."[2] Injustice and intemperance, and all other vices, are as contrary to his temper and constitution as the basest actions are to the most generous spirit, and impudence and scurrility to those who are naturally modest.

By this time I hope it appears that religion is, with a great deal of reason, termed a life, or vital principle; and that it is very necessary to distinguish between it and that obedience which is constrained and depends on external causes. It may be called a divine life, not only in regard to its fountain and original, having God for its author, and being wrought in the souls of men by the power of his Holy Spirit; but also in regard to its nature, being a resemblance of the divine perfections, the image of the Almighty shining in the soul of man. It is a real participation of his nature, a beam of the eternal light, a drop of that infinite ocean of goodness. They who are endued with it may be said to have God dwelling in their souls and Christ formed within them.

That life which is hid with Christ in God[3] has no glorious show or appearance in the world, and to the natural man will seem a mean and insipid notion. The root of the divine life is faith. The chief branches are, love to God, love to man, purity and humility. These names may be common and vulgar, and make no extraordinary sound. Yet they do carry such a mighty sense, that the tongue of man or angel can pronounce nothing more weighty or excellent.

Faith has the same place in the divine life that sense has in the natural, being indeed nothing else but a kind of feeling persuasion of spiritual things. It extends itself to all divine truths; but in our lapsed estate, it has a peculiar relation to the declarations of God's mercy and reconcilableness to sinners through a Mediator. Therefore, receiving its denomination from that principal object, it is ordinarily termed faith in Jesus Christ.

The love of God is a delightful and affectionate sense of the divine perfections, which makes the soul resign and sacrifice itself wholly unto him, desiring above all things to please him, and delighting in nothing so much as in fellowship and communion with him, and being ready to do or suffer anything for his sake or at his pleasure.

A soul thus possessed with divine love must needs be enlarged toward all mankind in a sincere and unbounded affection, because of the relation they have to God, being his creatures, and having something of his image stamped upon them. This is that love I named as the second branch of religion, and under which all the parts of justice, all the duties we owe to our neighbor, are eminently comprehended. For he who does truly love all the world will be nearly concerned in the interest of everyone, and so far from wronging or injuring any person, he will resent any evil that befalls others as if it happened to himself.

By purity I understand a due abstractedness from the body, and mastery over the inferior appetites. It is such a temper and disposition of mind as makes a man despise and abstain from all pleasures and delights of sense or fancy which are sinful in themselves or tend to extinguish or lesson our relish of more divine and intellectual pleasures. It also infers a resoluteness to undergo all those hardships he may meet with in the performance of his duty. So that not only chastity and temperance, but also Christian courage and magnanimity may come under this head.

Humility imports a deep sense of our own weakness with a hearty and affectionate acknowledgement of our owing all that we are to the divine bounty. It is always accompanied by a profound submission to the will of God, and great deadness toward the glory of the world and applause of men.

These are the highest perfections that either men or angels are capable of. They are the very foundation of Heaven laid in the soul. He who has attained them needs not to desire to pry into the hidden rolls of

God's decrees, or search the volumes of Heaven, to know what is determined about his everlasting condition. His love to God may give him assurance of God's favor to him.

And now, my dear friend, having discovered the nature of true religion, let us descend into a nearer and more particular view. Let us consider that love and affection wherewith holy souls are united to God, that we may see what excellency is involved in it. Love is that powerful and prevalent passion by which all the faculties and inclinations of the soul are determined, and on which both its perfection and happiness depend.

The worth and excellency of a soul is to be measured by the object of its love. He who loves mean and sordid things thereby becomes base and vile; but a noble and well-placed affection advances and improves the spirit into a conformity with what it loves. Thus we see how easily lovers or friends slide into the imitation of the persons they affect, and how, even before they are aware, they begin to resemble them, not only in their deportment, but also in their voice and gesture, their mien and air. In the same way we transcribe the virtues and inward beauties of the soul, if they were the object and motive of our love.

Love is the greatest and most excellent thing we are masters of. Therefore it is folly and baseness to bestow it unworthily. It is indeed the only thing we can call our own. Other things may be taken from us by violence, but none can ravish our love. Certainly love is the worthiest present we can offer unto God. Nothing can be more clear than that the happiness of love depends on the return it meets with. Here the divine lover has unspeakably the advantage. He has placed his affection on him whose nature is love, whose goodness is as infinite as his being.

God's mercy went before us when we were his enemies; therefore he cannot choose to but embrace us when we are become his friends. It is utterly impossible that God should deny his love to a soul wholly devoted to him, and which desires nothing so much as to serve and please him. He cannot disdain his own image, nor the heart in which it is engraven. Love is all the tribute which we can pay him, and it is the sacrifice which he will not despise.

Something which disturbs the pleasure of love, and renders it a miserable and unquiet passion, is absence and separation from those we love. It is sad to be deprived of that society which is so delightful. Our life becomes tedious, being spent in an impatient expectation of the happy hour in which we may meet again.

But O, how happy are those who have placed their love on him who can never be absent from them! They need but open their eyes, and they shall everywhere behold the traces of his presence and glory, and converse with him whom their soul loves. And this makes the darkest prison, or the wildest desert, not only supportable, but delightful to them.

If God were the object of our love, we should share in an infinite happiness, without any mixture or possibility of diminution. Behold, on what sure foundations his happiness is built, whose soul is possessed with divine love; whose will is transformed into the will of God, and whose greatest desire is that his Maker should be pleased. O the peace, the rest, the satisfaction that attends such a temper of mind!

The exercises of religion, which to others are insipid and tedious, yield the highest pleasure and delight to souls possessed with divine love. They rejoice when they are called to "go up to the house of the Lord," that they may "see his power and his glory, as they have formerly seen it in his sanctuary."[4] They never think themselves so happy as when, having retired from the world, and become free from the noise and hurry of affairs, and silenced all their clamorous passions (those troublesome guests within), they have placed themselves in the presence of God, and entertain fellowship and communion with him.

They delight to adore his perfections, and recount his favors, and to protest their affection to him, and tell him a thousand times that they love him; to lay out their troubles or wants before him, and disburden their hearts in his bosom. Repentance itself is a delightful exercise, when it flows from the principle of love. There is a secret sweetness which accompanies those tears of remorse, those meltings and relentings of a soul returning to God and lamenting its former unkindness.

The severities of a holy life, and that constant watch which we are obliged to keep over our hearts and ways, are very troublesome to those who are overruled and acted upon by an external law, and have no law in their minds inclining them to the performance of duty. But where divine love possessed the soul, it stands as sentinel to keep out everything that may offend the beloved, and disdainfully repulses those temptations which assault it. It complies cheerfully, not only with explicit commands, but with the most secret notices of the beloved's pleasure. It is ingenious in discovering what will be most grateful and acceptable to him. It makes mortification and self-denial change their harsh and dreadful names, and become easy, sweet and delightful things.

The next branch of the divine life is a universal charity and love. The excellency of this grace will be easily acknowledged. For what can be more noble and generous than a heart enlarged to embrace the whole world, whose wishes and designs are leveled at the good and welfare of the universe, which considers every man's interest as its own?

He who loves his neighbor as himself can never entertain any base or injurious thought, or be wanting in expressions of bounty. He had rather suffer a thousand wrongs than be guilty of one; and never counts himself happy but when someone or other has been benefited by him. The malice or ingratitude of man is not able to resist his love. He overlooks their injuries and pities their folly, and overcomes their evil with good. He never designs any other revenge against his most bitter and malicious enemies than to put all the obligations he can upon them, whether they will or not.

Is it any wonder that such a person be reverenced and admired, and accounted the darling of mankind? This inward goodness and benignity of spirit reflects a certain sweetness and serenity upon the very countenance, and makes it amiable and lovely. It inspires the soul with a noble resolution and courage, and makes it capable of enterprising and effecting the highest things. Those heroic actions which we are wont to read with admiration have been for the most part the effects of the love of one's country, or of particular friendships; and certainly a more extensive and universal affection must be much more powerful and efficacious.

Again, as love flows from a noble and excellent temper, so it is accompanied with the greatest satisfaction and pleasure. It delights the soul to feel itself thus enlarged, and to be delivered from those disquieting as well as deformed passions: malice, hatred and envy; and become gentle, sweet and benign. Had I my choice of all things that might tend to my present felicity, I would pitch upon this, to have my heart possessed with the greatest kindness and affection toward all men in the world.

I am sure this would make me partake in all the happiness of others, their inward endowments and outward prosperity; everything that did benefit and advantage them would afford me comfort and pleasure. And though I should frequently meet with occasions of grief and compassion, yet there is a sweetness in commiseration, which makes it infinitely more desirable than a stupid insensibility; and the consideration of that infinite goodness and wisdom which governs the world might repress any excessive trouble for particular calamities that happen in it; and the hopes or possibility of men's after-happiness might moderate their sorrow for their present misfortunes.

Certainly next to the love and enjoyment of God, that ardent love and affection wherewith blessed souls do embrace one another is justly to be reckoned as the greatest felicity of those regions above; and did it universally prevail in the world, it would anticipate that blessedness and make us taste of the joys of Heaven upon earth.

Any person engaged in a violent and passionate affection will easily forget his ordinary gratifications. He will be little curious about his diet, or his bodily ease, or the divertissements he was wont to delight in. No wonder, then, if souls overpowered with divine love despise inferior pleasures, and be almost ready to grudge the body its necessary attendance for the common accommodations of life, judging all these impertinent to their main happiness and those higher enjoyments they are pursuing. As for the hardships they meet with, they rejoice in them as opportunities to exercise and testify their affection. Since they are able to do so little for God, they are glad of the honor to suffer for him.

Purity, which I named as a third branch of religion, is accompanied with a great deal of pleasure. Whatsoever defiles the soul disturbs it too. All impure delights have a sting in them, and leave smart and trouble behind them. There is no slavery so base as that whereby a man becomes a drudge to his own lusts; nor is any victory so glorious as that which is obtained over them.

The last branch of religion is humility. However abject and base this quality may appear to vulgar and carnal eyes, yet really the soul of man is not capable of a higher and more noble endowment. It is a silly ignorance that begets pride. Humility rises from a nearer acquaintance with excellent things, which keeps men from doting on trifles, or admiring themselves because of some petty attainments.

Noble and well-educated souls have no such high opinion of riches, beauty, strength and other such like advantages, as to value them for themselves, or despise those that lack them. As for inward worth and real goodness, the sense they have of the divine perfections makes them think very meanly of anything they have hitherto attained, and be still endeavoring to surmount themselves, and make nearer approaches to those infinite excellencies which they admire.

I know not what thoughts people may have of humility, but I see almost every person pretending to it, and shunning such expressions and actions as may make them be accounted arrogant and presumptuous, so that those who are most desirous of praise will be loth to commend themselves. What are all those compliments and modes of civility so frequent in our ordinary conversation, but so many protestations of the esteem of others, and the low thoughts we have of ourselves? Must not that humility be a noble and excellent endowment, when the very shadows of it are accounted so necessary a part of good breeding?

Again, this grace is accompanied with a great deal of happiness and tranquility. The proud and arrogant person is a trouble to all who converse with him, but most of all to himself. Everything is enough to vex him, but scarcely anything is sufficient to content and please him.

He is ready to quarrel with everything that falls out, as if he himself were such a considerable person that God Almighty should do everything to gratify him, and all the creatures of Heaven and earth should wait upon him and obey his will.

The leaves of high trees shake with every blast of wind, and every breath, every evil word will disquiet and torment an arrogant man; but the humble person has the advantage when he is despised, that none can think more meanly of him than he does of himself. Therefore he is not troubled at the matter, but can easily bear those reproaches which wound the other to the soul.

As he is less affected with injuries, so he is less obnoxious to them. "Contention, which cometh of pride,"[5] betrays a man into a thousand inconveniences, which those of a meek and lowly temper seldom meet with. True and genuine humility begets both a veneration and love among all wise and discerning persons, while pride defeats its own design, and deprives a man of that honor it makes him pretend to.

But as the chief exercises of humility are those which relate to Almighty God, so these are accompanied with the greatest satisfaction and sweetness. It is impossible to express the great pleasure and delight which religious persons feel in the lowest prostration of their souls before God, when, having a deep sense of the divine majesty and glory, they sink (if I may so speak) to the bottom of their beings, and vanish and disappear in the presence of God, by a serious and affectionate acknowledgement of their own nothingness, and the shortness and imperfections of their attainments. Then they understand the full sense and emphasis of the Psalmist's exclamation, "Lord, what is Man!"[6] and can utter it with the same affection.

Never did any haughty and ambitious person receive the praises and applause of men with so much pleasure as the humble and religious do renounce them: "Not unto us, O Lord, not unto us, but unto thy name, give glory."[7]

It is true, religion in the souls of men is the immediate work of God, and all our natural endeavors can neither produce it alone, nor merit those supernatural aids by which it must be wrought. The Holy Spirit must come upon us, and the power of the Highest must overshadow us, before that holy thing can be begotten, and Christ be formed in us.

But yet we must not expect that this whole work should be done without any concurring endeavors of our own. We must not lie loitering in the ditch, and wait until Omnipotence pulls us out. No, no, we must bestir ourselves, and actuate those powers which we have already received. We must put forth ourselves to our utmost capacities, and then we may hope that "our labor shall not be in vain in the Lord."[8]

Nothing is more powerful to engage our affection than to find that we are beloved. Expressions of kindness are always pleasing and acceptable to us, though the person should be otherwise mean and contemptible. But to have the love of one who is altogether lovely, to know that the glorious Majesty of Heaven has any regard to us—how it must astonish and delight us! How it must overcome our spirits, and melt our hearts, and put our whole soul into a flame!

The Word of God is full of the expressions of his love toward man, and all his works do loudly proclaim it. He gave us our being, and by preserving us in it, he renews the donation every moment. He has placed us in a rich and well-furnished world, and has liberally provided for all our necessities. He rains down blessings from Heaven upon us, and causes the earth to bring forth our provision. He gives us our food and raiment, and while we are spending the productions of one year, he is preparing for us against another.

He sweetens our lives with innumerable comforts, and gratifies every faculty with suitable objects. The eye of his Providence is always upon us, and he watches for our safety when we are fast asleep, neither minding him nor ourselves.

But lest we should think these testimonies of his kindness less considerable, because they are the easy issues of his omnipotent power, and do not put him to any trouble or pain, he has taken a more wonderful method to endear himself to us. He has testified his affection to us by suffering as well as by doing; and because he could not suffer in his own nature, he assumed ours.

The eternal Son of God did clothe himself with the infirmities of our flesh, and left the company of those innocent and blessed spirits, who knew well how to love and adore him, that he might dwell among men, and wrestle with the obstinacy of that rebellious race, to reduce them to their allegiance and fidelity, and then to offer himself up as a sacrifice and propitiation for them.

I remember one of the poets has an ingenious fancy to express the passion by which he found himself overcome after a long resistance: "That the god of love had shot all his golden arrows at him, but could never pierce his heart, till at length he put himself into the bow, and darted himself straight into his breast." In some way this adumbrates God's method of dealing with men. He had long contended with a stubborn world, and thrown down many a blessing upon them. Then when all his other gifts could not prevail, he at last made a gift of himself, to testify his affection and engage theirs.

The account we have of our Savior's life in the Gospel presents us all along with the story of his life: all the pains that he took, and the troubles that he endured, were the wonderful effects and the uncontrollable evidences of it. But O, that last dismal scene! Is it possible to remember it and question his kindness, or deny him ours? Here it is that we should fix our most serious and solemn thoughts, that Christ may dwell in our hearts by faith, and that we, being rooted and grounded in love, may be able to comprehend with all saints what is the breadth, and length, and depth, and height, and to know the love of Christ which passes knowledge, that we may be filled with all the fullness of God.[9]

We ought frequently to reflect on those particular tokens of favor and love which God has bestowed on ourselves—how long he has borne with our follies and sins, and waited to be gracious unto us, wrestling as it were the stubbornness of our hearts, and essaying every method to reclaim us. We should keep a register in our minds of all the eminent blessings and deliverances we have met with. Some have been so conveyed that we might clearly perceive they were not the issues of chance, but the gracious effects of the divine favor and the signal returns of our prayers.

Nor ought we to embitter the thoughts of these things with any harsh or unworthy suspicion, as if they were designed on purpose to enhance our guilt, and heighten our eternal damnation. No, no, my friend, God is love, and he has no pleasure in the ruin of his creatures. If they abuse his goodness, and turn his grace into wantonness, and thereby plunge themselves into greater depths of guilt and misery, this is the effect of their obstinate wickedness, and not the design of those benefits which he bestows.

We shall find our hearts enlarged in charity toward men by considering the relation wherein they stand to God, and the impresses of his image which are stamped upon them. They are not only his creatures, the workmanship of his hands, but such of whom he takes special care, and for whom he has a very dear and tender regard. He laid the design of their happiness before the foundations of the world, and was willing to live and converse with them to all the ages of eternity.

The meanest and most contemptible person we behold is the offspring of Heaven, one of the children of the Most High. However unworthy he might behave himself in that relation, so long as God has not abdicated and disowned him by a final sentence, he will have us to acknowledge him as one of his, and as such to embrace him with a sincere and cordial affection.

You know what a great concern we are wont to have for those that do in any wise belong to the person whom we love; how gladly we lay hold on every opportunity to gratify the child or servant of a friend; and sure our love toward God would as naturally spring forth in love toward men, did we mind the interest that he is pleased to take in them, and consider that every soul is dearer to him than all the material world; and that he did not account the blood of his Son too great a price for their redemption.

As all men stand in a near relation to God, so they have still so much of his image stamped upon them, as may oblige and excite us to love them. In some this image is more eminent and conspicuous, and we can discern the lovely traces of wisdom and goodness. Though in others it is miserably sullied and defaced, yet it is not altogether erased. Some lineaments at least do still remain.

All men are endued with rational and immortal souls, with understandings and will capable of the highest and most excellent things. If they be at present disordered and put out of tune by wickedness and folly, this may indeed move our compassion, but ought not in reason to extinguish our love.

When we see a person in a rugged humor and perverse disposition, full of malice and dissimulation, very foolish and very proud, it is hard to fall in love with an object that presents itself to us under an idea so little graceful and lovely. But when we shall consider these evil qualities as the diseases and distempers of a soul, which is itself capable of all that wisdom and goodness with which the best of saints have ever been adorned, and which may one day come to be raised to such heights of perfection as shall render it a fit companion for the holy angels, this will turn our aversion into pity.

It will make us behold him with such resentments as we should have when we look upon a beautiful body that was mangled with wounds, or disfigured by some disease. However we hate the vices, we shall not cease to love the man.

Notes

1. Galatians 4:19.
2. Cf. Isaiah 32:8.
3. Colossians 3:3.
4. Psalm 63:2.
5. Proverbs 13:10.
6. Cf. Psalm 8:4.
7. Psalm 115:1.
8. 1 Corinthians 15:58.
9. Ephesians 3:17-19.

Selection from *The Life of God in the Soul of Man* taken from *The Works of the Rev. Henry Scougal, Together with His Funeral Sermon by the Rev. Dr. Gairden; and an Account of His Life and Writings*, published 1846 by Robert Carter, New York. The passages are from pages 14-23, 30-43, 48-49, 65-69.

François de Salignac de la Mothe Fénélon (1661–1715) was a French Roman Catholic archbishop whose writings have blessed millions of Christians throughout the world. After all these years his popularity remains undiminished. His deep spirituality, his love for the Lord, his common sense, his high moral qualities, his gracious and generous nature shine through his works. We find ourselves wishing that we, too, might have been guests at his table and heard his wise discourses.

But Fénélon also had a facility for making enemies. He sowed hostility among the Huguenots, whom he was sent to try to convert; among the Jansenists, whom he persecuted; among the church leaders in the court of King Louis XIV, who were responsible for having the pope condemn Fénélon's writings and for having the court banish him from Paris. Thus, after a rapid rise in the priesthood to the archbishopric of Cambrai, and after becoming internationally known through his brilliant religious writings, Fénélon was permanently exiled to his own diocese where he lived the remaining eighteen years of his life. The pope wept at news of Fénélon's death because he had not made him a cardinal.

Part of Fénélon's problem stemmed from his sympathy for and championing of the views of Madame Guyon, some of whose writing appears in Chapter Twelve of this volume. Our purpose here is not to discuss the strengths and weaknesses of "Quietism," as the views of Fénélon and Madame Guyon were labeled, or to defend the various actions of the archbishop, or to decide what kind of person he was. Fénélon obviously was not an evangelical; yet evangelicals and other Christians have received inspiration and positive help from the Letters of Spiritual Counsel *he wrote to various friends. You will probably see for yourself just why Fénélon is so admired, both for himself and his writings.*

5

From Letters of Spiritual Counsel by *François de la Mothe Fénélon*

Humility

All the saints are convinced that sincere humility is the foundation of all virtues. This is because humility is the daughter of pure love, and humility is nothing else but truth. There are only two truths in the world, that God is all, and the creature nothing. In order that humility be true, we need to give continual homage to God in our lowliness, and to stay in our place, which is to love being nothing.

Jesus Christ said that we must be meek and humble of heart.[1] Meekness is the daughter of humility, as anger is the daughter of pride. Only Jesus Christ can give that true humility of heart which comes from him. It is born of the unction of his grace. It does not consist, as one imagines, in performing exterior acts of humility, although that is good, but in keeping one's place.

He who has a high opinion of himself is not truly humble. He who wants something for himself is no more so. But he who so completely forgets himself that he never thinks of self; who has no turning back on himself; who within is only lowliness; not wounded by anything; without affecting patience on the outside; who speaks of himself as he would speak of someone else; who does not affect forgetting self when he is all full of it; who gives himself up to love without noticing whether it is humility or pride to act in that way; who is quite content to pass as being not humble at all; finally he who is full of love, is really humble.

He who does not seek his own interest, but the interest of God alone in time and for eternity, is humble. The more we love purely, the more perfect is our humility. Then let us not measure humility by the fabricated exterior. Let us not make it depend on one action or another, but on pure love. Pure love divests man of himself. It reclothes him with Jesus Chri˙t. That is in what true humility consists. It makes us live no longer for ourselves but lets Jesus Christ live in us.

We are always trying to be something. Often we are conspicuous in devotion. Why? Because we want to be distinguished in every condition. But he who is humble seeks nothing. It is the same to him to be praised or scorned, because he assumes nothing for himself and does not care how he is treated. Wherever he is placed, he stays. It does not even occur to him that he should be somewhere else.

There are plenty of people who practice sincere humility, but who are very far from that humility of heart of which I have just spoken. Outer humility, which does not have its source in pure love, is a false humility. The more we think we are lowering ourselves, the more we are persuaded of our elevation. He who is conscious of lowering himself is not yet in his place, which is beneath all lowering. People who think they are lowering themselves have a good deal of conceit. Also, at bottom, that kind of humility is often a subtle seeking of conceit.

That kind of humility will not enter into Heaven unless it is reduced to pure love, source of true humility, alone worthy of God, which he takes pleasure in filling with himself. Those who are full of it can neither humble themselves nor lower themselves before anyone. They find themselves beneath all abasement. If they wanted to lower themselves, they would have to raise themselves first, and in that way leave the state which is proper to them.

Also they are so persuaded that to "humiliate" themselves, they must place themselves higher than they are, and leave their own place, that they think they could never do it. They do not feel at all humiliated by the scorn and condemnation of men. They only stay in their place. They do not even take any part in the applause which could be given them. They deserve nothing. They expect nothing. They take part in nothing. They understand that it is only the Word of God who, in becoming incarnate, was lowered beneath what he was. That is why Scripture says that he became nothing, which it does not say of any creature.

Many misunderstand themselves at this point, keeping up their humility by their own will; and failing in the resignation and the perfect renunciation of themselves, they offend divine love. They believe themselves to favor a humility which nevertheless is not humility, if it is not compatible with love.

If we had the light to discern it, we should see clearly that when we think we are humbling ourselves we are exalting ourselves; when we think we are annihilating ourselves we are seeking our own life; and then finally we enjoy and possess the glory of humility as a comtemptible virtue in the acts of humility which we practice.

The truly humble does nothing, and objects to nothing. He lets himself be conducted and led where anyone wishes. He believes that God can do everything in him; thus that he can make everything of chaff, and that there is more humility in doing these things and in giving ourselves to them than in opposing, under the pretense of humility, the designs of God.

He who prefers abuse to exaltation is not yet truly humble, although he has a taste for humility. He who lets himself be placed and led where anyone wishes, high or low; who does not feel any difference; who does not notice if he is being praised or blamed, nor if what is being said to him is to his advantage or disadvantage, is truly humble, although he may not appear so to the eyes of men who do not judge true virtue by what it is in itself, but entirely by what people think of it.

The truly humble is perfectly obedient because he has renounced his own will. He lets himself be led to where he is wanted in one way or another. He yields to everything and resists nothing, because he would not be humble if he had a choice and a will or an argument over what was ordered for him. He has no leaning for any one thing, but he lets himself be bent from whatever side anyone pleases. He wants nothing, asks nothing, not from the habit of not asking anything, but because he is in such profound self-forgetfulness and is so completely separated from self, that he does not know what is most suitable for himself.

The truly humble is one of those children of whom Jesus Christ has said that the Kingdom of Heaven belongs to them. A child does not know what he needs. He can do nothing. He thinks of nothing, but he lets himself be led. Let us abandon ourselves then with courage. If God makes nothing of us, he will give us justice, because we are good for nothing; and if he makes great things, the glory will be his. We shall say with Mary that he has done great things in us, because he has regarded our low estate.[2]

Self-renunciation

If you really wish to understand what it means to renounce self, you have only to remember the difficulty which you felt within you and which you should quite naturally feel, when I said never to consider at all this "ego" which is so dear to us. Self-renunciation is to count oneself as nothing. Whoever feels the difficulty of doing this has already understood what the renunciation which revolts his whole nature consists of. Since you have felt this blow, it has shown the tender spot in your heart. Now it is up to you to allow the all-powerful hand of God to operate. He will know how to take you away from yourself.

The source of our trouble is that we love ourselves with a blind love which reaches the point of idolatry. All that we love outside we love for self alone. We must free ourselves from all these generous friendships, in which we seem to forget ourselves so that we think only of the interests of the people to whom we are attached. It is capable of poisoning us by the better nourishing of our self-love in us.

We seek in the world the glory of unselfishness and generosity. We seek to be loved by our friends although we do not seek to use them. We hope that they will be charmed by everything that we do for them without reversion to self, and thus we find again the reversion to self which we seem to have left. For what is sweeter and more flattering to a sensitive and delicate self-love than seeing itself praised as though it were not self-love?

We see a person who seemed to be all for others and not at all for himself, who is the delight of sincere people, a person who seems self-disciplined, self-forgetting. The self-oblivion is so great that self-love even tries to imitate it, and to find no glory equal to that of not appearing to seek any. This moderation and self-detachment, which would be the death of our nature if it were real, becomes on the contrary a more subtle and imperceptible food for a pride which scorns every ordinary means of exalting itself, and which wants to trample beneath its feet all the cruder kinds of vanity which puff up the rest of mankind.

But it is easy to unmask this modest pride which does not appear to be pride in any manner. If it is criticized, it is impatient of criticism. If the people whom it loves and helps do not repay it in friendship, respect and confidence, it is hurt to the quick. You see, it is not disinterested, although it forces itself to appear to be. It does not need dull praises, nor money, nor success in receiving place and honor. It does however want to be repaid. It is hungry for the esteem of good people. It wants to love so that it will be loved, and so that others will be impressed by its unselfishness. It only seems to forget itself in order to make itself more interesting to everyone.

Not that it would think all this through in a logical manner. It does not say, "I want to fool the world by my unselfishness, so that everyone will love me and admire me." No, it would not dare say such crude and unworthy things to itself. But it fools itself in fooling others. It admires complacently its own disinterestedness, like a lovely woman before her own glass. It is impressed with itself, seeing itself more sincere and more disinterested than other people. The illusion which it spreads for others comes back on itself. It only gives itself to others for what it believes itself to be, that is, for the sake of being unselfish. That is what flatters it the most.

However little we revert to ourselves to consider something which saddens or flatters us, we will easily recognize that pride has different tastes, according to whether it is cruder or more sensitive. But pride, whatever good taste you give it, is always pride, and that which appears the most reasonable is the most diabolic. For in valuing itself it suspects others. It pities the people who repay themselves with foolish vanities. It recognizes the emptiness of grandeur of the highest type. It cannot endure people who become intoxicated with their good fortune. It wishes by its moderation to be even above success, and thus to reach a new height, and leave at its feet all the false glory of humankind. It wants, like Lucifer, to become like the All-Highest.[3] It wants to be a kind of divinity above the passions and interests of men. It does not see that it is by this deceitful pride which blinds us that it places itself above other men.

Let us come to the conclusion that it is only the love of God which can make us get out of ourselves. If the powerful hand of God did not sustain us, we should not know where to get a foothold to take a step outside of ourselves. There is no middle way. We must refer everything to God or to ourselves. If we refer everything to ourselves, we have no other God except this "ego." If on the contrary we refer everything to God, we are in his order. Then, not regarding ourselves more than his other creatures, without self-interest and with the one object of accomplishing the will of God, we shall commence that self-renunciation which you hope to know well.

Involuntary Selfishness

But when we are really free of self, you say, can we involuntarily have our eyes on self-interest? To that I answer that it is rarely that a soul truly free of self, and devoted to God, still seeks its own interest purposely. But in order to feel relieved, and to stop being continually tormented, we must know once for all that involuntary reversions to selfishness do not make us displeasing to God, any more than do the other temptations to which we have given no consent.

A Friendship in God

There is a veil of mercy behind which God hides from us what we should not be able to bear. We have a certain amount of impatient eagerness for our own perfection. We should like to see everything and sacrifice everything at once. But a humble waiting under the hand of God, and a quiet bearing ourselves in this state of darkness and dependence, are infinitely more useful to help us die to ourselves than all our restless efforts to advance our own perfection.

Let us then be content to follow, without looking ahead, all the light which is given us from one moment to another. This is the daily bread. God only gives it for each day. It is still the manna. He who tries to take a double amount, and to make provision for the next day, makes a great mistake. It will spoil in his hands. He cannot keep any more of it than the person who has only taken enough for one day.

It is this dependence of a child toward his father to which God wishes to bend us, even in spiritual things. He gives us light within, as a wise mother would give her young girl work to do. She would not give her new work until the first is finished. When you have finished all that God has put before you, at that very instant he will give you new work, because he never leaves the soul idle and without growth in detachment.

If on the contrary you have not yet finished the first work, he hides what is to follow. A traveler who is marching across a vast plain sees nothing ahead of him but a slight rise which ends the distant horizon. When he tops this rise, he finds a new stretch of country as vast as the first. Thus in the way of self-renunciation we think we see everything at once. We think that we are holding nothing back, and that we are not clinging to ourselves or to anything else. We should rather die than hesitate to make a complete sacrifice. But in the daily round God constantly shows us new countries. We find in our hearts a thousand things which we would have sworn were not there. God only shows them to us as he makes them appear.

I am not speaking now of those whose hearts are gangrenous with enormous vices. I am speaking of the souls which seem honest and pure. We should see a foolish vanity which does not dare to come out in the open. We should see self-complacencies, heights of pride, subtle selfishness, and a thousand windings within, which are as real as they are inexplicable. We only see them as God begins to make them emerge.

Stop, he will say to you, see what corruption there was in the deep abyss of your soul! Then let God act, and let us be content to be faithful to the light of the present moment. It carries with it all that we need to prepare us for the light of the moment to follow. And this sequence of blessings, which connects one with another like the links of a chain, prepares us unconsciously for the further sacrifices which we have not even glimpsed.

This death to ourselves, and to all that we love, when we have pierced the surface of it, will penetrate to the center. It will leave nothing to the creature. It will push out, relentlessly, all that is not good.

Otherwise, be persuaded on the word of others, while waiting for experience to make you taste and feel, that this detachment from self and from all that you love, far from withering good friendships and hardening your heart, produces on the contrary a friendship in God, not only pure and firm, but completely cordial, faithful, affectionate, full of a sweet relationship. And we find there all the fullness of friendship which human nature seeks for its consolation.

Imitation

We must imitate Jesus. This is to live as he lived, to think as he thought, to conform ourselves to his image, which is the seal of our sanctification.

What a difference of behavior! The nothing believes itself something, and the All-Powerful makes himself nothing. I make myself nothing with you, Lord. I make you the entire sacrifice of my pride, of the vanity which possesses me up to the present. Help my good intention. Keep from me the occasions of my falling. "Turn my eyes that I see not vanity," that I see only you, and that I see myself before you. Then I shall know what I am and what you are.

Jesus Christ is born in a stable. He has to flee into Egypt. He passes thirty years of his life in the shop of a craftsman. He suffers hunger, thirst, weariness. He is poor, scorned and abject. He teaches the doctrine of Heaven, and no one listens to him. All the great and the wise pursue him, take him, and make him suffer frightful torments. They treat him like a slave, make him die between two thieves after having preferred a thief to him. That was the life that Jesus Christ chose, and we—we have a horror of every sort of humiliation! The slightest contempt is unbearable to us.

Let us compare our life to that of Jesus Christ. Let us remember that he is all-powerful and we are only weakness. He lowers himself and we raise ourselves. Can we with justice feel contempt for others and dwell on their faults, when we are full of them ourselves? Let us commence to walk on the road which Jesus Christ has marked for us, since it is the only one which can lead us to him.

And how can we find Jesus Christ if we do not seek him in the conditions of his mortal life? The saints find him in Heaven, in the splendor of glory and ineffable joy, but it is after having lived with him on earth in shame, suffering and humiliation. To be Christians is to be imitators of Jesus Christ. In what can we imitate him except in his humiliations?[4] Nothing else can draw us to him. As all-powerful, we ought to adore him; as just, we ought to respect him; as good and merciful, we ought to love him with all our strength; as humble, submissive, lowly and faithful unto death, we ought to imitate him.

Let us not pretend to be able to reach this state by our own strength. Everything in us resists it. But let us console ourselves in the presence of God. Jesus Christ has wanted to feel all our weaknesses. Let us then find all our strength in him who voluntarily became weak to strengthen us. Let us enrich ourselves by his poverty, and let us say with confidence, "I can do all things in him who strengthens me."[5]

Jesus, I want to follow the road you have taken. I want to imitate you; I can only do so by your grace. O Savior, may I learn the lesson which is incomprehensible to the human spirit, which is to die to self by mortification and true humility.

Let us put our hand to the work, and change this so hard and so rebellious heart into the heart of Jesus Christ. May he inspire our own hearts. O Jesus, who suffered so much shame for love of me, print respect and love for you deeply within my heart, and make me desire their practice.

Abandonment

Salvation does not depend only on the doing of no evil; to it must be added the doing of good. The Kingdom of Heaven is too great a prize to be given to a slavish fear which only refrains from sin because it does not dare commit any. God wants children who love his goodness, and not slaves who only serve him for fear of his power. So we must love him and do all which inspires true love.

Plenty of well-intentioned people are mistaken about this. Their mistake comes from not knowing either God or themselves. They are jealous of their liberty and fear to lose it by yielding too much to piety. But they ought to realize that they do not belong to themselves. They belong to God who, having made them for himself alone, and not for themselves, ought to lead them as he pleases with an absolute authority. They ought to belong entirely to him without condition and without reservation.

Properly speaking, we have not even the right to give ourselves to God, because we have not any right over ourselves. But if we did not yield ourselves to God as a thing which is of its nature wholly his, we should commit a sacrilegious theft, which would reverse the order of nature and violate the essential law of the creature.

So it is not for us to reason about the law which God imposes on us. It is for us to receive it, adore it, follow it. God knows better than we do what is right for us. If we were making the Gospel, perhaps we should be tempted to water it down to accommodate our own weakness. But God did not consult us when he made it. He gave it to us ready-made, and leaves us no hope of salvation except by fulfilling this supreme law which is the same under all conditions.

"Heaven and earth will pass away, but my words will not pass away." We cannot deduct one word or the least letter. "Woe to the blind man who leads another blind man," as the Son of God said. "Both will fall over the precipice."[6]

Then let the pride of man be stilled. He thinks he is free, and he is not. It is for him to carry the yoke of the law and to hope that God will give him strength in proportion to this yoke. Indeed, he who has this supreme power of command over his creature gives him by his grace within, the will to do what he commands.

Joy

Those who are God's are always glad, when they are not divided, because they only want what God wants, and want to do for him all that he wishes. Peace of conscience, liberty of heart, the sweetness of abandoning ourselves in the hands of God, the joy of seeing the light grow in our hearts, finally freedom from the fears and insatiable desires of the times, multiply a hundredfold the happiness which the true children of God possess in the midst of their crosses, if they are faithful.

What God asks of us is a will which is no longer divided between him and any creature. It is a will pliant in his hands, which neither seeks nor rejects anything, which wants without reserve whatever he wants, and which never wants under any pretext anything which he does not want. When we are in this disposition all is well, and the most idle amusements turn to good works.

Happy the man who gives himself to God! He is delivered from his passions, from the judgments of men, from their malice, from the tyranny of their sayings, from their cold and wretched mocking, from the misfortunes which the world distributes to wealth, from the unfaithfulness and inconstancy of friends, from the wiles and snares of enemies, from our own weakness, from the misery and brevity of life, from the cruel remorse attached to wicked pleasures, and in the end from the eternal condemnation of God.

He is delivered from this mass of evils because, placing his will entirely in the hands of God, he wants only what God wants, and thus he finds his consolation in faith, and hope in the midst of all his sufferings. What weakness it would be then to fear to give ourselves to God, and to undertake so desirable a state.

Happy are they who throw themselves with bowed head and closed eyes into the arms of the Father of mercies and the God of all consolation, as St. Paul said.[7] Then we desire nothing so much as to know what we owe to God, and fear nothing more than not to see enough what he is asking for.

As soon as we discover a new insight into our faith, we are transported with joy. What folly to fear to be entirely God's! It is to fear to be too happy. It is to fear to love God's will in all things. It is to fear to have too much courage in the crosses which are inevitable, too much comfort in God's love, and too much detachment from the passions which make us miserable.

Jesus Christ said to all Christians without exception, "Let him who would be my disciple carry his cross and follow me."[8] The broad way leads to perdition. We must follow the narrow way which few enter. Only those who destroy themselves deserve the Kingdom of Heaven. We must be born again, renounce ourselves, become a child, be poor in spirit, and not be of the world, which is cursed because of its scandals.

These truths frighten many people, because they only know what religion exacts without knowing what it offers, and they ignore the spirit of love which makes everything easy. They do not know that it leads to the highest perfection by a feeling of peace and love which sweetens all the struggle.

How dangerous it is for our salvation, how unworthy of God and of ourselves, how pernicious even for the peace of our hearts, to want always to stay where we are! Our whole life was given us to advance by great strides toward our heavenly country. The world escapes like a delusive shadow. Eternity already advances to receive us. Why do we delay while the light of the Father of mercies shines for us?

There is only one way to love God; that is not to take one step without him, and to follow with a brave heart wherever he leads. All those who live in denial, and yet would like very much to keep a little in with the world, run great risk of being among the lukewarm who, they say, will be "vomited up."[9]

God has little patience with those weak souls who say to themselves, "I shall go this far and no farther." Is it up to the creature to make the law for his Creator? What would a king say of a subject who only served him in his own way, who feared to care too much for his interests, and who was embarrassed in public because of belonging to him? Still more what will the King of kings say if we act like these cowardly servants?

We must learn not only God's will in general but also what his will is in each thing. We are only truly reasonable insofar as we consult God's will, to make ours conform to it. This is the true light which we should follow. Every other light is illusory and false.

God is so good that he only awaits our desire to overwhelm us with this gift which is himself. He says in the Scriptures, the cry will not yet be formed in your mouth when I, who see it before it is born in your heart, will grant it before it is made.[10] When we see during prayer that our minds wander, we have only to bring them back quietly, without ever being discouraged by the annoyance of these so stubborn distractions. While they are involuntary they can do no harm. On the contrary they will help us more than a prayer accompanied by ardent feeling, because they humiliate us, mortify us and accustom us to seek God purely for himself without the mingling of any pleasure.

Besides these prayers for which we ought to reserve special times (because our occupations, however necessary they are, never go to the point of not allowing us time to eat our daily bread), we must accustom ourselves to short, simple and frequent liftings of the heart to God. A word of a psalm, or of the Gospel, or of Scripture, which is apt to touch us, suffices for this. In this way we can lift our hearts in the midst of people who are with us, without anyone noticing it. They usually do more good than prayers following a certain subject.

It is good, for instance, to make a resolution to make brief prayers in the morning as well as in the afternoon, to think of God every time we see certain things or certain people, to anticipate our actions, and to go over them. This is the true way to act in the presence of God, and to become familiar with it.

For it is in seeing God that we see the nothingness of the world, which will vanish in a little while like smoke. All the grandeurs, and their paraphernalia, will flee away like a dream. All height will be brought low, all power will be crushed, every superb head will be bowed beneath the weight of the eternal majesty of God. In the day when he will judge men, he will obliterate with one look all that shines in the present night, as the sun in rising puts out the stars. We shall see only God everywhere, so great he will be. We shall seek in vain; we shall find only him, so shall he fill all things.

"Where have they gone," we shall say, "those things which charmed our hearts? What is left of them? Where were they?" Not even the marks of the place where they have been remain. They have passed like a shadow which the sun dissolves.

The time draws near. It comes. It is here. Let us hasten to be ready for it. Let us love the eternal beauty which does not grow old, and which stops from growing old those who love it only. What has become of the great actors who filled the scene thirty years ago? Without going so far, how many of them have died in the last seven or eight years? Soon we shall follow them. Is this then the world to which we are so devoted? We only pass through it. We are on our way out. It is only a phantom, a passing figure, as St. Paul said.[11]

O world so frail and so mad! Is it you in which we are made to believe? With what boldness do you hope to impose on us a vain and fantastic form which passes and disappears? You are only a dream, and you want us to believe in you. Even in possessing you, we feel that you are nothing real to fill our hearts.

Are you not ashamed to give magnificent names to the showy miseries by which you dazzle those who are attached to you? The moment you offer yourself to us with a smiling face, you cause us a thousand pains. The same moment you are going to disappear, you dare promise to make us happy. Happy only is he who sees his nothingness in the light of Jesus Christ!

But what is terrible is that thousands of people blind themselves, fleeing the light which shows them their nothingness, and which condemns their dark deeds. As they want to live like beasts, they do not want to know any other life than that of beasts, and they degrade themselves to stifle all decency and all remorse.

They mock those who think seriously of eternity. They treat as weakness the religious feeling by which we wish to avoid being ungrateful to God, from whom we receive all. Relations with such men should be avoided, and we should flee them carefully. It is important to break without delay with these people whom we know to be dangerous. The more we are exposed to them, the more we ought to watch over ourselves, redouble our efforts, be faithful in the reading of books of devotion, in prayer and in frequent use of the sacraments, without which we weaken, exposed to every temptation.

Let us accustom ourselves little by little to conquer ourselves, to practice virtue, to turn to God in simple, short prayers, but made with our whole heart. The enjoyment of what we have loved will vanish unnoticed. A new taste for grace will at last possess our hearts. We will be hungry for Jesus Christ, who is to feed us eternally. We shall be like a vessel in full sail with a fair wind. Happy are they who are in this state, or at least who wish to be so.

Mortification

The rule for finding the right balance between mortification and social relationships depends on the inner and outer state of each person. We should not be able to make a general rule for what depends on the particular circumstances of each. We must measure ourselves by our weakness, by our need to guard ourselves, by our inner compunction, by the signs of Providence in exterior things, by the time we have to spend, and by the state of our health.

Let us come to examples. It is not right to stay with a person to whom we could be of no use, when we could be meeting others productively. We should get rid of him, after having done what is proper to treat him honorably. The argument of mortifying self ought not to apply in these cases. We will find enough to mortify ourselves by entertaining contrary to our taste the people whom we cannot get rid of, and by being tied down by all our real duties.

Your eagerness to mortify yourself should never turn you from solitude, nor tear you away from external affairs. You must show yourself and hide yourself in turn, and speak and be still. God has not placed you under a bushel, but on a candlestick, so that you may light all those who are in the house.[12] So you must shine in the eyes of the world, although your self-love may take satisfaction in this state in spite of yourself. But you ought to reserve hours for reading, prayer and resting your mind and body in the presence of God.

Do not anticipate crosses. You would perhaps seek some which God would not want to give you, and which would be incompatible with his plans for you. But embrace unhesitatingly all those which his hand offers you every moment. There is a providence for crosses, as for the necessities of life. It is the daily bread which feeds the soul, and which God never fails to distribute to us.

I beg you to stay in peace in this right and simple conduct. In depriving yourself of this liberty by straining after far-fetched mortifications, you would lose those which God is jealous of preparing for you himself, and you would harm yourself under the pretext of advancing.

Be free, gay, simple, a child. But be a sturdy child, who fears nothing, who speaks out frankly, who lets himself be led; in a word, one who knows nothing, can do nothing, can anticipate and change nothing, but who has a freedom and a strength forbidden to the great. This childhood baffles the wise, and God himself speaks by the mouth of such children.

Crosses

God is ingenious in making us crosses. He makes them of iron and of lead, which are heavy in themselves. He makes them of straw which seems to weigh nothing, and which are no less difficult to carry. He makes them of gold and of precious stones which dazzle the spectators, which excite the envy of the public, but which crucify no less than the crosses which are most despised. He makes them of all the things which we like best, and turns them to bitterness. Favor brings vexation and importunity. It gives what we do not want, and takes away what we should like.

Suffering is only a matter of enduring and being silent before God. "I am still," said David, "because you have acted."[13] It is God who sends the humors, the fevers, the mental torments, the weaknesses, the exhaustions, the importunities, the annoyances. It is he who sends even the grandeur with all its torments and its cursed gear. It is he who brings to birth within us the dryness, the impatience, the discouragement, to humiliate us by temptation and to show us ourselves such as we are. It is he who does all. We have only to see him and to adore him in all.

We must not be in a hurry to obtain an artificial presence of God and his truths. It is enough to live simply in this disposition of heart, to wish to be crucified; most of all a simple, effortless life, which we renew every time we are turned from it within by some memory, which is a kind of awakening of the heart.

Thus the difficulties of "being the rage," the pains of sickness, even the imperfections within, if they are endured peacefully and with littleness, are an antidote to a state which is in itself so dangerous. In apparent prosperity there is nothing good except the hidden cross. O cross! O good cross! I embrace thee. I adore in thee the dying Jesus, with whom I must die.

Notes

1. Matthew 11:29.
2. Luke 1:48, 49.
3. Isaiah 14:12ff.
4. Philippians 2:5–7.
5. Philippians 4:13.
6. Matthew 15:14.
7. 2 Corinthians 1:3.

8. Mark 8:34.
9. Revelation 3:16.
10. Isaiah 65:24.
11. 2 Corinthians 4:18, cf. James 4:14.
12. Matthew 5:15.
13. Psalm 39:9.

Excerpts taken from *Christian Perfection*, a collection of Fenelon's letters translated by Mildred Stillman, edited by Charles F. Whisted and published by Harper and Row © 1947. The passages are taken by permission from 'Crosses' pp. 16–18; 'Mortification and Recollection' pp. 19–21; 'Abandonment to God' pp. 62, 63; 'Joy of Abandonment to God' pp. 64–73; 'Imitation of Jesus Christ' pp. 43, 44; 'Self-renunciation' pp. 178–80; 'Self-renunciation, Continued' pp. 189, 191–93; 'Humility' pp. 205–8.

If there is any one man who could be said to represent seventeenth-century England at its best, that man perhaps is Richard Baxter (1615-1691). Amid the conflict of a land torn by civil war, Baxter's steady hand kept the nation from foundering. His clear mind, strong Christian convictions, gentle spirit, and modern Puritan outlook made him a man for all situations.

Although himself a controversialist, Baxter favored toleration, as did Taylor and Fuller who appear elsewhere in this volume. He sided with Parliament against one king; yet he boldly preferred another king to Cromwell. He was known as a Presbyterian, but was offered a bishopric in the Church of England. He defended nonconformity, yet welcomed back Charles II to the English throne. His ministry in the Kidderminster parish among poor weavers was so effective that it has been studied as a model by student pastors ever since.

He is best remembered today for two devotional classics he wrote, Call to the Unconverted *and* The Saints' Everlasting Rest. *Our excerpts from the latter reveal not a mild-mannered man of the cloth but a flaming evangelist, a man of passion and zeal who would not rest while there were still people to be won to Christ. His message was for one and all; Baxter was indifferent to denominational labels. He applied himself to bringing everyone—the great and the lowly, the high churchman and the independent—together in Christ.*

6

From The Saints' Everlasting Rest
by Richard Baxter

Is there a glorious rest so near at hand, and shall no one enjoy it but the people of God? What does the rest of the world mean, then, by living so contentedly without any assurance of their interest in this rest, and by neglecting to try their title to it?

Most men I meet with say they believe this word of God to be true. How then can they sit still in such utter uncertainty as to whether they shall live in rest or not? Lord, what a wonderful madness is this. Here are men who know they must presently enter upon unchangeable joy or pain; yet they live as uncertain as to what shall be their doom as if they had never heard of any such state.

Not only that, they live as quietly and merrily in this uncertainty as if all were made sure, and there were no danger! Are these men alive or dead? Are they awake or asleep? What do they think about? Where are their hearts?

If they have a weighty suit at law, how careful they are to know whether it will go with them or against them. If they were to be tried for their lives in an earthly court, how careful they would be to know whether they would be saved or condemned—especially if their carefulness might make the difference. If they are dangerously sick, they will inquire of the physician, "What do you think, sir? Shall I escape or not?" But for the business of their salvation they are content to be uncertain.

If you ask most men "a reason of the hope that is in them," they will say, "Because God is merciful, and Christ died for sinners" and similar general reasons—which any man in the world might give as well as they. But put them to prove their interest in Christ, and in the saving mercy of God, and they can say nothing at all; at least nothing out of their hearts and experience.

Men are desirous to know all things save God and themselves. They will travel over sea and land to know the situation of countries and the customs of the world. They will go to schools and universities, and turn over multitudes of books, and read and study from year to year to know the creatures and to excel in the sciences. Yet they never read the book of conscience, or study the state of their own souls, that they may make sure of living forever.

The Scripture would never make such a wide difference between the righteous and the wicked, the children of God and the children of the devil, and set forth so largely the happiness of the one and the misery of the other, if a man could not know which of these two estates he is in. To what purpose should we be so earnestly urged to examine and prove and try ourselves, whether we be in the faith, if we cannot attain to some degree of certainty in the matter?

We cannot doubt but Satan will do his part to hinder us from examining ourselves. The devil knows well that if he cannot keep men from judging their state and knowing their misery, he will hardly be able to keep them from repentance and salvation. He therefore labors to keep them from a searching ministry; or to keep the minister from helping them to search; or to take off the edge of the Word, that it may not pierce their hearts.

Wicked men are great hindrances to others examining themselves. When a sinner sees all his friends and neighbors do as he does, and live quietly in the same state with himself, the rich and learned as well as others, this is a great temptation to him to sleep on in his security.

Besides, God scarcely ever opens the eyes of a sinner to see the danger of his state, but presently his friends and acquaintances are ready to flatter him and settle him again in the quiet possession of his former peace. "What!" they say, "do you doubt your salvation, you who have lived so well, and have done nobody any harm, and have been beloved by all? What do you think has become of all your forefathers? And what will become of all your friends and neighbors that live as you do?"

Let me entreat you to consider that it is Christ, and not your fathers or mothers, your neighbors or friends, who shall judge you at last; and if Christ condemn you, they cannot save you.

The great hindrances to self-examination are men's own hearts. Some are so ignorant that they know not what self-examination is. They think every man is bound to believe that God is his Father, and that his sins are pardoned. They do not think that assurance can be attained, or that there is any such great difference between one man and another, but that we are all Christians, and therefore need not trouble ourselves any further.

Some are so possessed with self-love and pride that they will not so much as suspect any danger to themselves. Some are so guilty that they dare not try themselves. Some are so much in love with sin, and have so much dislike to the ways of God, that they dare not venture on the trial of their state, lest they be forced from the course they love.

Most men are so taken up with their worldly affairs, and are so busy providing for themselves and their families, that they plead a lack of time to attend to the concerns of eternity. Most are so slothful that they will not be persuaded to be at the pains necessary to know their own hearts. But the most common and dangerous impediment is that false hope commonly called presumption, which bears up the hearts of most men and keeps them from suspecting their danger.

If however a man breaks through all these impediments, he still does not always attain a correct knowledge of his own state and character. Many are deceived and miscarry. There is such darkness and confusion in the soul of man, especially of an unregenerate man, that he can scarcely tell what he does or what is in him. The heart of a sinner is like an obscure cave or dungeon. Most men are strangers to themselves, and are little taken up with observing the temper and motions of their own hearts.

Many engage in the work but forestall the conclusion. They are resolved what to judge before they try. Most men are partial in their own cause. They are ready to think their great sins small, and their small sins to be none at all. The first common excellency which they meet with in themselves so dazzles their eyes that they are at once satisfied that all is well and look no further.

Because the comfort of a Christian consists so much in his assurance of God's special love, I will open to you some hindrances which prevent true Christians from attaining comfortable certainty as to their state and character.

One common cause of doubting and uncertainty is the weakness and small measure of our grace. Most Christians content themselves with a small measure of grace. They believe so weakly, and love God so little, that they can scarcely discover whether they believe and love at all.

Christians often mistake or confound assurance with the joy that sometimes accompanies it. When therefore they lack the joy of assurance, they are as much cast down as if they wanted assurance itself. Dr.

Sibbes[1] says well that as we cannot have grace except by the work of the Spirit, so must there be a further act to make us know that we have that grace; and when we know we have grace, yet must there be a further act of the Spirit to give us comfort in that knowledge.

This these complaining souls understand not; and therefore though they cannot deny their willingness to have Christ, yet because they do not feel their spirits replenished with comforts, they throw away all as if they had nothing.

Another great and common cause of doubting and discomfort is the secret indulgence of some known sin. When a man lives in some unwarrantable practice, and God has often touched him for it, and conscience is galled, yet he perseveres in it—it is no wonder if he be destitute of both assurance and comfort. I have known too many such, that would complain and yet sin, and accuse themselves, and yet sin still. All arguments and means could not keep them from the willful committing of that sin again and again.

The cherishing of sin hinders assurance in obscuring that which it destroys not. It puts out or dims the eye of the soul so that it cannot see its own condition; and it benumbs and stupefies the heart so that it cannot feel its own case. Especially it provokes God to withdraw the assistance of his Spirit, without which we may search long enough before we have assurance. God has made a separation between sin and peace.

Another common cause of want of assurance and comfort is that men grow sluggish in the spiritual part of duty. Dr. Sibbes says truly, "It is the lazy Christian commonly that lacks assurance." The way of painful duty is the way of fullest comfort. Christ carries all our comforts in his hand. If we are out of that way where Christ is to be met, we are out of the way where comfort is to be had.

The fire that lies still in the flint is neither seen nor felt; but when you smite it and force it into action, it is easily discerned. The greatest action forces the greatest observation. So long as a Christian has his graces in lively action, so long, for the most part, he is assured of them. The very act of loving God brings inexpressible sweetness with it into the soul. The soul that is best furnished with grace, when it is not in action, is like a lute well tuned, which, while it lies still, makes no more music than a common piece of wood. When it is taken up and handled by a skillful musician, the melody is most delightful.

Such doctrine teaches us why the people of God suffer so much affliction in this life. Afflictions are exceedingly useful to us, to keep us from mistaking our resting place. The most dangerous mistake our souls are capable of, is to mistake the creature for God, and earth for Heaven. Yet how common is this! Go to a man who has the world at his beck and call and tell him, "This is not your happiness; you have higher things to look after," and how little will he regard you! But when affliction comes, it speaks convincingly, and will be heard when preachers cannot.

Afflictions are a powerful means to keep us from wandering out of the way to our rest. If God had not set a hedge of thorns on the right hand, and another on the left, we would hardly keep the way to Heaven. If there be but one gap open without these thorns, how ready are we to find it and turn out at it! But when we cannot go astray without these thorns pricking us, perhaps we will be content to hold on our way.

Every Christian as well as Luther may call affliction one of his best schoolmasters. Many as well as David may say by experience, "Before I was afflicted I went astray; but now have I kept thy word."[2] When we have prosperity we grow secure and sinful. Then God afflicts us and, like Israel of old, we cry for mercy and purpose reformation. But after we have a little rest, we do evil again, till God take up the rod again that he may bring us back.

Afflictions are a powerful means to make us quicken our pace in the way to our rest. They are God's rod and spur. What a difference is there between our prayers in health and in sickness; between our prosperity and our adversity repentings! Even innocent Adam is likelier to forget God in a paradise, than Joseph in a prison, or Job upon a dunghill. Solomon fell in the midst of pleasure and prosperity, while wicked Manasseh was recovered in his irons.

God seldom gives his people so sweet a foretaste of their future rest, as in their deep afflictions. He keeps his most precious cordials for the time of our greatest faintings and dangers. Even the best saints seldom taste of the delights of God, pure, spiritual, unmixed joys, in the time of their prosperity, as they do in their deepest troubles.

Especially, when our sufferings are more directly for his cause, then God seldom fails of sweetening the bitter cup. Therefore have the martyrs been possessors of the highest joys. I question if Paul and Silas ever sang more joyfully than when they were thrust into the inner prison, their backs sore with scourgings, and their feet made fast in the stocks. We may never be put to the suffering of martyrdom; yet God knows that in our natural sufferings we need support and comfort.

But let us hear a little what it is that the flesh objects to:

Objection 1: "Oh," says one, "I could bear any other affliction but this. If God had touched me in anything else, I could have undergone it patiently; but it is my dearest friend, or child, or wife, or my health that suffers."

Answer: It seems God has hit the right vein. It is his constant course to pull down men's idols. If God had taken from you that which you can let go for him, and not that which you cannot; or had afflicted you where you can bear it, and not where you cannot, your idol would neither have been discovered nor removed.

Objection 2: "Oh," says another, "if God would only deliver me out of it at last, I could be content to bear it. But I have an incurable sickness; or I am likely to live and die in poverty, or disgrace, or a like distress."

Answer: Is it nothing that he has promised it will "work for your good," and that with the affliction he will "make a way to escape"? That he will be with you in it, and will deliver you in the fittest manner and season?

Objection 3: "Oh," says another, "if my affliction did not disable me for duty, I could bear it; but it makes me useless and utterly un-profitable."

Answer: For that duty which concerns your own personal benefit, it does not disable you, but is the greatest quickening help you could expect. As for duty to others, and service to the church, it is not your duty when God disables you. Must God do all his work by you? Has he not many others as dear to him and as fit for the employment? Is this any wrong to you?

What deceitfulness there is in our hearts! When we have time and health and opportunity to work, then we loiter and do our Master but very poor service. But when he lays affliction upon us, then we com-plain that he disables us for his work, and yet perhaps we are still negli-gent in that part of the work which we can do. So when we are in health and prosperity we forget our public duty, and are careless of other men's miseries and wants and mind almost nothing but ourselves. But when God afflicts us, we complain that he disables us for our duty to others. As if all of a sudden we were grown so charitable that we regard other men's souls far more than our own! But is not the hand of the flesh in all this dissimulation, secretly pleading its own cause?

Objection 4: "Oh," says another, "it is the godly who afflict, dis-claim, censure and slander me, and look upon me with a disdainful eye. If it were ungodly men I could easily bear it. I look for no better at their hands. But when those who were my delight are as thorns in my sides, how can I bear it?"

Answer: Whoever is the instrument, the affliction is from God, and the provoking cause from yourself. Were it not fitter, then, that you look more to God and yourself? Do you not know that the best men are still sinful in part, and that their hearts are naturally deceitful and des-perately wicked, as well as others'? So far, the best of them is as a brier, and the most upright of them sharper than a thorny hedge. Learn therefore to look less to men and more to God.

Perhaps you have given that love and confidence to saints, which are due only to God. Then it is no wonder if God chastises you by them. If we would use our friends as friends, God would make them our helps and comforts. But when once we make them our gods by excessive love, delight and trust, then he suffers them to prove adversaries to us, and to be our accusers and tormentors.

I confess it is a pity that saints should suffer from saints. It is quite contrary to their holy nature, and their Master's laws, who has left them his peace, and has made love to be the characteristic of his disciples, and to be the first and great and new commandment. I know that there is much difference between them and the world in this respect. But yet, as I said before, they are saints only in part, and therefore Paul and Barnabas may so fall out as to part asunder; and upright Asa may imprison the prophet.[3] Call it persecution or what you please. In fact, your own nature is as bad as theirs, and you are as likely to be yourself a grief to others.

Objection 5: "Oh, if I had but that consolation which you say God reserves for our suffering times, I would suffer more contentedly; but I do not enjoy any such thing."

Answer: The more you suffer for righteousness' sake, the more of this blessing you may expect. The more you suffer for your own evildoing, the longer you may expect to wait till that sweetness come. When by our folly we have provoked God to chastise us, shall we look that he should immediately fill us with comfort? That were to make affliction to be no affliction.

Are you overlooking or neglecting the comforts which you desire? God has filled precepts and promises and other providences with matter of comfort. If you will overlook all these and make nothing of them, and always pore upon your sufferings, and make more of one cross than a thousand mercies—who makes you uncomfortable but yourself?

Have your afflictions wrought kindly with you, and fitted you for comfort? Have they humbled you? Have they weaned your heart from its former idols, and brought you unfeignedly to take God for your portion and rest? It is not mere suffering that prepares you for comfort, but the fruit of suffering being produced in your heart.

Has God set before us such a glorious prize as this everlasting rest of the saints, and has he made man capable of such an inconceivable happiness? Why then do not all the children of the Kingdom bestir themselves more to help others to the enjoyment of it? How little are the souls around us indebted to the most of us! We see the glory of the

Kingdom and they do not. We see the misery and torment of the unconverted and they do not. We see them wandering out of the way and know if they hold on, they can never come into the Kingdom, and they discern not this themselves. And yet we will not speak to them seriously and show them their error and danger and help to bring them into the Way that they may live.

The duty that I would press upon you consists in the following:

1. Get your hearts affected with the misery of your brethren's souls. Be compassionate toward them. Yearn after their salvation. If you earnestly long for their conversion, and your hearts are fully set on doing them good, it will excite you to the work, and God will usually bless it.

2. Embrace all opportunities which you possibly can of conferring with them privately about their state, and instructing and helping them to attain salvation. If he be an ignorant person with whom you have to deal, who is an utter stranger to the principles of religion, the first thing you have to do is acquaint him with the primary truths of the Gospel.

Labor to make him understand wherein man's chief happiness consists, and how far he was once possessed of it, and what covenant God then made with him, and how he broke it, and what penalty he incurred and into what misery he brought himself thereby. Teach him what need men had of a Redeemer, and how Christ in mercy interposed and bore the penalty, and what is the only way in which salvation can now be attained, and what course Christ takes to draw men to himself, and what are the riches and privileges that believers have in him.

If when he understands all this, you find his soul enthralled in presumption and false hopes, persuading himself that he is a true believer, pardoned and reconciled, and all this upon false grounds, then urge him to examine his state. Produce from Scripture some undeniable evidences of a state of grace, and ask him whether he ever found such workings or dispositions in his heart. Urge him to a rational answer. Do not leave him till you have convinced him of his misery, and then wisely and seasonably show him the remedy.

If you perceive him possessed with any prejudices against the godly and the way of holiness, show him their falsehood, and with wisdom and meekness answer his objections. Because in all works the manner of doing them is of peculiar moment, and the right performance of them greatly furthers the success, I will here add a few directions.

3. Set about the work with right intentions. Let your aim be the glory of God and the salvation of your fellowmen. Do not do it to get a

name or esteem to yourself, or to bring men to depend upon you, or to get you followers.

4. Do it speedily. You have long been purposing to speak to such a neighbor, and yet you have never done it. While you delay, he runs on the score all the while. Sin is taking root. Conscience grows seared, and the heart hardened. The devil rules and rejoices. Christ is shut out. The Spirit is repulsed. God is dishonored. The law is violated. Time runs on. The day of visitation hastens away. Opportunities do not always last.

5. Do it from compassion and love. We have many reprovers, but their manner shows too plainly that they are not influenced by love. Pride bids men to reprove others, and they do it proudly, censoriously and contemptuously. Passion bids them reprove others, and they do it passionately. Vilifying or reproaching a man for his faults is not likely to work his reformation or convert him to God. Men will consider people who so deal with them to be enemies, and the words of an enemy are not very persuasive.

Go to sinners with tears in your eyes. Let them see that your very bowels yearn over them, and that it is the earnest desire of your heart to do them good. Let them perceive that you have no other end in view but their everlasting happiness, and that it is your love to their souls that forces you to speak. I know it must be God that changes men's hearts, but I know also that God works by means, and when he means to prevail with men he usually suits the means to the end, and stirs up men to plead with them in a kindly way, and so makes it successful.

6. Be wise in using the apt expressions. Many a minister delivers most excellent and useful matter in such harsh language that it makes the hearers loathe the food they should live by, and laugh at a sermon that might make them quake. So it is in private exhortation as well as public. If you clothe the most amiable truth in sordid language, you will make men disdain it as monstrous and deformed.

And now, Christian reader, seeing it is a duty that God has laid on every man according to his ability, thus to exhort and reprove, and with all possible diligence to labor after the salvation of all about him, judge for yourself whether this work is generally and conscientiously performed by us. Alas! Where shall we find the man among us that engages in this duty with all his might, that sets his heart upon the souls of his brethren, that they may be saved?

Let us enquire what are the causes of the general neglect of this duty, that the hindrances being discovered, they may the more easily be overcome.

1. Men's own gracelessness and guiltiness. They have not felt the wickedness of their own natures, nor their lost condition, nor their need of Christ, nor the transforming work of the Spirit; how then can they discover these to others? They have not been themselves exalted with the heavenly delights; how then should they draw others so earnestly to seek them? Men are also guilty themselves of the sins they should reprove, and this stops their mouths and makes them ashamed, as well indeed it may.

2. The secret infidelity of men's hearts. Brethren, we surely do not believe men's misery; we surely do not believe the truth of God's threatenings. This secret unbelief of the truth of Scripture consumes the vigor of each grace and duty.

3. Lack of charity and compassion to men's souls. Like the priest and the Levite, we look on the wounded man and pass by. Alas! What pitiful sights do we see daily! You will pray to God for them in customary duties, that he would open the eyes and turn the hearts of your unconverted friends and neighbors. But why do you not endeavor their conversion if you desire it? And if you do not desire it, why do you ask it? If you should see your neighbor fallen into a pit, and should immediately fall down on your knees and pray God to help him out, but would neither put forth your hand to help, nor persuade or direct him to help himself, would you not deserve to be set down as cruel and hypocritical?

4. A man-pleasing disposition. We are so loath to displease men, and so desirous to keep in favor with them, that it makes us neglect our known duty. To win them we must indeed become "all things to all men";[4] but to please them to their destruction and let them perish, just so we may maintain our credit with them, is a barbarously cruel course.

5. Bashfulness. We blush to tell people of their sin. Bashfulness is unseemly in cases of absolute necessity. To obey God in persuading men from their sins to Christ, and helping to save their souls, is not a business at which a man should blush. And yet what abundance of souls have been neglected through the prevalence of this sin! Most of us are in this respect heinously guilty.

6. Indolence and impatience. This is a work that seldom succeeds at the first, unless it be followed with wisdom and unweariedness. Now this is a tedious course to the flesh and few will bear it. Woe to us if God had been as impatient with us as we are with our fellowmen!

7. Self-seeking and self-minding. Men are all for themselves. "All mind their own things," few "the things of Christ"[5] and their brethren. Many Christians think only where they may enjoy the purest

ordinances; but where they may have the fairest opportunity to win the souls of others, or to do good, these things they little or nothing regard.

8. Pride. They would speak to a great man, provided it would not displease him. But to go among the multitude, to take pains with a company of mean persons, to sit with them in their humble houses and there to instruct them, where is the person who will do this? These men little consider how low Christ stooped for us, when the God of glory comes down in flesh and goes preaching among them from city to city. Few rich, and noble, and wise, and mighty are called. It is the poor chiefly who receive the glad tidings of the Gospel.

9. Ignorance. Some are hindered from performing their duty because they either do not know it to be a duty, or they do not know it to be *their* duty. If this be your case, then I hope that now you are acquainted with your duty, you will set about it without further delay.

"But," says one, "I have such weak parts and gifts that I am unable to manage an exhortation, especially to men of understanding." Use faithfully that ability which you have in instructing those who are more ignorant than yourself. If you cannot speak well yourself, still you can tell them what God speaks in his Word. It is not the excellency of speech that wins souls, but the authority of God manifested by that speech, and the power of his Word in the mouth of the speaker.

"But it is my superiors that need my exhortation and advice; and is it fit for me to teach or reprove them? Must the wife teach the husband, of whom the Scripture bids her learn? Or must children teach their parents, whose duty it is to instruct them?" It is fit that husbands should be able to teach their wives and parents their children, and God expects they should do so. But if they, through their own negligence or wickedness, bring their souls into such danger as that they have the greatest need of advice and reproof themselves, then it is themselves, and not you, that break God's order. Matters of mere order and manners must be dispensed with in cases of absolute necessity. But let me give you this caution: when necessity calls for your exhortation and advice, give it with all humility and modesty and meekness. By the humble manner of your address, let them perceive that you do it not out of a mere teaching humor or proud self-conceitedness. What father, or master, or husband, could take this ill?

"But the party is so ignorant, or stupid, or careless, or rooted in sin, and has so often been exhorted in vain, that there is no hope." How do you know when there is no hope? Can God not yet cure him? Should not a merciful physician use means while there is life? What if you had been so given up when you were ignorant?

"Oh, but it is a friend on whom I have all my dependence, and if I tell him of his sin and misery, I may lose his love." Is the love of your friend, then, to be more valued than his safety? Or your own benefit by him than the salvation of his soul? Is this your requital of his kindness?

"But we must not 'cast pearls before swine, nor give that which is holy to dogs.' "[6] This language indicates a dispensation of Christ for your safety. When you are in danger to be torn in pieces, Christ would have you forbear. But what is that to you who are in no such danger? As long as they will hear, you have encouragement to speak and may not cast them off.

Finally, let all your exhortations be backed with the authority of God. Let the sinner be convinced that you speak not from yourself, or out of your own head. Show them the very words of Scripture for what you say. Turn them to the chapter and verse where sin is condemned and duty is commanded. Press them with the truth and authority of God. Ask them whether they believe that this is his Word and whether his Word be true. They can and may reject your words, but they cannot, they dare not, reject the words of the Almighty. Be sure therefore to make them know that you speak nothing but what God has spoken before you. So much of God as appears in our words, so much will they carry power with them.

My Christian friends, I have here lined out for you a heavenly precious work. Would you but do it, it would make you happy indeed. To delight in God is the work of angels, and the contrary is the work of devils. If God would persuade you now to make conscience of this duty, and help you in it by the blessed influence of his Spirit, you would not change your lives with the greatest prince on earth.

But I am afraid, if I may judge of your hearts by the backwardness of my own, that it will prove a hard thing to persuade you to the work, and that much of my labor will be lost. Pardon my jealousy: it is raised upon too many sad experiments. What do you say? Will you resolve on this heavenly course or no? Will you let go all your sinful pleasures and daily seek after these higher delights? I pray you, reader, here shut the book and consider this matter; and resolve on the duty before you go further.

*   *   *

The world is passing away. Its pleasures are fading, its honors are leaving you, its profits will prove unprofitable to you. Heaven and Hell are a little before you. God is just and jealous. Your time runs on. Your lives are uncertain. You are far behind-hand. You have loitered long.

Your case is dangerous. Your souls are far gone in sin. You are strange to God. You are hardened in evil customs. You have no assurance of pardon to show.

If you die tomorrow, how unready are you? And with what terrors will your souls go out of your bodies? And do you yet loiter for all this? Will you sit still and trifle? Stop and think a moment. God stands all this time awaiting your leisure. His patience bears up. His justice forbears. His mercy entreats you. Christ stands offering you his blood and merits. You may have him freely, and life with him.

The Spirit is persuading you. Conscience is accusing and urging you. Ministers are praying for you and calling upon you. Satan stands waiting when Justice will cut off your lives, that he may have you. This is your time. Now or never!

Notes

1. Richard Sibbes (1577–1635), English Puritan writer.
2. Psalm 119:67.
3. Acts 15:37ff., 2 Chronicles 16:10.
4. 1 Corinthians 9:22.
5. Philippians 2:21.
6. Matthew 7:6.

Baxter's work has been reprinted many times since it was first published. The excerpts have been collated (with slight changes of expression and spelling) from the following four editions: *The Saints' Everlasting Rest: or, A Treatise of the Blessed State of the Saints in Their Enjoyment of God in Glory*, published before 1900 by Carlton and Lanahan, New York. It claims to have been 'extracted from the works of Mr Richard Baxter by John Wesley, M.A., late fellow of Lincoln College, Oxford'.

The Saints' Everlasting Rest, by the Rev. Richard Baxter, abridged 1759 by Benjamin Fawcett, A.M. Published before 1900 by the American Tract Society.

The Saints' Everlasting Rest, Fawcett's abridgement, Reunion edition, edited by M. Monckton, published London, 1928.

The Saints' Everlasting Rest, abridged by John T. Wilkinson, Epworth Press, London, 1962. The passages are found in the American Tract Society edition as chapter 8, 'How to Discern Our Title to the Saints' Rest'; chapter 9, 'The Duty of the People of God to Excite Others to Seek the Rest'; and chapter 10, 'The Saints' Rest is not to be Expected on Earth'.

Many Americans identify Roger Williams (1603–1683) as the founder of Rhode Island, a champion of religious liberty, and the organizer of the first Baptist congregation in America. However correct, none of these achievements properly reveals the inner depth of Williams' devotion to Jesus Christ and his love for his fellow human beings.

Williams was born in London, educated at Cambridge, and ordained in the Church of England. Because he opposed Archbishop Laud's harsh policy toward nonconformists, Williams emigrated to New England with Mary, his wife, in 1631. Having arrived in Massachusetts, he propounded the principle of separation of church and state, a view that led to his eventual banishment from the colony.

As an exile in Indian country, Williams established friendly relations with the Indians and learned their tribal languages. He bought land from them and set up a settlement which he named Providence. Returning to England, Williams published his protests against religious intolerance and secured from Cromwell's government a permanent charter for the colony of Rhode Island.

In America Williams also went on extended trading trips, during which he lived with the Indians. During his absence on one of these journeys his wife became ill back in Providence. His letter in response to news of her illness and recovery is included in this volume. Written about 1650, it was later printed in London under the title, "Experiments of Spiritual Life & Health and their Preservatives, in which the weakest Child of God may get Assurance of his Spiritual Life and Blessednesse, and the Strongest may find proportionable Discoveries of his Christian Growth, and the means of it."

This letter portrays the true charm of Puritan faith at its best. The depth of Williams' sincerity, his affection for his wife, his remarkable gifts both of perceptiveness in observation and scholarship, and his heart-yearning for God are all evident. Of particular interest today is the unusual recognition Williams gave in this letter to "Christian women," both in Scripture and in church history—a tribute that undoubtedly was not lost on his wife. Reading the "Experiments" (here abridged) gives one a fresh appreciation of the quality of intellectual and spiritual leadership that was enjoyed by colonial America.

7

From Experiments of Spiritual Life and Health
by Roger Williams

My dearest love and companion in this vale of tears: Your late sudden and dangerous sickness, and the Lord's most gracious and speedy raising you up from the gates and jaws of death, were wonderful in your own and others' eyes. So I hope and earnestly desire that [these events] may ever be in our thoughts as a warning from Heaven to make ready for a sudden call to be gone from hence.

Thus we may live the rest of our short, uncertain span more as strangers, longing and breathing after another home and country. We may cast off our great cares and fears and desires and joys about the candle of this vain life that is so soon blown out, and trust in the living God, of whose wonderful power and mercy you have had so much and so late experience.

My dear Love, since it pleases the Lord so to dispose of me and of my affairs at present that I cannot often see you, I desire often to send to you. Your holy and humble desires are strong, but I know your writing is slow, and that you will gladly accept of this, my poor help, which with thankfulness and praise to the Lord I humbly tender to his holy service, and yours in him.

I send you now (though in winter) a handful of flowers, made up in a little posy, for your dear self and our dear children to look on and smell on, when I as the grass of the field shall be gone and withered.

We know how it pleases the Spirit of God to distinguish between the outward and the inner man.[1] It has pleased the Most High to cast down your outward man, and again graciously to lift him up, and thereby to teach us both to examine and try the health and strength and welfare of the inner. This inner man has his tempers and distempers, his health and sickness, as well as the outward man, this body of clay.

The Holy Scripture mentions a three-fold person in all that are born again: first, the body of flesh and clay, this outward natural being. Second, the body of corruption, or old man, which being deadly wounded by the Son of God already in all that are his, shall shortly give up the ghost and rot and never rise again. Third, this holy, heavenly inner man, of whose health and daily renewing I now discourse, who is born of an immortal seed and therefore can no more die than Christ himself.[2]

Now as this outward man desires not only life and being, but also health and cheerfulness, so requires the inward and spiritual man a healthful and cheerful temper. For as the Lord loves a cheerful giver, so he loves also a cheerful preacher, a cheerful hearer, a cheerful prayer, and a cheerful sufferer for his Name's sake. He loves that the shoes of preparation be on our feet ready to run (all ways and weathers) the paths of his commandments.[3] Like a vessel, our leaks are to be stopped and our whole soul ready in a holy trim and tightness for all his holy employments of us in the great tempests. Like heavenly soldiers, our arms are to be fixed. Like an instrument, the strings of our affections and parts are to be all in tune, to make heavenly music in the holy ears of our heavenly Lord and King.

As it is between a loving couple (and as it was in the church at Ephesus),[4] it is not easy to keep the first flame of love fresh and equal, although the fire of the truth and the sincerity of marriage love never dies or is extinguished. I propose therefore with the assistance of God's Holy Spirit to examine three particulars:

First, what are the arguments of that measure of spiritual life in Christ which yet may stand with great spiritual weaknesses and diseases?

Second, what is the measure of the grace of Christ Jesus which may be called the health and cheerful temper and disposition of the inner man?

Third, what are those spiritual preservatives which may keep the soul in a healthy temper, free from spiritual sicknesses and distempers?

In these examinations I profess two things: first, not to oppress your thoughts and memory with any long discourse. I intend only to send you after your sickness a little posy fit and easy for your meditation and refreshing. Second, all my flowers shall be some choice example or speech of some son or daughter of God, picked out from the garden of the Holy Scriptures for our spiritual refreshing and consolation.

I begin therefore with such trials and arguments as declare the true life of the inner man, notwithstanding spiritual weakness, sickness and distempers.

First, when the Spirit of the Lord in Job 1:2 describes the several ages and growths of this inward man (a child, a strong man, and an old man), it pleased him to describe the young or little one by this difference, that he knows the Lord so as to look upon him as to a Father; that he fears him, loves him, obeys him, and calls on him as on a Father.

Second, where spiritual life is, there is always a professed willingness to get more and more knowledge of this heavenly Father, of his name, of his works, of his Christ, of his Spirit, his saints and ordinances.

A third trial of spiritual life is a vehement hunger and longing after the ordinance of the Word preached.

A fourth argument of the life of the inner man is to do that which it finds it cannot do, but falls short in doing or suffering the will of God.

A fifth trial of true life is a constant resisting and fighting against all known sin, as sin.

Sixth, a child of God though overwhelmed with many weaknesses or temptations, cannot possibly be brought to an ill opinion or thought of God, but is always ready to take his part, to speak well of him. He endures not, with a quiet mind, to hear his name dishonored.

A seventh argument of the true life of grace I observe to be a humble acknowledgement of, and a submitting to, the correcting and afflicting hand of God, in sicknesses, crosses, losses, etc.

An eighth trial of true life is a true, though faint, willingness and inclination to enjoy more and more of Christ Jesus in the society of his saints, after his own appointment, although it is with hardship and difficulty attained to.

A ninth discovery of true spiritual life I find to be a painful and restless mind, in temptations to sin, in yielding to sin, and lying in sin, the breach not being made up with the Lord in humble confession and suit for mercy in the blood of a Savior. So that as a fish out of the water (its element), as a bone broken or disjointed, is the troubled mind of a child of God upon his discovered or (strongly) suspected sinful way or practice.

A tenth trial of the true life of the inner man is a discerning and liking and secret wishing for that beauty and shining of the grace of Christ Jesus which appears in others of God's children, and which we see wanting in ourselves. Hence many of God's dear saints in Queen Mary's time, and other bloody days in our own and other countries, have praised God for and have been ravished with the beauties of the heavenly love and zeal and patience in *others* of God's servants, which they have seen wanting in *themselves.* Such a beauty (doubtless) did many of God's children apprehend in those who suffered for the Lord's ordinances in England, but who yet found not strength themselves to stand and suffer for and with them. Thus they left much and fled to New England, hoping to enjoy there (though with too much weak desire of peace and liberty) the ordinances of Christ Jesus, their souls' Beloved.

Objection: But did not Balaam see the beauty and excellency of God's saints when he cried out, let me die the death of the righteous?[5]

I answer, Balaam desired the death and blessedness of the righteous, but not the life and righteousness of the righteous.

Objection: Balaam seems to have seen the beauty of righteousness.

I answer, he might see and like the end and fruit of righteousness, and yet not the true nature and beauty of it. For then he would have desired the life as well as the death of the righteous. These Indians among whom I write these lines see the excellency of the English industry, joined with plenty and a better condition than their own. But they endure not that life of labor and endeavor wherein that plenty and better state is found.

These and many more discoveries of the life of Christ Jesus in the soul (though in the midst of weaknesses and spiritual sicknesses) I hope, my dear love and faithful companion, you discern in truth in yourself, and I and others have discerned in you. But oh, search diligently in the Lord's holy Presence, and humbly beg his help, that as the Spirit of God admonishes, you may have rejoicing in yourself, and not in another's good opinion of you.

Next to the discovery of spiritual life, all that are born of God must try their spiritual strength and health and cheerful temper, the particular instances whereof I shall pick, and gather, and bind up, for both our encouragement and comfort. These particulars are as a holy looking-glass for us to discover our souls' spots and blemishes. They are also sweet cordial flowers, to refresh and encourage our drooping spirits. The several particular trials of spiritual health and cheerfulness I shall bind up into three parcels, as sometimes we see sweet flowers bound up into smaller bundles, to make up at last one larger bundle or posy.

The three parcels, according to the division of the Holy Spirit by Paul to Titus, are: respecting our communion with God in Christ Jesus, respecting others, and respecting our private selves and persons.[6]

First, then, it is an argument of the strength and healthful temper of the inner man:

When our apprehensions of God are always such as bring us to holy wonderment and amazement at the nature of incomprehensible God, at his properties and works, from the sun in the firmament to the poorest worm; at his wonderful dispensing of his justice and mercy, and disposing and ruling all things in Heaven, earth, and seas, from the highest angels in Heaven to the lowest devils in Hell.

When the hallowing, the magnifying, and glorifying of the name of God is our great work and business in this world, beside which all the businesses and works we have in hand in the world give way.

When we perform actions of godliness with a single and upright eye unto God himself in secret.

When the Spirit of prayer breathes forth frequently, and constantly, and fervently to God in us.

Objection: But may not hypocrites be frequent and fervent in prayer to God? Did not the Pharisees and Jews pray and fast often? Do not the very Turks solemnly pray five times each twenty-four hours? And the Papists not only keep their solemn morning and evening times of prayer, but many other solemn prayers to which the several orders of friars, monks and nuns bind themselves. And how easy it is by worldly engines to wheel about the Indians of America to become frequent prayers unto God.

I answer: Many are the differences between the true prayers of God's children, and the false of dissemblers and hypocrites.

[It is an argument of spiritual health and strength when there is:] A constant holy sense of our own unworthiness, vileness and baseness in God's presence.

When the affections work strong and lifely after God, after God for himself, after God as a portion and inheritance, after God as a Husband: when as the hart panteth after the waterbrooks, so pant our hearts after God; when as the thirsty ground longs for the showers of rain, so long our souls after God; when his words are sweeter than the honey and honeycomb, and of more esteem than thousands of gold and silver.

When the holy commandments of God are not grievous, but pleasant and delightful to us; when we can say as the Lord Jesus said, it is our meat and drink to do our heavenly Father's will.[7]

[When there is] a humble, patient and thankful submission to the afflicting and chastising hand of God.

[When there is] a humble free confession, and giving glory to God, in the rising up or recovering out of any scandalous transgression against God.

[When we] maintain or recover a holy, vehement longing after the enjoyment of God and of Christ in a visible and open profession of his own holy worship and ordinances, separate from all false worships, gods and christs.

Hence it is that in the heavenly Love Song [the Song of Solomon] the love of Christians to Christ Jesus in his ordinances is most elegantly set forth by a similitude taken from the strong affection of married persons.[8] Hence it pleases the Spirit of God to resemble his worship to the marriage bed, which satisfies not the heavenly Spouse when the Husband Christ Jesus is not spiritually embraced therein, but absent.[9]

When the heart is fixed and readily prepared for all the holy pleasure of God. Hence this readiness and preparation of mind is compared to the shoes on our feet, without which we are unfit for traveling or walking, and with which we are ready for any spiritual employment.

Objection: What is the reason that God's children are sometimes brought on to difficult services and duties?

I answer: Unreadiness and unfitness is a spiritual sickness or distemper. When God's children recover out of it, then they say as the Lord Jesus did in Psalm 41: "Lord, my heart is willing and my heart is ready to do thy will, O my God."[10] And they say to Christ Jesus, as his holy servant John Bradford said of Queen Mary: "If she keep me in prison, I will thank her; if she release me, I will thank her; if she burn me, I will still thank her."[11]

When God's children walk in a continual sense of their own insufficiencies and distempers, and when they discern the evil inclination of their own spirits and the excellency and sufficiency of God's most Holy Spirit.

These and many more are the trials of spiritual strength, and health, and cheerfulness, in matters concerning God. We now come to the second head of trials of spiritual health and strength in matters concerning ourselves.

First, then, it is an argument of spiritual health and strength when (especially) after known sins committed, our hearts are in a broken frame and temper; when our spirits are as it were contrite, and pounded like spice in a mortar, then yielding the most delightful smell and savor to God.

Second: when we make it our work to observe, watch and kill our own corruptions and rebellions, and labor to keep under and beat down our body to a holy fitness and readiness for God's service, in fasting and prayer against temptations.

Third: when we so look upon our sins and our sinful dispositions that we not only loathe our sins, but also loathe ourselves for them.

Fourth: when we lay down ourselves at the feet of God; when our wills are subdued to the Lord's will, when the Lord is become our self, when his ends are our ends, which give us content and pleasure. Hence Epaphroditus, to further the work of the Lord, regarded not his health and consequently not his life, as a true soldier in the service of his heavenly King and Captain.[12]

Fifth: when we are cordially willing to go from hence that we may be with Christ; yet for the service of Christ and his saints, we are cordially willing to stay in hard and difficult service.

Sixth: when we are in a healthful frame of grace, when God has brought down our hearts to be content with the changes of his right hand upon us. When we have learned to be content with food and raiment, without pride, or security, or trust in earthly things, and want all outward mercies with quietness and contentation.

Seventh: when we are not only willing to suffer for the name of Christ Jesus, but when we also conceive a kind of pleasure in it.

Eighth: when we use this world and all the comforts of it with a weaned eye and mind, as if we used it not: as English travelers that lodge in an Indian house use all the wild Indian comforts with a strange affection, willing and ready to be gone. Or as passengers in a ship, willing and ready (when God will) to land, and go ashore in our own country, to our own House, and comforts in the Heavens.

Ninth: when we see God, and mind his name and praise. Hence the poorest Christian, able to contribute, observes weekly and therefore daily the dispensations of God toward him. He observes the givings and takings of God's hand, and walks with him though in the poorest and meanest calling and condition.

Objection: But may not hypocrites observe God's blessing in worldly things, in fair winds, good voyages, in the increase of children, corn, wine and cattle?

I answer: Natural conviction enforces even pagans to confess a Manitou, an invisible Deity and Godhead in these visible things. But to make it a work and business in all these earthly things to see and glorify God, to walk with him, and to be full of his praise all the day long: this is only the character of God's children, who only truly see his hand and love his name and glory.

Tenth: It is an argument of strength and vigor of grace to keep a constant watch and bridle on our lips and tongue, that no words pass but such as are seasoned with salt, to the glorifying of our Maker with our glory, and the edifying or benefiting of others.

Lastly, it argues strength and life and grace in Christ when our hearts, by God's Spirit, are wrought to such a degree of hatred of sin that we not only abhor the acts thereof, but also fly and shun the looks and appearance of it; so that we not only fly pride and passion and covetousness and uncleanness, but also the appearance of them.

I come now to the third head of the trials of spiritual health and strength, and that respects our conversation with men.

First, I argue that it is a strong argument of a strong constitutional and spiritual health when we can make it our work and trade to aim at glorifying our Maker in doing good to men. Thus our great example Christ Jesus made it his work and trade to go about to do good, which he did abundantly to the souls and bodies of men.

Objection: Christ Jesus and his apostles and messengers were endued with power from on high, not only to preach the Word for conversion, but also with power of casting out devils and healing bodily diseases.

I answer: A woman, as a holy witness of Jesus Christ, once answered a bishop, "I am a member of Christ Jesus as well as Peter himself." The least believer and follower of Jesus partakes of the nature and Spirit of him, their holy Head and Husband, as well as the strongest and holiest that ever did or suffered for his holy name. Therefore it is that we read not only of the service of those great master-builders and workmen of Christ Jesus, the apostles, but also the service and help of Christian women, for instance Phoebe, Priscilla, Mary, Persis.[13] They were eminently noted for helping forward the work of Christ Jesus, to wit, the glorifying of God in the saving of the poor sons of men.

A third trial of spiritual health and strength is a compassionate and pitiful, melting heart over the afflicted or miserable: yea, although our enemies, or enemies of their own salvation.

Fourthly, It is a good evidence of spiritual health respecting others, when we endure not sin to lie upon them, or rather them to lie in the pit of sin, but endeavor to help them out by wise, and loving, and seasonable reproof, and exhortation.

Fifth: when a soul is able to withstand, resist and repel such sins unto which the opportunity of temptation solicits and invites us.

Sixth: when we can patiently and thankfully bear a reproof and admonition, when we can esteem a reproof for our evil words, or ways, not as a blow or stroke on the head, but as a sweet and precious ointment poured on us.

Lastly, with reference to our walking with others, it is an argument of great strength of grace when the glory of the Lord and the salvation of God's people is so great and so dear in our eyes, that we can wish on their behalf that we might not only lose our temporal, but also our eternal state and welfare. Hence those two famous and wonderful speeches of those two glorious stars, Moses and Paul: "Blot me out of your book," says Moses, and "I could wish to be accursed from Christ," says Paul, "for Israel's sake."[14]

I am now come, dear Love, to the third and last head proposed, which is some few means of recovering and preserving of Christian health and cheerfulness, and the preventing of spiritual sicknesses and diseases. In this I shall desire to be brief, lest by too long a discourse I discourage your reading, and hinder your use and improvement of it.

First, then, holy consideration of our estate, a deep and frequent examination of our spiritual condition, is an excellent means of Christian health and temper. This holy practice ought to be frequent, especially when the hand and rods of the Lord are upon us. For then (as Job says) God softens our hearts, and we are most likely to be as the ground, mollified by a thaw, fit to be broken up; or like the ground moistened with storms and showers from Heaven, in some hopeful turn for the Lord's most gracious seed and heavenly planting.

Secondly, maintain an earnest longing, and endeavor to enjoy Christ Jesus, who is our soul's life in every holy ordinance which he has appointed. If it be possible, let us never rest from being planted into the holy society of God's children, gathered into the order of Christ Jesus according to his most holy will and testament. Remember that Christian health, growth and flourishing are promised to the trees planted in Jehovah's house, and that the holy ordinances are the Lord's provisions and soul meals.

Especially be much in holy prayer and fasting before the Lord. If it be possible practice this duty with others.

Thirdly, as ever we would preserve our spiritual health, let us carefully take heed of spiritual colds and obstructions. For as it is in the natural man, a cold itself is a great distemper, and the ground and beginning of others. So is it much more in the spiritual when our heavenly spirits are stopped by damp colds and obstructions of unnecessary frequenting of cold societies and places destitute of the life of the Sun of Righteousness, Christ Jesus.

Fourthly, take heed of spiritual surfeits, that the feeding too much upon the comforts of yokefellows, children, credit, profit (though sweet and wholesome as honey) turn not to bitterness and loathing. Remember that these worldly goods and comforts are the common portion of the men of this perishing world, who must perish together with them.

Fifthly, to maintain a spiritual health and cheerfulness it is of no small use to lay hold (says Paul to Timothy) of eternal life.[15] As the soldier meditates upon the glory of his victories; the sick passenger at sea upon his sweet refreshings on shore; the traveler upon his journey's end and comforts at his home; the laborer and the hireling on his wages, the husbandman on his harvest, the merchant on his gain, the woman in travail on her fruit: so let us sometimes warm and revive our cold hearts and fainting spirits with the assured hope of those victories, those crowns, those harvests, those refreshings and fruits, which God has prepared for those that love him.

God gives his servants a taste in this life, yet the harvest and the vintage are to come, when they that suffer with Christ Jesus shall reign with him, and they that have sown in tears shall reap the never-ending harvest of inconceivable joys.

Sixthly, as it is in the restoring of the body to health, or in the preserving of it in a healthful condition, it is often necessary to use the help of sharp and bitter things—bitter pills, bitter potions, bitter medicine, sweatings, purgings—so it is with our souls and spirits, and preservation of the health and cheerfulness of the spiritual and inner man.

The Word of God, and all his holy ordinances, are not only of a feeding and nourishing, but also of a purging and cleansing nature, of a preserving and restoring quality. It is so evident that although Christ Jesus' blood has quenched the fire of God's eternal wrath toward his people, and sweetened the bitter cup of all present judgments and afflictions; yet for his name and the sake of justice in this world, God's children have temporally felt the fearful strokes of his displeasure. Judgment must begin at the house of God.[16]

Let us also cast our eyes abroad and behold the direful signs and tokens of God's severe justice executed at present in the world. How lamentably do we see before our eyes the daily and continued effects of that first wrath upon mankind in so many sorrows of all sorts for the first transgression.

Let us consider the great constant reproach and misery over all the nations of the world, by reason of God's righteous sentence in the division of so many tongues and languages. How many hundreds of thousands of men, women and children have of late years been swept away in the world by wars, famines and pestilences?

And since we are commanded to weep with them that weep: O that our heads were fountains, and our eyes rivers of waters, that we might weep with Germany, weep with Ireland, yea, weep day and night with England and Scotland (to speak nothing of other remote nations) in laying again and again to heart the strokes of God's most righteous judgments in their most fearful slaughters and desolations.

To speak nothing of whole nations and kingdoms that know not at all the true and living God. Who can but wonder and tremble at so many hundred thousand and millions of men given up for so long a time to those two monstrously bewitching worships of Mohammedanism and anti-Christianism, the dire effects of God's most righteous judgments upon the eastern and western professors of the knowledge of God in Christ Jesus?

Add to these that most fearful and deplorable captivity of the souls and consciences of God's own people for so many hundred years under false and superstitious worships. And (to come to the full period and final sentence of the most righteous Judge of the whole world) with what horrors and terrors shall these heavens and earth pass away, this earth with the works thereof being consumed and burnt up? How inconceivably direful will the last eternal judgment be when two worlds of men (the former destroyed by water, and this by fire) shall appear before the most glorious tribunal of the Son of God?

Yet we may adore God's righteous judgments and (working out salvation with fear and trembling) make sure of a Jesus, a Savior, to deliver us from the wrath that is to come.

My dear Love, let us go down together by the steps of holy meditation into the valley of the shadow of death. It is of excellent use to walk often into Golgotha. It is of great and sweet use against the bitter-sweet delusions of this world, daily to think each day our last. To think it the day of our last farewell, the day of the splitting of this vessel, the breaking of this bubble, the quenching of this candle.

How weaned, how sober, how temperate, how mortified should be our spirits, our affections, our desires, when we remember that we are but strangers, converse with strange companies, dwell in strange houses, lodge in strange beds. We know not whether this day, this night shall be our final change of this strange place for one far stranger, dark and doleful except as enlightened by the death and life of the Son of God.

How contented we should be with any pittance, any allowance of bread, of clothes, of friendship, of respect. How thankful to God and man should we poor strangers be for the least crumb or drop or rag vouchsafed to us, when we remember we are but strangers in an inn, passengers in a ship. Though we dream of long summer days, yet our very life and being is but a swift, short passage from the bank of time to the other side or bank of a doleful eternity.

How patient should our minds and bodies be under the hand of our all-powerful Maker, of our most gracious Father, when we remember that this is the short span of our purging and fitting for an eternal glory; and that when we are judged, we are chastened of the Lord, that we should not be condemned with the world!

How quietly should we bear the daily injuries, reproaches, persecutings from the hands of men who pass away and wither (it may be before night) like grass, or as the smoke on the chimney's top; and their love and hatred shall quickly perish!

Yes, how busy, how diligent, how solicitious should we be (like strangers upon a strange coast), waiting for a wind or passage to get dispatched what we have to do before we hear that final call, "Away, away, let us be gone from hence!"

How should we plan to get aboard that which will pass, and turn to blessed account in our own country?

How should we overlook and despise this world's trash which (as the holy woman going to be burnt for Christ said of money) will not pass in Heaven?

How zealous for the true God, the true Christ, his praise, his truth, his worship; how faithful in a humble witness against the lies and cozening delusions of the father of lies, even though they are gilded over the truth, and that by the hands of the highest or holiest upon the earth?

How frequent, how constant (like Christ Jesus our Founder and Example) in doing good, especially to the souls of all men, especially to the household of faith; yea, even to our enemies, when we remember that this is our seed time, of which every minute is precious? As our sowing is, so must be our eternal harvest, for so says the Spirit by Paul to the Galatians: "He that soweth to the flesh, shall of the flesh reap corruption or rottenness, and he that soweth to the Spirit, shall of the Spirit reap life everlasting."[17]

Notes

1. 2 Corinthians 4.
2. Romans 6.
3. 2 Corinthians 9:7, Ephesians 6:15.
4. Revelation 2:4.
5. Numbers 23:10.
6. Cf. Titus 3.
7. John 4:34.
8. Cf. Song of Solomon 4.
9. Ephesians 5:23, 24.
10. Actually Psalm 40:7, 8.
11. John Bradford (1510–1555) was martyred for his faith, being burnt at the stake at Smithfield in the reign of Mary Tudor.

12. Philippians 2:25-30.
13. Romans 16:1, Acts 18:2, Acts 1:14, Romans 16:12.
14. Exodus 32:32, Romans 9:3.
15. 1 Timothy 6:12.
16. 1 Peter 4:17.
17. Galatians 6:8.

Williams' letter is taken by permission from *The Complete Writings of Roger Williams*, volume 7, edited by Perry Miller, published by Russell and Russell Inc, New York, 1963.

Probably no finer Christian literature has come out of Scotland than the letters of Samuel Rutherford (1600–1661) which he wrote from Aberdeen, where he was exiled, to his congregation at Anwoth. These epistles have become Christian classics. Vibrant with the love of Jesus Christ, they have captured the admiration of millions of readers.

Yet Rutherford seems hardly to have thought of himself as a devotional writer. After a stint as professor of Latin at Edinburgh University, he was ordained as a Presbyterian minister. His theological writings, being strongly Calvinistic in nature, enveloped him in controversy and caused him to be deposed (after a nine-year ministry) from his Anwoth pulpit in 1636. By order of the High Commission he was confined "during the king's pleasure" to the city of Aberdeen. The order was rescinded nearly two years later.

After his release, Rutherford went to London in 1643 as one of the Scottish commissioners to the Westminster Assembly. There he helped to write the Westminster Confession and Catechisms. He also wrote Lex Rex, a political essay which was considered an attack on the restored monarchy of Charles II. It was publicly burned in 1660, and Rutherford would have been executed for high treason had he not died before the king's officers arrived to take him to London.

To fellow-pastors who visited him during his final illness, Rutherford said, "Dear brethren, pray for Christ. Preach for Christ. Do all for Christ; beware of men-pleasing." The political and ecclesiastical battles of the seventeenth century are long gone, but Rutherford's beautiful letters remain.

Behind the unique imagery of the letters, the careful reader will be able to discern a certain spiritual progression. Rutherford lived through one of Britain's worst times, and some of the letters reflect the struggles of the people. The last letter to be included is addressed to the Reverend James Guthrie, a genuine Scottish martyr for his faith who was executed by the officers of King Charles II at Tolbooth prison, Edinburgh, June 1, 1661. Rutherford wrote this touching letter in February of that year, and himself died a month later.

To make a selection from Rutherford's 365 extant letters has been difficult. (Not all reproduced here were written from Aberdeen.) Only excerpts are used in many cases, for some of the letters are quite long. Footnotes provide a glossary for unfamiliar words in the text.

8

From Letters *of* *Samuel Rutherford*

To Lady Kenmure, 1630

Madam—I have longed exceedingly to hear of your life and health, and growth in the grace of God. I entreat you, Madam, let me have two lines from you concerning your present condition. I know you are in grief and heaviness; and if it were not so, you might be afraid, because then your way should not be so like the way that (our Lord says) leads to the New Jerusalem.

If God has given you the earnest of the Spirit as part of payment of God's principal sum, you have to rejoice; for our Lord will not lose his earnest, neither will he go back or repent him of the bargain. Peace of conscience, liberty of prayer, the doors of God's treasure cast up to the soul, and a clear sight of himself looking out and saying, with a smiling countenance, "Welcome to me, afflicted soul"; this is the earnest that he gives sometimes, and which makes glad the heart, and is an evidence that the bargain will hold.

I have neither tongue nor pen to express to you the happiness of such as are in Christ. I wonder that your heart should ever be cast down if you believe this truth. Believe, then, believe and be saved. Think it not hard if you do not get your will or your delights in this life. God will have you to rejoice in nothing but himself.

Our church, Madam, is decaying. She is like Ephraim's cake (Hosea 7:8). Her wine is sour and corrupted. The power and life of religion is away. It were time for us by prayer to put upon our master-pilot, Jesus, and to cry, "Master, save us; we perish." Grace, grace be with you.

Yours in the Lord,
S.R.

(7)

To Lady Kenmure, 1630

Worthy and dear lady, in the strength of Christ, fight and overcome. You are now alone, but you may have for the seeking, three always in your company, the Father, Son and Holy Spirit. I trust in God that, carrying this temple about with you, you shall see Jehovah's beauty in his house.

We are in great fears of a great and fearful trial to come upon the kirk[1] of God. Our King [has drawn] hard and dangerous conclusions against such as are termed Puritans, for the rooting of them out. Our prelates (the Lord take the keys of his house from these bastard porters!) assure us that for such as will not conform there is nothing but imprisonment and deprivation.

All sorts of crying sins without controlment abound in our land. The glory of the Lord is departing from Israel. Corrupt and false doctrine is openly preached by the idol-shepherds of the land. For myself, I have daily griefs. I was summoned before the High Commission by a profligate person in this parish, convicted of incest. Upon the day of my appearance, the sea and winds refused to give passage to the Bishop of St. Andrews. The Lord Jesus be with your spirit.

(11)   S.R.

To Lady Kenmure, 1636

Noble and Elect Lady—The honor I have prayed for these sixteen years, with submission to my Lord's will, my kind Lord has now bestowed upon me, even to suffer for my royal and princely King Jesus, and for his kingly crown, and the freedom of his kingdom that his Father has given him.

The forbidden lords have sentenced me with deprivation and confinement within the town of Aberdeen. I am charged in the King's name to enter against the 20th day of August next, and there to remain during the King's pleasure, as they have given it out. Howbeit Christ's green cross, newly laid upon me, be somewhat heavy, I call to mind with faith that the Lord hears the sighing of a prisoner, with undoubted hope (as sure as my Lord lives) after this night to see daylight, and Christ's sky to clear up again upon me, and his poor kirk.

My dear worthy lady, I give it to your ladyship, under my own hand, my heart writing as well as my hand—welcome, welcome, sweet, sweet and glorious cross of Christ; welcome, sweet Jesus, with your light cross. I purpose to obey the King, who has power of my body; and rebellion to kings is unbeseeming Christ's ministers. I will look that your ladyship and that good lady [Lady Mar] will be mindful to God of the Lord's prisoner, not for my cause, but for the Gospel's sake. I am yours in his own sweetest Lord Jesus,

(61) S.R.

To Mr. Hugh M'Kail, 1636

Reverend and Dear Brother—I thank you for your letter. I cannot but show you, that as I never expected anything from Christ but much good and kindness, so he has made me to find it in the house of my pilgrimage. And believe me, brother, whoso looks to the white side of Christ's cross, and can take it up handsomely with faith and courage, shall find it such a burden as sails are to a ship, or wings to a bird.

I find that my Lord has overgilded that black tree, and has perfumed it, and oiled it with joy and consolation. I am taught in this ill weather to go on the lee-side of Christ, and put him in between me and the storm; and (I thank God) I walk on the sunny side of the brae.

I am not out of the house yet. A letter were a work of charity to me. Grace be with you. Pray for me.

Your brother and Christ's prisoner,

(71) S.R.

To Lady Culross, 1636

Madam—Grace, mercy and peace be multiplied upon you. I am now (all honor and glory to the King eternal, immortal and invisible!) in better terms with Christ than I was. Like a fool, I libelled unkindness against my Lord; but now I pass from that foolish pursuit; I give over the plea. He is God, and I am man.

I see grace grows best in winter. The poor persecuted kirk, this lily among thorns, shall blossom, and laugh upon the gardener. I know no other way how to glorify Christ, but to make an open proclamation of his love, and of his fidelity to such as suffer for him. Grace, grace be with you.

(74) S.R.

To Mr. John Meine, 1637

Worthy and dear brother—Grace, mercy and peace be to you. I am here waiting, if the fair wind will turn upon Christ's sails in Scotland, and if deliverance be breaking out to this overclouded and be-nighted kirk.

I have little of Christ in this prison but groanings and longings and desires. All my stock of Christ is some hunger for him, and yet I cannot say but I am rich in that. But blessed be my Lord, who takes me light, and clipped, and naughty, and feckless as I am.[2] I see that Christ will not prig with me,[3] nor stand upon stepping-stones; but comes in broadside without ceremonies, or making it nice, to make a poor, ran-somed one his own.

Remember my love in Christ to your father, and help me with your prayers. Grace be with you.

(81)   S.R.

To Robert Gordon, 1637

My very worthy and dear friend—Grace, mercy and peace be to you. My dear brother, I cannot show you how matters go betwixt Christ and me. I find my Lord going and coming seven times a day. His visits are short; but they are both frequent and sweet. I am like a hungry man that wants teeth, or a weak stomach having a sharp appetite. I can let Christ grip me, but I cannot grip him. I love to sit on Christ's knee, but I cannot set my feet to the ground, for afflictions bring the cramp upon my faith. All that I can do is hold out a lame faith to Christ, like a beg-gar holding out a stump instead of an arm or leg, and cry, "Lord Jesus, work a miracle!"

Oh, what would I give to have hands and arms to grip strongly and fold heartsomely about Christ's neck, and to have my claim made good with real possession! I think that my love to Christ has feet in abundance, and runs swiftly to be near him, but it wants hands and fingers to apprehend him. Oh, to have as much faith as I have love and hunger.

I see that mortification, and to be crucified to the world, is not so highly accounted of by us as it should be. I see men lying about the world, as nobles about a king's court, and I wonder what they are all doing there. This world can take little from me, and just as little can it give me. I recommend mortification to you above anything. We chase feathers flying in the air, and tire our own spirits for the froth and gilded clay of a dying life.

I have no cause to say that I am pinched with penury, or that the consolations of Christ are dried up, for he has poured down rivers upon a dry wilderness. In my very swoonings, he holds up my head, and stays

me with flagons of wine, and comforts me with apples (Song of Solomon 2:5). My house and bed are strewed with kisses of love. Praise, praise with me. Oh, if you and I betwixt us could lift up Christ upon his throne, even if all Scotland should cast him down to the ground! The prisoner's prayers and blessings come upon you. Grace be with you.
(92)   S.R.

To Mr. Matthew Mowat, 1637

Reverend and Dear Brother—You desire me "not to mistake Christ under a mask." I bless you and thank God for it. But alas! masked or barefaced, kissing or glooming, I mistake him. Yea, I mistake him the farthest when the mask is off; for then I play with his sweetness. I am like a child that has a gilded book, that plays with the ribbons and the gilding, and the picture on the first page, but reads not the contents of it. My poor weakness makes me lie behind the bush and hide me.

When I came to Christ's camp, I had not so much free gear as to buy a sword. I wonder that Christ should not laugh at such a soldier. I am no better yet; but faith lives and spends upon our Captain's charges, who is able to pay for all. We need not pity him, he is rich enough. The Lord Jesus be with your spirit.
(120)   S.R.

To Mr. John Osburn, provost of Ayr, 1637

Much honored sir—Grace, mercy and peace be to you. I have nothing to say but that Christ, in that honorable place he has put you in, has intrusted you with a dear pledge, which is his own glory. Make a good account of it to God. Be not afraid of men. Serve Christ. Back him. Let his cause be your cause. Give not a hairbreadth of truth away, for it is not yours, but God's.

I have cause to say this, because I find him truth itself. In my sad days, Christ laughs cheerfully and says, "All will be well!" Would to God that all this kingdom, and all that know God, knew what is betwixt Christ and me in this prison—what kisses, embracements and love communion! I take his cross in my arms with joy; I bless it, I rejoice in it. Suffering for Christ is my garland. I would not exchange Christ for ten thousand worlds; nay, if the comparison could stand, I would not exchange Christ with Heaven. Grace be with you.
(149)   S.R.

To Lady Mar, 1637

My very noble and dear lady—Grace, mercy and peace be to you. I received your ladyship's letter, which has comforted my soul. God give you to find mercy in the day of Christ.

I am in as good terms and court with Christ as an exiled, oppressed prisoner of Christ can be. I am still welcome to his house. He knows my knock, and lets in a poor friend. Under this black, rough tree of the cross of Christ, he has ravished me with his love, and taken my heart to Heaven with him.

Well and long may he brook it. I would not niffer Christ[4] with all the joys that man or angel can devise beside him. Who has such cause to speak honorably of Christ as I have? Oh, the depth of Christ's love. It has neither brim nor bottom. Oh, if this blind world saw his beauty. Grace, grace be with you.

(150)   S.R.

To James MacAdam, 1637

My very dear and worthy friend—Grace, mercy and peace be to you. It will be the joy of my heart to hear that you hold your face up the brae, and wade through temptations without fearing what man can do.

For myself, I am as well as Christ's prisoner can be; for by him I am master and king of all my crosses. I am above the prison, and the lash of men's tongues; Christ triumphs in me. I have been cast down and heavy with fears and haunted with challenges. I was swimming in the depths, but Christ had his hand under my chin all the time, and took good heed that I should not lose breath; and now I have got my feet again.

Oh, my short arms cannot fathom his love. I beseech you, I charge you, to help me to praise. Yours, in his sweet Lord Jesus,

(151)   S.R.

To John Gordon of Cardoness, 1637

Much honored sir—I long to hear how your soul prospers. I wonder that you write not to me, for the Holy Spirit bears me witness that I cannot, I dare not forget you.

Love Heaven; let your heart be on it. Up, up, and visit the new Land and view the fair City, and the white Throne, and the Lamb in his Bridegroom's clothes, sitting upon it. I beseech you by the wounds of your Redeemer, and by your compearance[5] before him, and by the salvation of your soul, lose no more time; run fast, for it is late.

The Lord is my witness above, that I write my heart to you. I never knew, by my nine years' preaching, so much of Christ's love as he has taught me in Aberdeen, by six months' imprisonment. He has made me to know now better than before, what it is to be crucified to the world.

The Lord has given you much, and therefore he will require much of you again. Number your talents, and see what you have to render back. You cannot be persuaded enough of the shortness of your time. Set forward up the mountain to meet with God; climb up, for your Savior calls on you. You have my love and the desires of my heart for your soul's welfare. Your affectionate and lawful pastor,
(166)   S.R.

To John Gordon of Cardoness, 1637

Much honored and dearest in my Lord—Grace, mercy and peace be to you. My soul longs exceedingly to hear how matters go betwixt you and Christ; and whether or not there be any work of Christ in that parish that will bide the trial of fire and water.

Sir, show the people this; for when I write to you, I think I write to you all, old and young. Fulfil my joy and seek the Lord. Sure I am that once I discovered my lovely, royal, princely Lord Jesus to you all. Woe, woe, woe shall be your part of it for evermore, if the Gospel be not the savor of life to you. Fit your accounts and order them. Lose not the last play, whatever you do, for in that play with death your precious soul is the prize. For the Lord's sake spill not the play and lose not such a treasure.

Examine yourself if you be in good earnest in Christ, for some are partakers of the Holy Ghost, and taste of the good word of God, and of the powers of the life to come, and yet have no part in Christ at all. Many think they believe, but never tremble: the devils are farther on than these (James 2:19). I never knew so well what sin was as since I came to Aberdeen.

Oh, if the heaven, and the heaven of heavens, were paper, and the sea ink, and the multitude of mountains pens of brass, and I able to write that paper within and without, full of the praises of my fairest, my dearest, my loveliest, my sweetest, my matchless, and my most marrowless and marvelous Well-beloved!

Oh, that people were wise! Oh, that people were wise! Oh, that people would speer out Christ and never rest until they find him.[6] Now, worthy sir, now my dear people, my joy and my crown in the Lord, let him be your fear. Seek the Lord and his face. Pray for me and praise for

me. The blessing of my God, the prayers and blessing of a poor prisoner and your lawful pastor, be upon you.
(180)   S.R.

To Mr. John Fergushill, 1637

Reverend and dear brother—Grace, mercy and peace be to you.
My longings and desires for a sight of the newly-builded tabernacle of
Christ again in Scotland has now taken some life again. I find the grief
of my silence swelling upon me. I wonder how I have passed a year and
a quarter's imprisonment without shaming my sweet Lord, to whom I
desire to be faithful.

Oh, that I were free of that idol which they call *myself;* and that
Christ were for *myself;* and *myself* a decourted cypher,[7] and a denied
and forsworn thing! But that proud thing, *myself,* will not play, except
it ride up side for side with Christ, or rather have place before him.
O *myself,* if you could give Christ the way, and take your own room,
which is to sit as low as nothing or corruption!

Oh, but we have much need to be ransomed and redeemed by
Christ from that master-tyrant, that cruel and lawless lord, *ourself.* Nay,
when I am seeking Christ, and am out of myself, I have the third part of
a squint eye upon that vain, vain thing, *myself, myself,* and something of
mine own.

Grace, grace, be (as it is) your portion,
(188)   S.R.

To Lady Cardoness, 1637

Mistress—I beseech you in the Lord Jesus to make every day
more and more of Christ. Learn daily both to possess and miss Christ.
He must go and come, because his infinite wisdom thinks it best for
you. We shall be together one day. We shall not need to borrow light
from sun, moon or candle.

Oh, blessed is the soul whose hope has a face looking straight out
to that day. It is not our part to make a treasure here; anything, under
the covering of heaven, which we can build upon, is but ill ground and
a sandy foundation. Every good thing, except God, wants a bottom, and
cannot stand alone; how then can it bear the weight of us?

Let us not lay a load on a windlestraw.[8] There shall nothing find
my weight, or found my happiness, but God. It is better to rest on God
than to sink or fall; and we weak souls must have a bottom and a being-
place, for we cannot stand our lone.

Now I can say no more. Remember me. I have God's right to that people; howbeit by the violence of men stronger than I, I am banished from you and chased away.

It may be that God will clear my sky again, but there is small appearance of my deliverance. But let him do with me what seems good in his own eyes. I am his clay; let my Potter frame and fashion me as he pleases. Grace be with you. Your lawful and loving pastor,
(192)   S.R.

To John Lennox, Laird of Cally, 1637

Worthy and dear sir, separate yourself, and bend yourself to the utmost of your strength and breath, in running fast for salvation. It cost Christ and all his followers sharp showers and hot sweats ere they won to the top of the mountain; but still our soft nature would have Heaven coming to our bedside when we are sleeping.

Oh, how loath are we to forego our packalds and burdens, that hinder us to run our race with patience.[9] Oh, what pains, and what a death is it to nature, to turn me, myself, my lust, my ease, my credit, over into "my Lord, my Savior, my King and my God, my Lord's will, my Lord's grace!"

What made Eve miscarry, and what hurried her headlong upon the forbidden fruit, but that wretched thing *herself?* What drew that brother-murderer to kill Abel? That wild *himself.* What drove the old world on to corrupt their ways? Who, but *themselves,* and their own pleasure? What was the cause of Solomon's falling into idolatry and multiplying of strange wives? What but *himself,* whom he would rather pleasure than God?

What was the hook that took David and snared him first in adultery, but his *self-lust?* And then in murder, but his *self-credit* and *self-honor?* What led Peter on to deny his Lord? Was it not a piece of *himself,* and *self-love* to a whole skin? What made Judas sell his Master for thirty pieces of money, but a piece of *self-love,* idolizing of avaricious *self?* What made Demas to go off the way of the Gospel, to embrace this present world? Even *self-love* and love of gain for himself.

Every man blames the devil for his sins, but the great devil, the house-devil of every man, the house-devil that eats and lies in every man's bosom, is that idol that kills all, *himself.* Oh, blessed are they who can deny themselves and put Christ in the room of themselves! Oh, would to the Lord that I had not a *myself,* but Christ; nor a *my lust,* but Christ; nor a *my ease,* but Christ; nor a *my honor,* but Christ! O sweet word: I live no more, but Christ lives in me! (Galatians 2:20).

Oh, if every one would put away himself, his own self, his own ease, his own pleasure, his own credit, and his own twenty things, his own hundred things which he sets up as idols, above Christ!

Worthy sir, pardon this my freedom of love; God is my witness that it is out of an earnest desire after your soul's eternal welfare that I use this freedom of speech. Stand now by Christ and his truth. Let me have power with you to confirm you in him. I think more of my Lord's sweet cross than of a crown of gold and a free kingdom lying to it.

Sir, I remember you in my prayers to the Lord, according to my promise. Grace, grace be with you.

(198)   S.R.

To the Lord of Cally, 1637

Worthy sir—Grace, mercy and peace be to you. My suit now to you, in paper, since I have no access to speak to you as formerly, is that you would lay the foundation sure in your youth. Surely you are now in the throng of temptations.[10] When youth is come to its fairest bloom, then the devil and the lusts of a deceiving world, and sin, are upon horseback and follow with upsails. If this were not so, Paul needed not to have written to a sanctified and holy youth, Timothy, a faithful preacher of the Gospel, to flee the lusts of youth (2 Timothy 2:22).

Give Christ your virgin love; you cannot put your love and heart into a better hand. Oh! if you knew him, and saw his beauty, your love, your liking, your heart, your desires would close with him and cleave to him. Love by nature, when it sees, cannot but cast out its spirit and strength upon amiable objects and good things, and things love-worthy; and what fairer thing than Christ?

O fair sun, and fair moon, and fair stars, and fair flowers, and fair roses, and fair lilies, and fair creatures; but O ten thousand times fairer Lord Jesus! Grace, grace be with you.

(202)   S.R.

To Mistress Stuart, 1637

Mistress—I am sorry that you take it so hardly that I have not written to you. I am judged to be that which I am not. I fear that if I were put into the fire, I should melt away, and fall down in shreds of painted nature; for truly I have little stuff at home that is worth the eye of God's servants.

If there be anything of Christ's in me, it is but a spunk of borrowed fire,[11] that can scarce warm myself and has little heat for standers-by. I would fain have that which you and others believe I have; but you are only witnesses to my outer side, and to some words on paper. Oh that he would give me more than paper-grace or tongue-grace! Were it not want that pains me, I should have a skailed house and gone a-begging long since.[12] But Christ has left me with some hunger. . . .

Grace, grace be with you.

(215) S.R.

To Mr. Hugh Mackail, 1637

Reverend and dear brother—Grace, mercy and peace to you. I received your letter. I bless you for it. My dry root would take more dew and summer's rain than it gets, were it not that Christ will have dryness and deadness in us to work upon. So that I am often thanking God, not for guiltiness, but for guiltiness for Christ to whet and sharpen his grace upon. I am half content to have boils for the sake of the plasters of my Lord Jesus. . . .

Grace be with you.

(216) S.R.

To Alexander Gordon, 1637

Dear brother—if Christ were as I am, I could not keep a covenant with him. But I find Christ to be Christ; and that is all our happiness. Sinners can do nothing but make wounds, that Christ may heal them; and make debts, that he may pay them; and make falls, that he may raise them; and make deaths, that he may quicken them; and spin out and dig hells for themselves, that he may ransom them.

It is neither shame nor pride for a drowning man to swim to a rock, nor for a shipbroken soul to run himself ashore upon Christ. But alas! My soul is like a ship run on ground through ebbness of water. I am sanded, and my love is stranded, and I find not how to bring it on float again.

It is so cold and dead that I see not how to bring it to a flame. Fy, fy upon the meeting that my love has given Christ. Woe, woe is me! I have a lover, Christ, and yet I want love for him. I have a lovely and desirable Lord, who is love-worthy and who begs my love and heart, and I have nothing to give him!

I forget you not; pray for me, that our Lord would be pleased to send me among you again, fraughted and full of Christ.

Grace, grace be with you.

(217) S.R.

To Mr. James Hamilton, 1637

Reverend and dear brother—Peace be to you. I am laid low when I remember what I am, and that my outside casts such a luster when I find so little within. It is a wonder that Christ's glory is not defiled, running through such an unclean and impure channel.

But I see that Christ will be Christ in the dreg and refuse of men. His art, his shining wisdom, his beauty, speak loudest in blackness, weakness, deadness, yea, in nothing. I see nothing, no money, no worth, no good, no life, no deserving, is the ground that Omnipotency delights to draw glory out of.

Oh, how sweet is the inner side of the walls of Christ's house, and a room beside himself! My distance from him makes me sad. Oh, that the middle things betwixt us were removed. I am like a low man looking up to a high mountain, whom weariness and fainting overcomes. I would climb up, but find that I do not advance in my journey as I would wish. Yet I trust he will take me home against night.

I am exceedingly distracted with letters and company that visit me. Excuse my brevity. I desire to be mindful of you. Grace, grace be with you.

(236)   S.R.

To Lady Kenmure, 1659

Madam—I should be glad that the Lord would be pleased to lengthen out more time to you. Though I was lately knocking at death's gate, yet could I not get in, but was sent back for a time.

Madam, these many years the Lord has let you see a clear difference betwixt those who serve God and love his name, and those who serve him not. True it is that many of us have fallen from our first love; but Christ has renewed his first love of our espousals to himself, and multiplied the seekers of God all the country over, even where Christ was scarce named, east and west, south and north, above the number that our fathers ever knew.

But ah, Madam, what shall be done or said of many fallen stars, and many near to God complying woefully and sailing to the nearest shore? Yea, and we are consumed in the furnace and not melted; burned, but not purged. Our dross is not removed, but our scum remains in us.

We pray not, but wonder that Christ comes not the higher way, by might, by power, by garments rolled in blood. What if he come the lower way? We put the book in his hand, as if we could teach the Almighty knowledge. We make haste; we believe not. Let the only wise God alone; he steers well. He draws straight lines, though we think and say they are crooked.

Madam, hoping, believing, patient praying is our life. He loses no time. The Lord Jesus be with your spirit.

(354)   S.R.

To Mr. James Guthrie, my Reverend and dear Brother, Christ's soldier in bonds, minister of the Gospel at Stirling, 1661

Dear brother—We are very often comforted with the word of promise, though we stumble not a little at the work of holy providence. Some earthly men flourish as a green herb, and the people of God are counted as sheep for the slaughter, and killed all the day long. And yet both word of promise and work of providence are from him whose ways are equal, straight, holy and spotless.

Think it not strange that men devise against you, whether it be to exile, the earth is the Lord's; or perpetual imprisonment, the Lord is your light and liberty; or a violent and public death, for the Kingdom of Heaven consists in a fair company of glorified martyrs and witnesses, of whom Jesus Christ is the chief witness.

The Lord will make the innocency and Christian loyalty of his defamed and despised witnesses in this land to shine to after-generations. Be not terrified; fret not. Forgive your enemies; bless, and curse not. Though you and I should be silent, sad and heavy is the judgment and indignation of the Lord that is abiding the unfaithful watchmen of the Church of Scotland. The souls under the altar are crying for justice, and there is an answer returned already. The Lord's salvation will not tarry.

Cast the burden of wife and children on the Lord Christ; he careth for you and them. Your blood is precious in his sight. The everlasting consolations of the Lord bear you up and give you hope; for your salvation (if not deliverance) is concluded.

Your own brother,

(362)   S.R.

Notes

1. Kirk = Church.
2. Clipped = a coin not of full weight; naughty = vile; feckless = worthless.
3. Prig = haggle.
4. Niffer = exchange.

5. Compearance = appearance in a judicial court.
6. Speer out = search out by questions.
7. Decourted = sent out of court; discarded.
8. Windlestraw = a mere trifle; literally a withered stalk of grass.
9. Packalds = things packed up; burdens.
10. Throng = multitude.
11. Spunk = spark.
12. Skailed = scattered.

Excerpts taken from *Letters of Samuel Rutherford*, edited by Rev. Andrew A. Bonar, D.D., fourth edition, published by Oliphant, Anderson and Ferrier, Edinburgh, 1891.

Of all the authors included in this collection, John Bunyan (1628–1688) was in many ways the most unusual. He was perhaps the least educated, yet produced the most widely-read book, Pilgrim's Progress. *He had an abundance of mental problems, yet in his latter years proved to be wiser and more mature than many in discerning the deceptive policies of a hostile government. Known for his strict Calvinism, he was denounced as a false brother by even stricter members of his church. Although a Baptist, he did not stress baptism unduly.*

Most amazing, however, is the latent creative genius in this Bedford tinsmith that enabled him, while in prison, to produce an allegory of the Christian life that has blessed the world. Bunyan considered this writing project just a "trifle," something he turned to only in spare moments when he was not working at his trade (making lace tags) or engaging in religious controversies. He had no model to work from; it was entirely a product of his own mind.

A brief segment of Pilgrim's Progress *can hardly convey the work's wealth of symbolism and images. Quagmires and pits, steep hills, dark and horrible glens, soft vales, sunny pastures, a gloomy castle, animals, devils and hypocritical human beings are found together with noble characters and, of course, the pilgrim himself; once called Graceless, but now Christian, he is on his way from the City of Destruction to Mount Zion, the Celestial City.*

The son of a tinker, John Bunyan had only a village school education. Beyond that, his knowledge of English came from reading the Bible. He served in Cromwell's army as a young man, a period marked by a variety of mental conflicts and pressures. He found no pleasure in his strict Puritanism, and was even convinced at one time of having sinned against the Holy Spirit. He was twice married and had four children.

It was persecution under King Charles II, during which Bunyan spent twelve years in the Bedford jail, that finally relieved him of many of his internal tensions. During a later, briefer imprisonment in 1676, he wrote his famous allegory that for the next 300 years became the best-selling book in the English language after the Bible, permanently affecting the character of the English-speaking world. By the time he died, Bunyan was a famous person and was preaching to great crowds in London. His victorious faith is still blessing humanity.

9

From Pilgrim's Progress *by John Bunyan*

Now, I saw in my dream that the highway up which Christian was to go was fenced on either side with a wall that was called Salvation.[1] Up this way, therefore, did burdened Christian run, but not without great difficulty, because of the load on his back.

He ran thus till he came to a place somewhat ascending; and upon that place stood a cross, and a little below, in the bottom, a sepulchre. So I saw in my dream that just as Christian came up with the cross, his burden loosed from off his shoulders, and fell from off his back, and began to tumble, and so continued to do till it came to the mouth of the sepulchre, where it fell in, and I saw it no more.

Then was Christian glad and lightsome, and said with a merry heart, "He hath given me rest by his sorrow, and life by his death." Then he stood still awhile to look and wonder; for it was very surprising to him that the sight of the cross should thus ease him of his burden. He looked, therefore, and looked again, even till the springs that were in his head sent the water down his cheeks.[2]

Now, as he was looking and weeping, three Shining Ones came to him and saluted him with, "Peace!"

So the first said to him, "Your sins be forgiven you."[3] The second stripped him of his rags and clothed him with a change of raiment.[4] The third also set a mark on his forehead,[5] and gave him a roll with a seal upon it, which he told him to look at as he ran; and that he should turn it in at the celestial gate. So they went their way.

Then Christian gave three leaps for joy and went on, singing:

> Thus far did I come laden with my sin;
> Nor could aught ease the grief that I was in,

Till I came hither: what a place is this!
Must here be the beginning of my bliss?
Must here the burden fall from off my back?
Must here the strings that bound it to me crack?
Blest cross! blest sepulchre! blest rather be
The Man that was there put to shame for me!

I saw then in my dream that he went on thus until he came to the bottom, where he saw, a little out of the way, three men fast asleep with fetters upon their heels. The name of one was Simple, of another Sloth, and of the third Presumption.

Christian, then, seeing them lie in this case, went to them, thinking he might awake them, and cried, "You are like them that sleep on the top of a mast,[6] for the deep sea is under you, a gulf that has no bottom. Awake, and come away; if you are willing, I will help you off with your irons." He also warned them, "If he that goes about like a roaring lion[7] comes by, you will certainly become a prey to his teeth."

At that, they looked at him and began replying in this fashion: Simple said, "I see no danger."

Sloth said, "A little more sleep."

Presumption said, "Every tub must stand on its own bottom." So they lay down to sleep again, and Christian went on his way.

It troubled him to think that men in such danger should esteem so lightly the kindness that was offered them, both by waking them up and counseling them, and by proffering to help them off with their irons. Just then he spied two men who came tumbling over the wall on the left side of the narrow way, and caught up with him. The name of one was Formalist and the other, Hypocrisy.

Christian said to them, "Gentlemen, where did you come from and where are you going?"

They replied, "We were born in the land of Vainglory, and we're going for praise to Mount Zion."

Christian then asked, "Why didn't you come in at the front gate? Don't you know that it is written, "He who comes not in by the door, but climbs up some other way, is a thief and a robber?"[8]

Their response was that to go around to the entrance gate was considered too far out of the way by all their countrymen. For that reason the usual way was to take a shortcut and climb over the wall.

"Won't that be considered trespassing against the Lord of the city we're bound for?" asked Christian. "It is a direct violation of his revealed will." They replied that he didn't need to trouble his head about it, for it was the custom, and they could produce testimony that it had been the custom for more than a thousand years. "But will it stand a trial at law?" Christian insisted.

Formalist and Hypocrisy told him that any impartial judge would no doubt consider a custom legal that had stood for a thousand years. "Besides," they added, "just so we get into the Way, what difference does it make how we get in? If we're in, we're in. You came in at the gate; we came tumbling over the wall. Just how is your condition better than ours?"

Christian replied, "I walk by the rule of my Master; you walk by the rude working of your fancies. You are counted thieves already by the Lord of the way; therefore I expect you will not be found true men at the end of the way. You come in by yourselves without his direction, and you shall go out by yourselves without his mercy."

To this they made him but little answer, bidding him look to himself. Then I saw that they went on, each man in his way, without much conferring one with another; save that these two men told Christian that as to law and ordinances, they doubted not but that they should observe them as conscientiously as he. "So," they said, "we can't see where you differ from us except by the coat on your back, which was probably given you by some of your neighbors to hide the shame of your nakedness."

Christian said to them, "By laws and ordinances you will not be saved, since you did not come in by the door.[9] And as for this coat on my back, it was given to me by the Lord of the place I am headed for. It was indeed given to cover my nakedness, and I take it as a token of his kindness to me, since I had nothing but rags before.

"I am comforted to think that when I arrive at the gate of the city, the Lord will recognize me since I have his coat on my back—a coat he gave me freely on the day he stripped me of my rags. Moreover, I have a mark on my forehead, which you may not have noticed. One of my Lord's most intimate associates fixed it there the day that my burden fell off my shoulders. And at the same time I was given a roll sealed, to comfort me by reading it as I go in the Way. I was told to hand it in at the celestial gate, before going in myself. All of these you lack because you did not come in at the gate."

The two men, Formalism and Hypocrisy, simply looked at each other and laughed. So they continued on their way, but Christian walked ahead, talking with no one but himself, and sometimes sighing, but sometimes in a more comfortable mood. Often he would be reading in the roll that one of the Shining Ones gave him, and was refreshed by it.

I beheld then that they came to the foot of the Hill Difficulty, at the bottom of which was a spring. In the same place were two other ways, one of which turned to the left, the other to the right, at the foot of the hill. There was also a narrow way that proceeded right up the hill. Christian now went to the spring[10] and drank to refresh himself, and started up the hill.

The other two also came to the foot of the hill, which they saw was steep and high. When they discovered there were two other ways to go, they supposed that these two ways might meet again with the other route on the other side of the hill; so they resolved to go those ways. So one took the way which is called Danger, which led him into a great wood; and the other took the way called Destruction, which led him into a wide field, full of dark mountains, where he stumbled and fell and rose no more.

I looked then after Christian, to see him climbing the hill, and I perceived that his pace went from running to walking, and from walking to clambering on his hands and knees because of the steepness of the grade. Halfway to the summit, however, a pleasant arbor had been erected by the Lord of the hill for the refreshment of weary travelers. When Christian reached it he sat down to rest, and pulled his roll out of his shirt and read to his comfort. He took a fresh look, too, at the coat or garment that had been given him as he stood by the cross.

Thus pleasing himself awhile, Christian at last fell into slumber and thence into a fast sleep, which detained him in that place until it was almost night; and in his sleep the roll fell out of his hand. But while he was sleeping someone came by and awakened him, saying, "Go to the ant, thou sluggard; consider her ways, and be wise."[11] With that, Christian suddenly started up and sped on his way until he came to the top of the hill.

When he reached the crest two men came running toward him: the name of one was Timorous, and the other Mistrust. Christian said to them, "Sirs, what's the matter? You run the wrong way."

Timorous replied that they were going to the City of Zion and had climbed up that difficult place—"but," he said, "the farther we go, the more danger we meet with, so we turned and are going back."

"Yes," added Mistrust, "just before us a couple of lions lay in the path. We don't know whether they were asleep or awake, but we couldn't help thinking that if we came within reach, they would quickly tear us to pieces."

Christian then said, "You make me afraid; but where shall I run to where I can be safe? If I go back to my own country, that is prepared for fire and brimstone and I shall certainly perish there. If I can get to the Celestial City, I am sure to be in safety there, so I must venture on. To go back is nothing but death; to go forward is fear of death, and life everlasting beyond it. I will yet go forward."

So Mistrust and Timorous ran down the hill, and Christian went on his way. But thinking again of what he had heard from the men, he felt in his shirt for his roll, and did not find it. Now he was in great distress, and didn't know what to do. He wanted very much that which used to relieve him, and which should have been his pass into the Celestial City. So he began to be much perplexed.

At last he remembered that he had slept in the arbor on the side of the hill, and falling upon his knees, he asked God's forgiveness for his foolish act. Then he went back to look for his roll. And on the way back, who can sufficiently set forth the sorrow of Christian's heart? He sighed, he wept, he chided himself for being so foolish as to fall asleep in that place, which was erected only for a little refreshment from weariness. So he went back, carefully looking on this side and on that all the way, hoping he might find his roll that had been his comfort so many times in his journey.

He went thus till he came again within sight of the arbor where he had sat and slept. That sight renewed his sorrow all the more by bringing again his evil of sleeping freshly to his mind.[12] He bewailed his sinful sleep, saying, "Oh, wretched man that I am that I should sleep in the daytime, and in the midst of difficulty! That I should so indulge the flesh as to use that rest for ease to my flesh which the Lord of the hill has erected only for the relief of the spirits of pilgrims. How many steps have I taken in vain! The same thing happened to the Israelites: for their sin they were sent back again by the way of the Red Sea; and I am made to tread those steps with sorrow which I might have trod with delight, had it not been for this sinful sleep. How far might I have been on my way by this time! I am made to tread those steps three times which I needed not to have trod but once. Also, the day is almost spent, and night is going to trap me here. Oh that I had not slept!"

By this time he had reached the arbor, where for awhile he sat down and wept. At last, as Providence would have it, looking sorrowfully down under the settle, he espied his roll, which he picked up with trembling and haste and put it into his bosom. But who can tell how joyful this man was when he had found his roll again? For this roll was the assurance of his life and acceptance at the desired haven. Therefore he tucked it away, giving thanks to God for directing his eye to the place where it lay, and with joy and tears betook himself again to his journey.

But oh, how nimbly now did he go up the rest of the hill! Yet before he reached the summit, the sun went down upon Christian; and this made him recall again the vanity of his sleeping. Thus he began again to condole himself: "O sinful sleep! Because of you, I am caught by the night. I must walk without the sun, darkness must cover the path of my feet, and I must listen to the noise of the doleful creatures, all because of you."

Christian also remembered the story Mistrust and Timorous had told him, of how they were frightened by the sight of the lions. He said to himself, "These beasts range in the night for their prey, and if they should meet me in the dark, how could I cope with them? How should I escape being torn in pieces?" So he went on his way, bewailing his unhappy miscarriage; but when he lifted up his eyes, he beheld a stately palace before him, the name of which was Beautiful. It was just at the side of the highway.

So I saw in my dream that he made haste and went forward, hoping he might find lodging there. Soon he entered a narrow passage which was some 200 yards from the porter's lodge; and looking closely before him as he walked, he discovered two lions in the way. "Now," he thought, "I see the dangers that drove back Mistrust and Timorous." (The lions were chained, but he did not see the chains.)

Now Christian was afraid, and was minded to turn around and go back with the others, for he was sure that nothing but death lay before him. But the porter at the lodge, whose name is Watchful, perceiving that Christian had halted as if he would go back, called out to him, "Is your strength so small?[13] Don't be afraid of the lions; they are chained and are placed there for the trial of faith where it exists, and for the discovering of those who have none. Keep in the middle of the path and no harm will come to you."

Then I saw that Christian went on, trembling for fear of the lions but taking good heed to the directions of the porter. He heard the lions roar, but they did not harm him. Then he clapped his hands and went on till he came and stood before the gate where the porter was. He said to the porter, "Sir, what house is this, and may I lodge here tonight?"

The porter answered, "This house was built by the Lord of the hill, and he built it for the relief and security of pilgrims." The porter also asked where he had come from and where he was bound.

"I come," said Christian, "from the City of Destruction, and am going to Mount Zion. But because the sun is now set, I desire if I may to lodge here tonight."

"What is your name?" asked the porter.

"My name is now Christian," he replied, "but at the first my name was Graceless. I came of the race of Japhet, whom God will persuade to dwell in the tents of Shem."[14]

"How does it happen," asked the porter, "that you come so late? The sun is set."

"I would have been here sooner," said Christian, "but wretched man that I am, I slept in the arbor that stands on the hillside. Notwithstanding that, I would have been here earlier but in my sleep I lost my evidence, and came without it to the brow of the hill. Then feeling for it and not finding it, I was forced with sorrow of heart to go back to the place where I slept, where I found it; and now I am come."

"Well," said the porter, "I will call out one of the virgins of this place. If she likes your talk, she will bring you in to the rest of the family, according to the rules of the house." So Watchful the porter rang a bell, at the sound of which there came out the door of the house a grave and beautiful damsel named Discretion. She asked why she was called.

The porter answered, "This man is on a journey from the City of Destruction to Mount Zion; but, being weary and overtaken by dark, he asked me if he might lodge here tonight. So I told him I would call for you and that after you had discourse with him you might do as seems best to you, according to the law of the house."

Discretion then asked where he had come from and which way he was going, and he told her. She asked him also how he got into the Way, and he told her. Then she asked him what he had seen and met with on the way, and he told her.

At last she asked his name. So he said, "It is Christian; and I have so much more a desire to lodge here tonight, because by what I perceive, the place was built by the Lord of the hill for the relief and security of pilgrims."

So she smiled, but the water stood in her eyes, and after a little pause she said, "I will call forth two or three of my family." So she ran to the door and called out Prudence, Piety and Charity, who, after a little more discourse with him, had him in to the family. Many of them, meeting him at the threshold of the house, said, "Come in, thou blessed of the Lord: this house was built by the Lord of the hill on purpose to entertain such pilgrims." So he bowed his head and followed them into the house.

When he had come in and sat down, they gave him something to drink. It was agreed among them that until supper was ready, some of them should have conversation with Christian for the best improvement of time. So they appointed Piety, Prudence and Charity to talk with him.

Piety said to him, "Come, good Christian, since we have been so loving to you to receive you into our house this night, let us talk with you of all things that have happened to you in your pilgrimage, so that perhaps we may better ourselves thereby."

"With a very good will," said Christian, "and I am glad that you are so well disposed."

"What moved you at first to betake yourself to a pilgrim's life?" Piety continued.

Christian replied, "I was driven out of my native country by a dreadful sound that was in my ears, telling me that unavoidable destruction would attend me if I abode in that place where I was."

"But how did it happen that you came out of your country this way?"

"It was as God would have it," said Christian. "When I was under the fears of destruction, I did not know which way to go; but by chance a man came to me as I was trembling and weeping, whose name is Evangelist. He directed me to the wicket gate, which I never would have otherwise found; and so set me in the way that led directly to this house."

"But did you not come by the house of the Interpreter?" asked Piety.

"Yes," said Christian, "and I saw things there, the memory of which will stick by me as long as I live. Especially three things: how Christ, in spite of Satan, maintains his work of grace in the heart; how a man sinned himself quite out of hope of God's mercy; and also the dream of a man who thought in his sleep that the day of judgment had come."

"Why, did you hear him tell his dream?" asked Piety.

"Yes, and a dreadful one it was. It made my heart ache as he was telling it, yet I am glad I heard it."

"Was that all you saw at the house of the Interpreter?" asked Piety.

"No. He took me to a stately palace, and showed me how the people in it were clad in gold, and how there came a venturous man who cut his way through the armed men that stood in the door to keep him out; and how he was then invited to come in and win eternal glory. The sight of such things ravished my heart. I would have stayed at that good man's house a year, but I knew I had farther to go."

"What else did you see on the way?" Piety continued.

"See? Why, I went only a little farther and I saw One, as I thought in my mind, hang bleeding upon a tree; and the very sight of him made my burden fall off my back; for I groaned under a very heavy burden, and then it fell down off me. It was a strange thing to me, for I never saw anything before like it. And while I stood looking up (for I could not stop looking) three Shining Ones came to me. One of them testified that my sins were forgiven me; another stripped me of my rags, and gave me this embroidered coat which you see; and the third set the mark which you see in my forehead, and gave me this sealed roll." (And with that he plucked it out of his shirt.)

"But you saw more than this, did you not?" asked Piety.

Christian replied, "The things that I have told you were the best; yet some other matters I saw. For example, I saw three men, Simple, Sloth, and Presumption, lying asleep, a little out of the way as I came, with irons upon their heels. But do you think I could wake them? I also saw Formalist and Hypocrisy come tumbling over the wall, on their way, as they pretended, to Zion. But they quickly got lost, just as I warned them they would, but they would not believe.

"I found it hard work climbing this hill, and it was hard getting past the lions' mouths. If it had not been for that good man, the porter, who stands at the gate, I don't know but what I might after all have gone back again. But now I thank God I am here, and I thank you for receiving me."

Prudence then wanted to ask him a few questions and get his answers. "Do you think sometimes," she asked, "of the country you came from?"

"Yes, but with much shame and detestation. Truly, if I had been mindful of that country I came out of, I might have had an opportunity to return; but now I desire a better country, that is, a heavenly one."[15]

"And don't you still find yourself afflicted with some of the things that bothered you then?"

"Yes," said Christian, "but greatly against my will. Especially that goes for my inward carnal thoughts, in which I, along with all my countrymen, used to delight myself. But now all those things are my grief. If I were to choose my own thoughts, I would choose never to think of those things again. But when I want to be doing that which is best, that which is worst is with me."[16]

Prudence asked, "But don't you find sometimes that those things are vanquished that at other times perplex you?"

"Yes," agreed Christian, "but that is but seldom. They are to me golden hours in which such things happen to me."

"And can you remember what means you used to find your annoyances as if they were vanquished?"

"Yes," said Christian. "When I think about what I saw at the cross, that will do it; and when I look upon my embroidered coat, that will do it; also when I look into the roll that I carry with me, that will do it; and when my thoughts wax warm about where I am going, that will do it."

"What makes you so desirous to go to Mount Zion?"

"Why," said Christian, "there I hope to see him alive that did hang dead on the cross; and there I hope to be rid of all those things that are to this day an annoyance to me, because they are in me. They say there is no death[17] there, and I shall dwell with such company as I like best. To tell you the truth, I love him because by him I was eased of my burden; and I am weary of my inward sickness. I would fain be where I shall die no more, with the company that shall continually cry, 'Holy, holy, holy!'"

Charity then spoke to Christian: "Have you a family? Are you a married man?"

"I have a wife and four small children," said Christian.

"And why did you not bring them along with you?"

Then Christian wept and said, "Oh, how willingly would I have done it! But they were all of them utterly averse to my going on pilgrimage."

"You should have talked to them," said Charity. "You should have endeavored to show them the danger of staying behind."

"I did," answered Christian. "I told them also what God had shown me about the coming destruction of our city; but I seemed to them as one that mocked; they did not believe me."[18]

"Did you pray to God that he would bless your counsel to them?" asked Charity.

"Yes," said Christian, "and that with much affection; for you must know that my wife and poor children were very dear to me."

"But did you tell them of your own sorrow and fear of destruction? For I suppose that destruction was visible enough to you."

"Yes, over and over," said Christian. "They might also see my fears in my countenance, in my tears, and also in my trembling under the apprehension of the judgment that did hang over our heads: but all was not sufficient to prevail with them to come with me."

"But what could they say for themselves why they came not?" asked Charity.

"Why," he replied, "my wife was afraid of losing this world, and my children were given to the foolish delights of youth; so, what by one thing, and what by another, they left me to wander in this manner alone."

"But did you not, with your vain life, damp all that you by words used by way of persuasion to bring them away with you?"

"Indeed," said Christian, "I cannot commend my life, for I am conscious to myself of many failings therein. I know, also, that a man by his conversation may soon overthrow what, by argument or persuasion, he labors to fasten upon others for their good. Yet this I can say, I was very wary of giving them occasion by any unseemly action, to make them averse to going on pilgrimage. They would tell me I was too precise, and that I denied myself things (for their sakes) in which they saw no evil. I may say that, if what they saw in me hindered them, it was my great tenderness lest I sin against God, or do any wrong to my neighbor."

Charity responded, "If your wife and children have taken offense over this, they show themselves to be implacable to good. You have delivered your soul from their blood."[19]

Now I saw in my dream that they sat talking until supper was ready. So when they had made ready, they sat down to meat. The table was furnished with fat things, and wine that was well refined; and all their talk at the table was about the Lord of the hill—about what he had done, and why he did what he did, and why he built the house. By what they said, I perceived that he had been a great warrior, and had fought with and slain him that had the power of death[20] but not without great danger to himself: which made me love him the more.

For as Christian said they told him, "He did it with the loss of much blood," and they added, "But what puts the glory of grace into all he did, was that he did it out of pure love to this country." Besides, some of the household told Christian they had seen and spoken with him since he died on the cross; and they attested that they had it from his own lips, that he is a lover of poor pilgrims such as is not to be found from east to west.

Moreover, they gave an instance of what they affirmed: that he had stripped himself of his glory, that he might do this for the poor; and that they had heard him say that he would not dwell in the mountains of Zion alone. Moreover, they said he had made many pilgrims princes, though by nature they were born beggars, and their original had been the dunghill.[21]

Thus they discoursed together till late at night; and after they had committed themselves to their Lord for protection, they betook themselves to rest. The Pilgrim they laid in a large upper chamber, whose window opened toward the sunrising. The name of the chamber was Peace.

Notes

1. Isaiah 26:1.
2. Zechariah 12:10.
3. Mark 2:5.
4. Zechariah 3:4.
5. Ephesians 1:13.
6. Proverbs 23:34.
7. 1 Peter 5:8.
8. John 10:1.
9. Galatians 2:16.
10. Isaiah 58:11.
11. Proverbs 6:6.
12. Revelation 2:5, 1 Thessalonians 5:6–8.
13. Mark 4:40.
14. Genesis 9:27.
15. Hebrews 11:15, 16.
16. Romans 7:15–21.
17. Isaiah 25:8, Revelation 21:4.
18. Genesis 19:14.
19. Ezekiel 3:19.
20. Hebrews 2:14, 15.
21. 1 Samuel 2:8, Psalm 113:7.

Excerpt taken from *Pilgrim's Progress*, published by John C. Winston Company, Philadelphia, 1933. The incidents narrated are found in chapter 3.

"Perhaps the most remarkable incident in modern history," wrote Thomas Carlyle, "is not the Diet of Worms, still less the Battle of Austerlitz, Waterloo, Peterloo, or any other battle; but an incident passed carelessly over by most historians, and treated with some degree of ridicule by others: namely, George Fox's making to himself a suit of leather."

Carlyle was not a Christian, and he looked upon Fox (1624-1691) as neither religious reformer nor saint, but rather as an apostle of the new individualism, one who represented the aspiring free spirit of true manhood and who rode the wave of the future—the leather suit being his *"tool."*

Fox wouldn't have known what Carlyle was talking about. He was an earnest young man who, having caught a vision of what the church should be, set out to do something about it in the north and west of England. His sincerity and devotion to Christ won him followers who were nicknamed *"Quakers."* Fox's blunt aggressiveness caused him to be attacked, however, by both Christians and non-Christians, and he languished in British prisons for six years.

People thought of Fox as a mystic and a dreamer, but he was a mystic with a purpose. He vigorously attacked the social ills of his time, taking the side of women, striving with jurists, arguing with Cromwell, reproving teachers and tax collectors, and demanding prison reform. He also lashed out often against the hypocrisy of the churches.

By the time he died there were 50,000 Quakers scattered throughout Britain, Holland, Germany, America and other places. Fox's stand against war brought his followers persecution, but they remained steadfast in their faith. It is impossible to estimate the impact made by Quakerism upon the Western world, notably in the struggle against slavery and the slave trade, but in many other areas of concern as well.

For all his influence in social matters, Fox, particularly in his early years, thought of himself as simply a Spirit-filled evangelist and proclaimer of *"the truth."* His followers were known as *"Friends of truth."*

Carlyle's assessment was correct in one respect: George Fox was a complete individualist. As he tells us himself, many of the characteristics of Quakerism in the following centuries—the silent meeting, the *"plain speech,"* the refusal to take oaths or doff the hat—were introduced by Fox to his followers.

Our excerpt from his famous Journal *portrays Fox as he saw himself.*

10

From the Journal *of George Fox*

About the beginning of the year 1647 I was moved of the Lord to go into Derbyshire, where I met with some friendly people and had many discourses with them. Traveling on through some parts of Nottingham-shire, I met with a tender people; but I was often under great tempta-tions. I fasted much, and walked abroad in solitary places many days, and often took my Bible and went and sat in hollow trees and lonesome places till night came on; and frequently, in the night, walked mourn-fully about by myself; for I was a man of sorrows[1] in the times of the first workings of the Lord in me.

During all this time I was never joined in profession of religion with any, but gave myself up to the Lord, having forsaken all evil com-pany, and taken leave of father and mother and all other relations. I traveled up and down as a stranger in the earth, which way the Lord inclined my heart; taking a chamber to myself in the town where I came, and tarrying sometimes a month more or less in a place. I durst not stay long in any place, being afraid both of professor and profane, lest being a tender young man I should be hurt by conversing much with either. For which reason I kept myself much as a stranger, seeking heavenly wisdom and getting knowledge from the Lord; and was brought off from outward things to rely wholly on the Lord alone.

Though my exercises and troubles were very great, yet they were not so continual but that I had some intermissions, and was sometimes brought into such a heavenly joy that I thought I had been in Abra-ham's bosom.[2] As I cannot declare the misery I was in, it was so great and heavy upon me; so neither can I set forth the mercies of God unto me in all my misery. O, the everlasting love of God to my soul, when I was in great distress! When my troubles and torments were great, then was his love exceedingly great.

Now after I received an opening from the Lord, that "to be bred at Oxford or Cambridge was not sufficient to fit a man to be a minister of Christ," I regarded the priests less, and looked more after the Dissenting people. Among them I saw there was some tenderness.

But as I had forsaken the priests, so I left the separate preachers also, and those esteemed the most experienced people; for I saw there was none among them all that could speak to my condition. When all my hopes in them and in all men were gone, so that I had nothing outwardly to help me, nor could I tell what to do; then, O! then I heard a voice which said, "There is one, even Christ Jesus, that can speak to thy condition"; and when I heard it, my heart did leap for joy.

Then the Lord let me see why there was none upon the earth that could speak to my condition, namely, that I might give him all the glory; for all are concluded under sin,[3] and shut up in unbelief, as I had been, that Jesus Christ might have the preeminence, who enlightens, and gives grace and faith and power. Thus when God doth work, who shall hinder it? And this I knew experimentally.

My desires after the Lord grew stronger, and zeal in the pure knowledge of God, and of Christ alone, without the help of any man, book or writing. For though I read the Scriptures that spoke of Christ and of God, yet I knew him not, but by revelation, as he who hath the key did open,[4] and as the Father of Life drew me to his Son by his Spirit.

Then the Lord gently led me along, and let me see his love, which was endless and eternal, surpassing all the knowledge that men have in their natural state, or can obtain from history or books; and that love let me see myself, as I was without him. When I myself was in the deep, shut up under all, I could not believe that I should ever overcome. My troubles, my sorrows and my temptations were so great that I thought many times I should have despaired, I was so tempted.

But when Christ opened to me how he was tempted by the same devil, and overcame him and bruised his head,[5] and through him and his power, light, grace, and Spirit, I should overcome also, I had confidence in him. So he it was that opened to me when I was shut up and had no hope nor faith. Christ, who had enlightened me, gave me his light to believe in.[6] He gave me hope, which he himself revealed in me, and he gave me his Spirit and grace, which I found sufficient in the deeps and in weakness.

I found that there were two thirsts in me: the one after the creatures, to get help and strength there; and the other after the Lord, the

Creator, and his Son Jesus Christ. I saw the great love of God, and I was filled with admiration at the infinitude of it; I saw what was cast out from God, and what entered into God's Kingdom; and how by Jesus, the opener of the door with his heavenly key, the entrance was given.

Yet it was so with me, that there seemed to be two pleading in me.[7] Questionings arose in my mind about gifts and prophecies; and I was tempted again to despair, as if I had sinned against the Holy Spirit. Then the spiritual discerning came into me, by which I did discern my own thoughts, groans and sighs. I discerned also the groans of the Spirit, which opened me, and made intercession to God. By this Spirit, in which the true sighing is, I saw over the false sighings and groanings.

A report went abroad of me, that I was a young man that had a discerning spirit,[8] whereupon many came to me from far and near, professors, priests and people. The Lord's power broke forth, and I had great openings and prophecies, and spoke to them of the things of God, which they heard with attention and silence, and went away, and spread the fame thereof. Then came the tempter, and set upon me again.

After this I went to Mansfield, where was a great meeting of professors and people; here I was moved to pray; and the Lord's power was so great that the house seemed to be shaken. When I had done, some of the professors said it was now as in the days of the apostles, when the house was shaken where they were.

Now after I had had some service in these parts, I went through Derbyshire into my own country, Leicestershire, and several tender people were convinced. Then I heard of a great meeting to be at Leicester, for a dispute, wherein Presbyterians, Independents, Baptists, and Common-prayer-men were said to be all concerned. The meeting was in a steeple-house, and thither I was moved by the Lord God to go, and be amongst them.

I heard their discourse and reasoning, some being in pews, and the priest in the pulpit; abundance of people being gathered together. At last one woman asked a question out of Peter, What that birth was, viz., a being born again of incorruptible seed, by the Word of God, that liveth and abideth for ever?[9]

The priest said to her, "I permit not a woman to speak in the church," though he had before given liberty for any to speak. Whereupon I was wrapped up, as in a rapture, in the Lord's power; and I stepped up and asked the priest, "Dost thou call this (the steeple-house) a church? Or dost thou call this mixed multitude a church?"

For the woman asking a question, he ought to have answered it, having given liberty for any to speak. But instead of answering me, he asked me what a church was. I told him, "The church was the pillar and ground of truth, made up of living stones, living members, a spiritual household, which Christ was the head of; but he was not the head of a mixed multitude, or of an old house made up of lime, stones and wood."[10]

This set them all on fire: the priest came down out of his pulpit, and others out of their pews, and the dispute there was marred. But I went to a great inn, and there disputed the thing with the priests and professors of all sorts; and they were all on a fire. But I maintained the true church, and the true head thereof, over the heads of them all, till they all gave out and fled away. Howbeit there were several convinced that day; and the woman that asked the question was convinced, and her family; and the Lord's power and glory shone over all.

Thus the work of the Lord went forward, and many were turned from the darkness to the light within the compass of these three years, 1646–1648. Divers meetings of Friends in several places were then gathered to God's teaching by his light, Spirit and power; for the Lord's power broke forth more and more wonderfully.

Now was I come up in Spirit through the flaming sword into the paradise of God. All things were new, and all the creation gave another smell unto me than before, beyond what words can utter.[11] I knew nothing but pureness and innocency and righteousness, being renewed into the image of God by Christ Jesus to the state of Adam, which he was in before he fell.

Great things did the Lord lead me into, and wonderful depths were opened unto me, beyond what can by words be declared;[12] but as people come into subjection to the Spirit of God, and grow up in the image and power of the Almighty, they may receive the Word of Wisdom that opens all things, and come to know the hidden unity in the Eternal Being.

Thus I traveled on in the Lord's service, as the Lord led me. And when I came to Nottingham, the mighty power of God was there among Friends. From thence I went to Clawson in Leicestershire, in the Vale of Beavor, and the mighty power of God was there also, in several towns and villages where Friends were gathered.

While I was there, the Lord opened to me three things relating to those three great professions in the world, physic, divinity (so called), and law. He showed me that the physicians were out of the wisdom of God, by which the creatures were made; and so knew not their virtues, because they were out of the Word of Wisdom, by which they were made.

He showed me that the priests were out of the true faith which Christ is the author of; the faith which purifies and gives victory, and brings people to have access to God, by which they please God; which mystery of faith is held in a pure conscience.

He showed me also that the lawyers were out of the equity, and out of the true justice, and out of the law of God, which went over the first transgression, and over all sin, and answered the Spirit of God that was grieved and transgressed in man.

And that these three, the physicians, the priests, and the lawyers, ruled the world out of the wisdom, out of the faith, and out of the equity and law of God: the one pretending the cure of the body, the other the cure of the soul, and the third the property of the people.

But I saw that they were all out of the wisdom, out of the faith, out of the equity and perfect law of God. And as the Lord opened these things unto me, I felt his power went forth over all, by which all might be reformed, if they would receive and bow unto it.

The priests might be reformed and brought into the true faith, which was the gift of God. The lawyers might be reformed and brought into the law of God, which answers that command of God, which is transgressed in every one, and brings one to love one's neighbor as himself. This lets man see, if he wrongs his neighbor he wrongs himself; and this teaches him to do unto others as he would they should do unto him.

The physicians might be reformed and brought into the wisdom of God, by which all things were made and created; that they might receive a right knowledge of them, and understand their virtues, which the Word of Wisdom, by which they were made and are upheld, hath given them.

I saw the state of those, both priests and people, who in reading the Scriptures cry out much against Cain, Esau, and Judas, and other wicked men of former times, mentioned in Holy Scriptures;[13] but do not see the nature of Cain, of Esau, of Judas and those others, in themselves.

These said it was they, they, they, that were the bad people; putting it off from themselves. But when some of these came with the light and Spirit of truth to see into themselves, then they came to say I, I, I, it is I myself, that have been the Ishmael, and the Esau. For then they came to see the nature of wild Ishmael in themselves; the nature of Cain, of Esau, of Korah, of Balaam, and of the son of perdition in themselves, sitting above all that is called God in them.

Now the Lord God opened to me by his invisible power "that every man was enlightened by the divine light of Christ," and I saw it shine through all; and that they that believed in it came out of condemnation to the light of life, and became the children of it; but they that hated it, and did not believe in it, were condemned by it, though they made a profession of Christ.

This I saw in the pure openings of the light, without the help of any man; neither did I then know where to find it in the Scriptures, though afterwards, searching the Scriptures, I found it.[14] For I saw in that Light and Spirit which was before the Scriptures were given forth, and which led the holy men of God to give them forth, that all must come to that Spirit if they would know God, or Christ, or the Scriptures aright, which they that gave them forth were led and taught by.

On a certain time as I was walking in the fields, the Lord said unto me, "Thy name is written in the Lamb's book of life, which was before the foundation of the world."[15] And as the Lord spoke it, I believed and saw it in the new birth. Then some time after, the Lord commanded me to go abroad into the world, which was like a briery, thorny wilderness.

When I came, in the Lord's mighty power, with the word of life into the world, the world swelled and made a noise like the great raging waves of the sea. Priests and professors, magistrates and people, were all like a sea, when I came to proclaim the day of the Lord amongst them, and to preach repentance to them.

I was sent to turn people from darkness to the light,[16] that they might receive Christ Jesus. I was to direct people to the Spirit that gave forth the Scriptures,[17] by which they might be led into all truth, and so up to Christ and God, as they had been who gave them forth.

Now, when the Lord God and his Son Jesus Christ sent me forth into the world to preach his everlasting Gospel and Kingdom, I was glad that I was commanded to turn people to that inward light, Spirit, and grace, by which all might know their salvation, and their way to God; even that Divine Spirit which would lead them into all truth.

With and by this divine power and Spirit of God, and the light of Jesus, I was to bring people off from all their own ways to Christ, the new and living way; and from their churches, which men had made and gathered, to the church in God, the general assembly written in Heaven, which Christ is the head of. I was to bring them off from the world's teachers, made by men, to learn of Christ, who is the way, the truth, and the life, of whom the Father said, "This is my beloved Son, hear ye him";[18] and off from all the world's worships, to know the Spirit of Truth in the inward parts, and to be led thereby.

And I was to bring people off from all the world's religions, which are vain; that they might know the pure religion, might visit the fatherless, the widows, and the strangers, and keep themselves from the spots of the world. Then there would not be so many beggars, the sight of whom often grieved my heart, as it denoted so much hard-heartedness amongst them that professed the name of Christ.

I was to bring them off from all the world's fellowships, and prayings, and singings, which stood in forms without power; that their fellowship might be in the Holy Spirit, and in the Eternal Spirit of God; that they might pray and sing in the Spirit, with the grace that comes by Jesus, making melody in their hearts to the Lord.

I was to bring people off from men's inventions and worldly doctrines, by which they blew the people about this way and the other way, from sect to sect; and from all their beggarly rudiments,[19] with their schools and colleges for making ministers of Christ, who are indeed ministers of their own making but not of Christ's. I was to bring them off from all their vain traditions,[20] which they had instituted since the apostles' days, which the Lord's power was against; in the dread and authority of which, I was moved to declare against them all.

Moreover, when the Lord sent me forth into the world, he forbade me to "put off my hat" to any, high or low; and I was required to "Thee and Thou" all men and women, without any respect to rich or poor, great or small. O! the rage and scorn, the heat and fury that arose! O! the blows, punchings, beatings and imprisonments that we underwent, for not putting off our hats to men!

About this time I was sorely exercised in going to their courts to cry for justice, and in speaking and writing to judges and justices to do justly. I warned such as kept public-houses for entertainment, that they should not let people have more drink than would do them good; and in testifying against their wakes or feasts, May-games, sports, plays, and shows, which trained up people to vanity and looseness, and led them from the fear of God. I warned that the days they had set forth for holydays were usually the times wherein they most dishonored God by these things.

In fairs, also, and in markets, I was made to declare against their deceitful merchandise, cheating and cozening; warning all to deal justly, to speak the truth, to let their yea be yea, and their nay be nay;[21] and to do unto others as they would have others do to them; forewarning them of the great and terrible day of the Lord which would come upon them all.[22]

I was also moved to cry against all sorts of music, and against the mountebanks playing tricks on their stages, for they burdened the pure life and stirred up people's minds to vanity. I was much exercised, too, with school-masters and school-mistresses, warning them to teach their children sobriety in the fear of the Lord, that they might not be nursed and trained up in lightness, vanity and wantonness.

Likewise I was made to warn masters and mistresses, fathers and mothers in private families, to take care that their children and servants might be trained up in the fear of the Lord; and that they themselves should be therein examples of sobriety and virtue to them.

I saw that all Christians, and all that made a profession of Christianity, ought to train up their children and servants in the new covenant of light, Christ Jesus, who is God's salvation to the ends of the earth, that all may know their salvation; and they ought to train them up in the law of life, the law of the Spirit, the law of love and of faith, that they might be made free from the law of sin and death.

Coming to Mansfield-Woodhouse, there was a distracted woman under a doctor's hand, with her hair loose all about her ears. He was about to bleed her, she being first bound, and many people being about her, holding her by violence; but he could get no blood from her. I desired them to unbind her and let her alone, for they could not touch the spirit in her by which she was tormented.

So they unbound her; and I was moved to speak to her, and in the name of the Lord to bid her be quiet and still; and she was so. The Lord's power settled her mind, and she mended; and afterwards she received the truth, and continued it to her death. The Lord's name was honored, to whom the glory of all his works belongs. Many great and wonderful things were wrought by the heavenly power in those days.

Now while I was at Mansfield-Woodhouse, I was moved to go to the steeple-house there, and declare the truth to the priest and people; but the people fell upon me in great rage, struck me down, and almost stifled and smothered me. I was cruelly beaten and bruised by them with their hands, Bibles and sticks.

Then they haled me out, though I was hardly able to stand, and put me into the stocks, where I sat some hours; and they brought dog-whips and horsewhips, threatening to whip me. After some time they had me before the magistrate, at a knight's house where there were many great persons; who, seeing how evilly I had been used, after much threatening set me at liberty. But the rude people stoned me out of the town for preaching the word of life to them.

I was scarcely able to move or stand, by reason of the ill usage I had received; yet with considerable effort I got about a mile from the town, and then I met with some people who gave me something to comfort me, because I was inwardly bruised; but the Lord's power soon healed me again. That day some people were convinced of the Lord's truth and turned to his teaching, at which I rejoiced.

As I traveled through markets, fairs and divers places, I saw death and darkness in all people, where the power of God had not shaken them. As I was passing on in Leicestershire, I came to Twy-Cross, where there were excise men. I was moved of the Lord to go to them and warn them to take heed of oppressing the poor; and people were much affected with it.

There was in that town a great man that had long lain sick, and was given up by the physicians; and some Friends in the town desired me to go to see him. I went up to him in his chamber, and spoke the word of life to him, and was moved to pray by him; and the Lord was entreated, and restored him to health.

But when I was come downstairs into a lower room, and was speaking to the servants and some people that were there, a serving-man of his came raving out of another room with a naked rapier in his hand, and set it just to my side. I looked steadfastly on him and said, "Alack for thee, poor creature! What wilt thou do with thy carnal weapon? It is no more to me than a straw."

The standers-by were much troubled, and he went away in a rage and full of wrath. But when the news of it came to his master, he turned him out of his service. Thus the Lord's power preserved me, and raised up the weak man, who afterwards was very loving to Friends; and when I came to that town again, both he and his wife came to see me.

There being many new soldiers raised, the commissioners would have made me captain over them; and the soldiers said they would have none but me. So the keeper of the house of correction was commanded to bring me before the commissioners and soldiers in the market-place of Derby; and there they offered me that preferment, as they called it, asking me if I would not take up arms for the Commonwealth against Charles Stuart?

I told them I knew from whence all wars arose, even from the lust, according to James' doctrine;[23] and that I lived in the virtue of that life and power that took away the occasion of all wars. But they courted me to accept their offer, and thought I did but compliment them. But I told them I was come into the covenant of peace, which was before wars and strifes were. They said they offered it in love and kindness to me, because of my virtue; and such like flattering words they used. But I told them if that was their love and kindness, I trampled it under my feet.

Then their rage got up and they said, "Take him away, jailer, and put him into the dungeon amongst the rogues and felons." So I was had away and put into a lousy, stinking place, without any bed, amongst thirty felons, where I was kept almost half a year; unless it were at times, for they would sometimes let me walk in the garden, having a belief that I would not go away.

In this time of my imprisonment I was exceedingly exercised about the proceedings of the judges and magistrates in their courts of judicature. I was moved to write to the judges concerning their putting men to death for cattle, and money, and small matters; and to show them how contrary it was to the law of God in old time; for I was under great suffering in my spirit because of it, and under the very sense of death. But standing in the will of God, a heavenly breathing arose in my soul to the Lord. Then did I see the heavens opened, and I rejoiced, and gave glory to God.

Moreover, I laid before the judges what a hurtful thing it was that prisoners should lie so long in jail; showing how they learned wickedness one of another in talking of their bad deeds: and therefore speedy justice should be done.

While I was here in prison, there was a young woman in the jail for robbing her master of some money. When she was to be tried for her life, I wrote to the judge and to the jury about her, showing them how it was contrary to the law of God in old time to put people to death for stealing,[24] and moving them to show mercy. Yet she was condemned to die, and a grave was made for her; and at the time appointed she was carried forth to execution.

Then I wrote a few words, warning all people to beware of greediness or covetousness, for it leads from God; and exhorting all to fear the Lord, to avoid all earthly lusts, and to prize their time while they have it. This I gave to be read at the gallows. And though they had her upon the ladder, with a cloth bound over her face, ready to be turned off, yet they did not put her to death, but brought her back again to prison; and in the prison she afterwards came to be convinced of God's everlasting truth.

The next First-day I went to Tickhill, whither the Friends of that side gathered together, and in the meeting a mighty brokenness by the power of God was amongst the people. I went out of the meeting, being moved of God to go to the steeple-house.

I found the priest and most of the chief of the parish together in the chancel. So I went up to them and began to speak; but they immediately fell upon me; and the clerk took up his Bible as I was speaking, and struck me on the face with it, so that it gushed out with blood, and I bled exceedingly in the steeple-house.

Then the people cried, "Let us have him out of the church," and when they had got me out they beat me exceedingly, and threw me down, and over a hedge; and afterwards they dragged me through a house into the street, stoning and beating me as they drew me along, so that I was besmeared all over with blood and dirt. They got my hat from me, which I never obtained again. Yet when I was got upon my legs again, I declared to them the word of life, and showed them the fruits of their teacher, and how they dishonored Christianity.

After awhile I got into the meeting again amongst Friends; and the priest and people coming by the house, I went forth with Friends into the yard, and there I spoke to the priest and people. The priest scoffed at us and called us Quakers. But the Lord's power was so over them, and the word of life was declared in such authority and dread to them, that the priest began trembling himself; and one of the people said, "Look how the priest trembles and shakes; he is turned a Quaker also."

When the meeting was over, Friends departed; and I went without my hat to Balby, about seven or eight miles. Friends were much abused that day by the priest and his people; insomuch that some moderate justices hearing of it, two or three of them came and sat at the town, to hear and examine the business. And he that had shed my blood was afraid of having his hand cut off for striking me in the church (as they called it); but I forgave him, and would not appear against him.

*   *   *

After I had finished my services for the Lord in England, the ship and the Friends that intended to go with me being ready, I went to Gravesend on the 12th of 6th month (1671), my wife and several friends accompanying me to the Downs; for it was upon me from the Lord to go beyond the seas to visit America.

We went from Wapping in a barge to the ship, which lay a little below Gravesend, and there we found the Friends that were bound for the voyage with me, who had gone down to the ship the night before. Early next morning the passengers and those Friends that intended to accompany us to the Downs, being come on board, we took our leave of those that came with us to Gravesend only, in great tenderness, and set sail about six in the morning for the Downs.

Having a fair wind, we out-sailed all the ships that were outward-bound and got thither by evening. The next afternoon, the wind serving, I took leave of my wife and other Friends and went on board. Being clear we set sail in the evening.

When we had been about three weeks at sea, one afternoon we spied a vessel about four leagues astern of us. Our master said it was a Sallee [Moorish pirate] man-of-war that seemed to give us chase. Our master said, "Come, let us go to supper, and when it grows dark we shall lose him." This he spoke to please and pacify the passengers, some of whom began to be very apprehensive of the danger.

But Friends were well satisfied in themselves, having faith in God and no fear upon their spirits. When the sun was gone down I saw the ship out of my cabin making toward us. When it grew dark, we altered our course to miss her; but she altered also, and gained upon us.

At night the master and others came into my cabin and asked me what they should do. I told them I was no mariner; and I asked them what they thought was best to do. They said there were but two ways, either to outrun him, or tack about and hold the same course we were going before.

I told them, if he were a thief they might be sure he would tack about too; and as for outrunning him, it was to no purpose to talk of that, for they saw he sailed faster than we.

They asked me again what they should do, for they said if the mariners had taken Paul's counsel they had not come to the damage they did.

I answered it was a trial of faith, and therefore the Lord was to be waited on for counsel. So retiring in spirit, the Lord showed me that his life and power was placed between us and the ship that pursued us. I told this to the master and the rest, and that the best way was to tack about and steer our right course. I desired them also to put out all their candles but the one they steered by, and to speak to all passengers to be still and quiet.

About eleven at night the watch called and said they were just upon us. That disquieted some of the passengers; whereupon I sat up in my cabin, and looking through the porthole, the moon being not quite down, I saw them very near us. I was getting up to go out of the cabin, but remembering the word of the Lord, that his life and power was placed between us and them, I lay down again.

The master and some of the seamen came again, and asked me if they might not steer such a point? I told them they might do as they would. By this time the moon was quite down, a fresh gale arose, and the Lord hid us from them; and we sailed briskly on and saw them no more.

The next day being the first day of the week, we had a public meeting in the ship, as we usually had on that day throughout the voyage, and the Lord's presence was greatly among us. And I desired the people to mind the mercies of the Lord, who had delivered them; for they might have been all in the Turks' hands by that time had not the Lord's hand saved them.

About a week after, the master and some of the seamen endeavored to persuade the passengers that it was not a Turkish pirate that chased us, but a merchantman going to the Canaries. When I heard of it

I asked them why, then, did they speak to me? Why did they trouble the passengers? And why did they tack about from him and alter their course? I told them they should take heed of slighting the mercies of God.

Afterward, while we were at Barbados, there came in a merchant from Morocco and told the people that "one of the Sallee men-of-war saw a monstrous yacht at sea, the greatest that ever he saw, and had her in chase, and was just upon her, but that there was a spirit in her that he could not take."

This confirmed us in the belief that it was a Sallee-man we saw make after us, and that it was the Lord that delivered us out of his hands.

Notes

1. Isaiah 53:3.
2. Luke 16:22, 23.
3. Romans 3:23.
4. Revelation 3:7.
5. Genesis 3:15.
6. Ephesians 5:14.
7. Romans 7:22, 23.
8. 1 Corinthians 12:10.
9. 1 Peter 1:23.
10. 1 Timothy 3:15, 1 Peter 2:5.
11. 2 Corinthians 5:17.
12. 2 Corinthians 12:3, 4.
13. Cf. Genesis 4, 25; Numbers 16, 22; Mark 14.
14. Psalm 119:98.
15. Revelation 17:8, 21:27.
16. Acts 26:18.
17. 2 Peter 1:21.
18. Mark 9:7.
19. Galatians 4:9.
20. Colossians 2:8.
21. Matthew 5:37.
22. Joel 2:31.
23. James 4:1.
24. Cf. Exodus 22:1ff.

Excerpt abridged from the much-longer original by Percy Livingstone Parker, published by Isbister and Company, London, 1903.

"No man is an island, entire of itself. Every man is a piece of the continent, a part of the main. If a clod be washed away by the sea, Europe is the less. . . . Any man's death diminishes me, because I am involved in mankind. And therefore never send to know for whom the bell tolls. It tolls for thee."

Those words, better than any latter-day tribute, tell why John Donne (1571–1631) is included in this collection. Brilliant, sensuous, devout, Donne (the man and the poet) stands in sharp contrast to the Puritans Bunyan, Baxter and Roger Williams. His poetry conveys a breathtaking beauty and the insight of pure genius.

But it is Donne the preacher who concerns us here. The son of a well-to-do ironmonger, he was brought up a Roman Catholic; but after attending Oxford, and later Cambridge, he left Rome and became an Anglican. His subsequent years have been described as "worldly" and "reckless." He studied law, entered military service, became a man about town, married his employer's niece, and fathered a large family. Eventually he lost his position and was thrown into poverty.

Donne's poems and religious writings had meanwhile attracted London's attention, even to the royal court, and one day he was urged by King James I to seek the Church of England ordination he had so long avoided. In 1621, at age fifty, he became dean of St. Paul's Cathedral, London, where he preached to vast audiences. Three hundred and sixty years later those sermons are still being reprinted.

We might have chosen other, better-known writings of this remarkable Englishman. It seemed appropriate, however, that a volume of seventeenth-century Christian writings should include an example of the expository preaching by Donne that drew the crowds to St. Paul's.

Such a sermon, if it does nothing else, will expose by contrast the shallowness of much of today's preaching. Yesterday's rhetoric is not ours, nor does flowery oratory necessarily carry in any age the convicting power of the Holy Spirit. The fact remains that to read a sermon such as this one by John Donne is like sitting through a Shakespearean tragedy—but one that has a better ending. It is an experience of the soul. It is small wonder that a revival of Donne studies has occurred in our century.

The message chosen for this volume, entitled, "On Prayer, Repentance and the Mercy of God: A Lenten Sermon," is built around an unusual passage in Job. It is distinguished for its homiletic artistry as well as its literary excellence.

11

From On Prayer, Repentance and the
Mercy of God: A Lenten Sermon
by John Donne

> Yet my hands have been free of violence
>   and my prayer is pure.
> O earth, do not cover my blood;
>   may my cry never be laid to rest!
> Even now my witness is in Heaven;
>   my advocate is on high.
>   —Job 16:17–19

Job's friends (as in civility we are obliged to call them, because they came upon a civil pretense, to visit him and to comfort him) had now done speaking. "I have heard many things like these," says Job to them; they are not new to me, and therefore "miserable comforters are you all," old and new. But, he adds, "Will your long-winded speeches"—your airy, your frothy words—"never end?"[1]

Now they have an end. Eliphas has ended his charge, and in this chapter Job begins to answer for himself. But how? By a middle way. Job does not justify himself; but yet he does not prevaricate, he does not betray his innocence neither. For there may be a pusillanimity even toward God. A man may overclog his own conscience, and belie himself in his confessions, out of a distempered jealousy and suspicion of God's purposes upon him. Job does not so.

Many men have troubled themselves more about how the soul comes into man, than about how it goes out. They wrangle whether it comes in by infusion from God, or by propagation from parents, and never consider whether it shall return to him that made it, or to him that marred it; to him that gave it, or to him that corrupted it. So many of our expositors upon this book of Job have spent themselves upon the person, and the place, and the time, who Job was, when Job was, where Job was, and whether there were ever any such person as Job or no, and have passed over too slightly the senses and doctrines of the book.

In this chapter and before this text, we have Job's anatomy, Job's skeleton, the ruins to which he was reduced. In the eighth verse he takes knowledge that God had filled him with leanness and wrinkles, and that those wrinkles and that leanness were witnesses against him. In the ninth verse, that they that hated him had torn him in pieces. In the eleventh verse, that God had delivered him over to the ungodly, and that God himself had shaken him in pieces and (in the twelfth verse) had set him up as a mark to shoot at. In the thirteenth verse, that God had cleft his reins and poured out his gall upon the ground. In the thirteenth and fourteenth, that he broke him, breach after breach, and ran over him as a giant, and at last, in the sixteenth verse, that foulness was upon his face and the shadow of death upon his eyelids.

Now let me ask in Job's behalf God's question to Ezekiel: "Do you believe that these bones can live?"[2] Can this anatomy, this skeleton, these ruins, this rubbish of Job speak? It can, it does in this text:

> Yet my hands have been free of violence
> and my prayer is pure.

These words deliver to us the confidence of a godly man. Do God what he will, and say if you will that because I am more afflicted than other men, therefore I am guilty of more heinous sins than other men; yet I know that whatsoever God's end be in this proceeding, it is not because of any injustice from my hands. "Also my prayer is pure."

These words deliver us, too, from that kind of infirm anguish and indignation, that half-distemper, that expostulation with God, which sometimes comes to an excess even in good and godly men: "O earth, do not cover my blood; may my cry never be laid to rest!" I desire not that anything should be concealed or disguised. Let all that I have ever done be written in my forehead and read by all men.

Finally these words deliver to us the foundation of his confidence, and the recovery from his infirmity, and from his excess in the manner of expressing it. "My witness is in heaven and my advocate is on high." He was not overbold. God is his witness that that which they charge him with is false, and what he says in his own discharge (in the sense that he says it) is true.

So in Job's protestation ("not guilty"), in Job's manifest ("I would that all the world knew all") and Job's establishment and consolidation ("My witness is in Heaven"), and in some fruits which we shall gather from them in passing, we shall determine all that appertains to these words.

*   *   *

I remember St. Gregory, in handling one text, says that he will endeavor to handle it so that the weakest understanding might comprehend the highest points, and the highest understanding not be weary to hear ordinary doctrines so delivered. It is a good art to deliver deep points in a holy plainness, and plain points in a holy delightfulness. Many times one part of our audience understands us not, when we have done, and so they are weary; and another part understands us before we began, and so they are weary. Today my humble petition must be that you will be content to hear plain things plainly delivered.

First, Job found himself under the oppression and calumny of that misinterpretation that kings themselves and states have not escaped:

The tower of Siloam fell and slew them, therefore they were the greater sinners in Jerusalem.[3]

This man prospers not in the world, therefore he proceeds not in the fear of God.

The heir wastes the estate, therefore the estate was ill-gotten.

These are hasty conclusions in *private* affairs.

Treasuries are empty, therefore there are unnecessary wastes.

Discontented persons murmur, therefore things are ill-carried.

Our neighbors prosper by action, therefore we perish by not appearing.

These are hasty conclusions in *state* affairs.

This man is affected when he hears a blasphemous oath, and when he looks upon the general liberty of sinning; therefore he is a Puritan.

That man loves the ancient forms and doctrines and disciplines of the church, and retains and delights in the reverend names of priest and altar and sacrifice; therefore he is a Papist.

These are hasty conclusions in *church* affairs.

When we do fall under these misinterpretations and ill applications of God's proceedings, we may say with Job, "I also could speak as you do. If your soul were in my soul's stead, I could heap up words against you and shake my head at you."[4] I could speak scornfully of you. But I will not; yet I will not betray myself. I will make my protestation, whatever end God propose to himself in this his proceeding. "My hands have been free of violence and my prayer is pure."

In these two, cleanness of hands and pureness of prayer, are all religious duties comprehended,[5] for clean hands denote justice and righteousness toward men, while pure prayer denotes devotion and the service and worship of God. Job protests for both. Therefore Origen says of Job, "I do verily believe and may be bold to say that for constancy and fidelity toward God, Job exceeded not only men but angels themselves."

Origen explains that Job did not only suffer without being guilty of those things to which his afflictions were imputed, but he said grace when he had no meat, when God gave him stones for bread and scorpions for fish.[6] He praised God as much for the affliction itself as for his former or his subsequent benefits and blessings. Not that Job was merely innocent, but that he was guilty of no such things as might confer those conclusions which, from his afflictions, his enemies raised.

"If I justify myself," says Job, "my own mouth shall condemn me."[7] *Every self-justification is a self-condemnation.* When I give judgment for myself I am therein a witness against myself. "If I say I am perfect," says Job in the same place, "even that proves me perverse." If I say I never go out of the way, I am out simply because I say so.

Job felt the hand of destruction upon him, and he felt the hand of preservation too; and it was all one hand. This is God's method and his alone: to preserve by destroying. Men of this world sometimes repair and recompense those whom they have oppressed before, but this is an after-recompense.

God's first intention even when he destroys is to preserve, as a physician's first intention, in the most distasteful physic, is health. Even God's demolitions are super-edifications; his anatomies, his dissections are so many recompactings, so many resurrections. God winds us off the skein, that he may weave us up into the whole piece, and he cuts us out of the whole piece into pieces, that he may make us up into a whole garment.

But for all these humiliations and confessions, Job does not waive his protest: "My righteousness I hold fast, and my heart shall not reproach me as long as I live."[8] Not that I shall never sin, but never leave any sin unrepented; and then my heart cannot reproach me of a repented sin, without reproaching God himself.

"The sun must not set upon my anger";[9] much less will I let the sun set upon the anger of God toward me, or sleep in an unrepented sin. Every night's sleep is a *nunc dimittis;* then the Lord lets his servant depart in peace. Your lying down is a valediction, a parting, a taking leave (shall I say so?), a shaking hands with God; and when you shake hands with God, let those hands be clean.

Enter into your grave, your metaphorical, your quotidian grave, your bed, as you entered into the church at first, by water, by baptism. Rebaptize yourself every night, in Job's snow water, in holy tears that may cool the inordinate lusts of your heart, and withhold unclean abuses of those hands even in that grave, your bed. And remember Job's fear and jealousy in that place, that when he had washed himself in snow water, "My own clothes will make me foul again."[10]

Your flesh is your clothes; and to this mischievous purpose of fouling your hands with your own clothes, you have most clothes on when you are naked; then in that nakedness you are in most danger of fouling your hands with your own clothes. Miserable man! that could have no use of hands nor any other organ of sense, if there were no other creature but yourself. And yet if there were no other creature but yourself, you could sin upon yourself and foul your hands with your own hands. How much more then, if you strike with those hands by oppression in your office, or shut up those hands and that which is due to another in them?

Sleep with clean hands, either kept clean all day by integrity, or washed clean at night by repentance. So when we wake, though all Job's messengers thunder about you, and all Job's friends multiply misinterpretations against you, yet Job's protestation shall be your protestation, whatever end God may have in this proceeding.

As clean hands denote all righteousness toward man, so do pure prayers all devotion and worship and service of God. For we are of the household of the faithful, and the service which we are to do, as his household servants, is prayer; for his house is the house of prayer. It is only possible to us to fulfil the commandment, "Pray continually,"[11] when we glorify God continually in all our familiar actions (whether we eat or drink, we do it to his glory); and every glorifying, every thanksgiving, is prayer.

There cannot be a more effectual prayer for the future than a thankful acknowledgement of former benefits. How often is that repeated in the Gospel and in the epistles? "Ask, and it shall be given you."[12] No grant without prayer, and no denial upon prayer.

It must be prayer, and my prayer. I must not rely upon the prayers of others. Not of angels, though they be ministering spirits, not only to God himself, but between God and man.[13] As they present our prayers, no doubt they pour out their own for us too; yet we must not rely upon the prayers of angels. Nor of saints, though they have a more personal and experimental sense of our miseries than angels have. No, nor upon the prayers of the congregation, though we see and hear them pray.

It must be my own prayer, and no prayer is so truly or so properly mine as that which the church has delivered and recommended to me. In sudden and unpremeditated prayer I am not always I; and when I am not myself, my prayer is not my prayer. Passions and affections sometimes, sometimes bodily infirmities, and sometimes a vain desire of being eloquent in prayer, alienates me, withdraws me from myself, and then that prayer is not my prayer.

As the law of the land is my law, and I have an inheritance in it, so the prayers of the church are my prayers, and I have an interest in them, because I am a son of that family. My baptism is mine, and my absolution is mine, because the church has given them to me, and so are her prayers mine. Men will study even for compliments; and princes and ambassadors will not speak to one another without thinking what they will say. Let us not speak to God so, not unadvisedly, inconsiderately. Prayer must be my prayer; and even in this kind, what have I that I have not received? So it is my prayer, and as Job's prayer was pure prayer, also my prayer is pure.

The Holy Spirit has so marshaled and disposed the qualification of prayer, that there is no pure prayer without clean hands. The lifting up of hands was the gesture of prayer, even among the heathen. Among the Jews, prayer and the lifting up of hands was one and the same thing: "Let the lifting up of my hands be an evening sacrifice."[14] This lifting up of my hands brings them into my sight. Then I can see them, and see whether they be clean or no. If I see impurity in my hands, God sees impurity in my prayer.

Can I think to receive ease from God with that hand that oppresses another? Mercy from God with that hand that exercises cruelty upon another? Or bounty from God with that hand that withholds right from another? Prayer is our hand, but it must be a clean hand, pure prayer.

The Emperor Constantine was coined praying. Other emperors were coined triumphing, in chariots, or preparing for triumphs, in battles and victories, but he, Constantine, was in that posture, kneeling, praying. He knew his coin would pass through every family, and to every family he desired to be an example of piety. Every piece of single money was a catechism, and testified to every subject. And yet this symbolical and catechistical coin of Constantine's was not so convincing, nor so irrefragable a testimony of his piety (for Constantine might be coined praying and yet never pray) as when we see a prince as great as he, actually, really, personally, daily, duly at prayer with us.

Let not your prayer be lucrative or vindictive. Pray not for temporal superfluities. Pray not for the confusion of them that differ from you in opinion or in manners. Condition your prayer, animate your prayer with the glory of God, and your own everlasting happiness, and the edification of others. This is Job's prayer, pure prayer.

*   *   *

Job says, I do no man wrong; my prayer is pure, I mock not God. But because he continued under such great afflictions, men would not believe this. So he proceeds perchance to some excess and inconsiderateness in desiring a manifestation of all his actions: "O earth, cover not my blood; may my cry never be laid to rest."

Blood in this text is the blood of the soul, exhausted by sin. For every sin is an incision of the soul, a lancination, a phlebotomy, a letting of the soul blood. A delight in sin is like going with open veins into a warm bath and bleeding to death. This will be the force of Job's imprecation: "O earth, do not cover my blood." I am content to stand as naked now as I shall do at the day of judgment, when all men shall see all men's actions. I desire no disguise. I deny, I excuse, I extenuate nothing that I ever did. I would that my enemies knew my worst, that they might study some reason of God's proceeding thus with me, other than those heinous sins which, from these afflictions, they will necessarily conclude against me.

But could Job have stood out this trial? Was Job so innocent as that he need not care, though all the world knew all? Perchance there may have been some excess, some inordinateness in his manner of expressing it. We cannot excuse the vehemence of some holy men in such expressions.

We cannot say that there was no excess in Moses' "Pardon this people or blot my name out of thy book," or that there was no excess in St. Paul's saying that he wished to be accursed, to be separated from Christ for his brethren.[15] But for Job we shall not need this excuse. Either we may restrain his words to those sins which they imputed to him; or, if we enlarge Job's words generally to all his sins, we must consider them to be spoken after his repentance and reconciliation to God thereupon. If they knew (Job may have said) how it stood between God and my soul, how earnestly I have repented, how fully he has forgiven, they would never say these afflictions proceeded from those sins.

Thus David protested to God, "Judge me, O Lord, according to my righteousness, according to my innocency, according to the cleanness of my hands."[16] (But his words were spoken not of all his sins, but rather of those which Saul pursued him for.) And truly so may I, so may every soul say that is rectified, refreshed, restored, reestablished by the seals of God's pardon and his mercy. So the world would take knowledge of the consequences of my sins, as well as of the sins themselves, and read my leaves on both sides, and hear the second part of my story as well as the first. So the world would look upon my temporal calamities, the bodily sicknesses, and the penuriousness of my fortune contracted by my sins, and upon my spiritual calamities, dejections of spirit, sadness of heart, declinations toward a diffidence and distrust in the mercy of God.

Then when the world sees me in agony and bloody sweat, it would also see the angels of Heaven ministering comforts unto me. So they would consider me in my earnest confessions, God in his powerful absolutions, me drawn out of one sea of blood, the blood of my own soul, and cast into another sea, the bottomless sea of the blood of Christ Jesus. Then they would know what God has done for my soul, as well as what my soul and body have done against my God.

As they would read me throughout, and look upon me altogether, I would join with Job in his confident adjuration, "O earth, do not cover my blood." Let all the world know all the sins of my youth, and of my age too, and I would not doubt but God should receive more glory, and the world more benefit, than if I had never sinned. This is that that exalts Job's confidence. He was guilty of nothing; that is, no such thing as they concluded upon, of nothing absolutely, because he had repented all. And from this, his confidence rises to a higher pitch than this: "O earth, do not cover my blood; may my cry never be laid to rest!"

What does Job mean in this? In the former part (Job's protest) he considered God and man: righteousness toward man in clean hands, devotion toward God in pure prayers. In this part (his manifest) he pursues the same method. He considers man and God. Though men knew all my sins, that should not trouble me, he says. Yes, though my cry find no place with God, that should not trouble me.

I should be content that God should seem not to hear my prayers, but rather laid me open to the ill interpretation of wicked men. "Tush, he prays, but the Lord hears him not. He cries, but God relieves him not." And yet when will you relieve me, O Reliever of men, if not upon my cries and my prayers? Yet St. Augustine has repeated more than once or twice, be not overjoyed when God grants you your prayer. The devil had his prayer granted (says that father) when he had leave to enter the herd of swine.

So it was when the devil obtained power from God against Job. But all this aggravated the devil's punishment; and so it may do yours to have some prayers granted. And just as it must not overjoy you to have your prayer granted, so it must not deject you if your prayer be not granted. God suffered St. Paul to pray and pray and pray; yet after his praying three times, God granted him not what he prayed for.[17] God suffered that "if it be possible" to let the cup pass from Christ himself, yet he granted it not.[18]

But in these cases some men more easily satisfy their minds than do other men. If God does not grant me my prayer, I recover quickly and lay hold upon the horns of the altar, and ride safely at that anchor. God saw that what I prayed for was not so good for him, nor so good for me. God may propose further glory to himself, more benefit to me, and more edification even to those who at first made ill constructions of his proceedings. So my satisfaction and acquiescence do not arise out of the opinion and interpretation of others. Rather, as Job says, "My witness is in Heaven; my advocate is on high." And that is our third and last consideration.

*   *   *

All that we are to consider is this: "My witness is in Heaven." And truly that is enough. I care not if all the world knows all my faults. I care not what they conclude about God's not granting my prayers. "My witness is in Heaven." To be condemned unjustly among men, to be ill interpreted in the acts of my religion, is a heavy case; yet I have a relief in all this. "My witness is in Heaven."

The first comfort is, he whom I rely upon is in Heaven. That is the foundation upon which our Savior erects that prayer which he has recommended to us: "Our Father which art in Heaven." When I lay hold upon him there, I pursue cheerfully and confidently all the other petitions: for daily bread, for forgiveness of sins, for deliverance from temptations. He is in Heaven and he sits in Heaven. I see him in that posture that Stephen saw him, standing at the right hand of the Father, in a readiness and willingness to come to my succor.[19]

But I might also contemplate him in a judiciary posture, a sovereign posture, sitting, and consider him as able and willing to relieve me. He is in Heaven and he sits in Heaven and he dwells in Heaven. He is, and he is always, there. Baal's priests could not always find him at home. Job's God, and our God, is never abroad. He dwells in the heavens and he dwells on high, so high that God humbles himself to behold the things that are in Heaven.

With what amazedness must we consider the humiliation of God in descending to the earth, and lower still, to Hell, when even his descending to Heaven is a humiliation! God humbles himself when he beholds anything lower than himself, whether cherubim or seraphim, whether the human nature, the body of his own and eternal Son; and yet he beholds, considers, and studies us, worms of the earth.

This is Job's and our first comfort, because he is in Heaven, and so sees all things. But then if God sees and says nothing, David apprehends it for a most dangerous condition. Therefore he says, "Be not silent, O Lord, lest if you be silent, I perish."[20] And again, "Hold not your peace, O God of my praise, for the mouth of the wicked is opened against me."[21] Lord, let your mercy be as forward as their malice.

The strictest examination that we put upon any witness is, that if he pretends to testify anything upon his knowledge, we ask how he came by that knowledge, and if he be a good witness that saw it. This is good evidence. Therefore, as God from that height sees all; as God is to this purpose all eye, so for our farther comfort, he descends to the office of being a witness. There is a witness in Heaven.

But God may be a witness and yet not be my witness, and in that there is small comfort, especially if God be a witness on my adversaries' side, and against me. "I know, and am a witness," says the Lord; that is, a witness of the sins which I know by you. Now, if our own heart and conscience condemn us, this is shrewd evidence, says St. John.[22] For my own conscience, by itself, is a thousand witnesses against me.

But then (says the Apostle) God is greater than the heart, for he knows all things.[23] He knows circumstances of sin as well as substance. He knows things we seldom take knowledge of. If then my own heart be a thousand, God, that is greater, is ten thousand witnesses, if he witness against me. But if he be my witness, a witness for me, as he always multiplies in his ways of mercy, he is thousands of thousands, millions of millions of witnesses in my behalf. "For there is no condemnation," no possible condemnation, "to them that are in him."

But will all this come home to Job's end and purpose? Will he no longer care that all men know all his faults, or that God has passed over his prayers, because God is his witness? And would the world believe that God testified in his behalf, when it sees his calamities multiplied upon him, and his prayers neglected?

If they will not, herein lies Job's and our final comfort: that he that is my witness is in the highest Heaven; there is no person above him; and therefore he that is my witness is my judge too. I shall not be tried by an arbitrary court, where it may be wisdom enough to follow a wise leader and think as he thinks. I shall not be tried by a jury that would rather that I suffered than that they fasted: that would rather I lost my life than that they lost a meal.

Nor will I be tried by peers, where honor shall be the Bible. But I shall be tried by the King himself, than which no man can propose a nobler trial. That King shall be the King of kings too; for he who in the first of the Revelation is called "the faithful Witness," is in the same place called "the Prince of the kings of the earth."[24] As he is there produced as a witness, so he is ordained to be the judge of the quick and the dead, and so all judgment is committed to him.

He that is my witness is my judge, and the same person is my Jesus, my Savior, my Redeemer, the one who has taken my nature and given me his blood. So that he is my witness in his own cause, and my judge, but of his own title; and he will in me preserve himself. He will not let that nature that he has invested perish, nor that treasure which he has poured out for me—his blood—be ineffectual. My witness is in Heaven, my Judge is in Heaven, my Redeemer is in Heaven, and in them, who are but One, I have not only a constant hope that I shall be there too, but an evident assurance that I am there already, in his Person. Go then in this peace, that you always study to preserve this testimony of the Spirit of God by outward evidences of sanctification.

You are naturally composed of four elements, and three of those four are evident and unquestioned [earth, air, water]. The fourth element, fire, is more problematical and disputable. Every good man, every true Christian, has four elements also; and three of those four are declared in this text:

First, a good name, the good opinion of good men, for honest dealing in the world, and discharge of duties toward God, that there be no injustice in our hands, also that our prayer be pure.

A second element is a good conscience in myself, that either a holy wariness before, or a holy repentance after, settle me so in God that I care not though all the world knew all my faults.

A third element is my hope in God, that my witness which is in Heaven will testify for me, as a witness in my behalf here, or acquit me as a merciful judge, hereafter.

Now there may be a fourth element, an infallibility of final perseverance, grounded upon the eternal knowledge of God. But this is like the element of fire, which may be, but is not so discernible or demonstrable as the rest.

Men argue about the element of fire, that whereas the other elements produce creatures in such abundance—the earth such herds of cattle, the waters such shoals of fish, the air such flocks of birds—it is worth considering whether there should be an element of fire since it produces no creatures.

So if your pretended element of infallibility produce no creatures, no good works, no holy actions, you may justly doubt that there is such an element in you. In all doubts that arise in you, still it will be a good rule to choose now that which you would later choose upon your deathbed. If a temptation to beauty, to riches, to honor be proposed to you upon such and such conditions, consider whether you would accept it upon those conditions upon your deathbed, when you must part with them in a few minutes.

So, when you doubt in what you should place your assurance in God, think seriously whether you shall not have more comfort then upon your deathbed in being able to say, "I have finished my course, I have fought a good fight, I have fulfilled the sufferings of Christ in my flesh," I have clothed him when he was naked, and fed him when he was poor—more comfort, I say, than in any other thing that you may conceive God to have done for you.[25]

And do all the way as you would do then. Prove your element of fire by the creatures it produces. Prove your election by your sanctification, for that is the right method, and shall deliver you over, infallibly, to everlasting glory at last. Amen.

Notes

1. Job 16:2.
2. Ezekiel 37:3.
3. Luke 13:4.
4. Job 16:4.
5. Psalm 24:4.
6. Luke 11:11.
7. Job 9:20.
8. Job 27:6.
9. Ephesians 4:26.
10. Job 9:31.
11. 1 Thessalonians 5:17.
12. Matthew 7:7.
13. Hebrews 1:14.
14. Psalm 141:2.
15. Exodus 32:32, Romans 9:3.
16. Psalm 7:8.
17. 2 Corinthians 12:7-10.
18. Mark 14:36.
19. Acts 7:56.
20. Psalm 28:1.
21. Psalm 109:2.
22. 1 John 3:21.
23. 1 John 3:20.
24. Revelation 19:11-15.
25. Cf. Matthew 25:36, 2 Timothy 4:7.

Sermon abridged by permission from *The Showing Forth of Christ, Sermons of John Donne*, edited by Edmund Fuller, published by Harper and Row, New York, 1964.

Madame Guyon (1648–1717) has been dead over two and a half centuries; yet she continues to evoke almost as much controversy today as during her lifetime. She has been called a quietist, a mystic, a saint, a neurotic, a hysterical degenerate. While her native land (France) and her church (Roman Catholic) have not always treated her memory kindly, an evangelical group in California declared as recently as 1975 that "Catholicism has never produced a woman more qualified to be canonized than Jeanne Guyon."

So opinions concerning the lady fluctuate, but the autobiography she wrote (at the insistence of her spiritual adviser) is still popular and has been translated into many languages. Her name lives on as one of France's great spiritual teachers.

Let the record show that even if thirty of Guyon's spiritual "propositions" were condemned by the Roman curia, her enemies in the church were hardly justified in forcing her into solitary confinement for many years. She spent four years of this period behind the twelve-feet-thick walls of the infamous Bastille in Paris.

Jeanne Marie Bouvier de la Mothe was born into a well-known French family. Married at sixteen to a man twenty-two years her senior and by whom she bore three children, she was left a widow in just twelve years. Always spiritually inclined, she then began studying devotional writings and lectured throughout France. The priest who accompanied her, Father LaCombe, was later arrested and imprisoned for many years in the Bastille, where he died insane.

After years of conflict with church authorities, including Pope Clement XI, and a lengthy imprisonment, Madame Guyon was banished from Paris in 1702 to her son's estate in Blois, where she died. Despite official church censure, forty volumes of her writings were published posthumously. Among her most enduring works is A Short Method of Prayer *(Moyen court et très facile de faire oraison), published in 1685 while she was still in royal and ecclesiastical favor. The work was later publicly burned. In after-years John Wesley, Jessie Penn-Lewis, Watchman Nee and other well-known Christians have acknowledged their indebtedness to this short book; its influence on the Quaker and Holiness movements in Britain and America is a matter of record.*

12

From A Short and Very Easy Method of Prayer
by Madame Guyon

Everybody is capable of prayer, and it is a dreadful misfortune that almost all the world has conceived the idea that it is not called to prayer. We are all called to prayer as we are called to salvation.

Prayer is nothing but the application of the heart to God and the internal exercise of love. St. Paul has told us to "pray without ceasing," and our Lord bids us watch and pray.[1] All therefore may and ought to practice prayer.

Let all pray. You should live by prayer as you should live by love. This is very easily obtained, much more easily than you can conceive. Come, you famishing souls who find nothing to satisfy you. Come, and you shall be filled. Come, you poor, afflicted ones, bending beneath your load of wretchedness and pain, and you shall be comforted! Come, you sick, to your physician, and don't be fearful of approaching him because you are filled with diseases. Show them, and they shall be healed!

Children, draw near to your Father and he will embrace you in the arms of love. Come, you poor, stray, wandering sheep, return to your Shepherd! Come, sinners, to your Savior! Come, you who are dull, ignorant and illiterate, and who think yourselves most incapable of prayer. You are most especially adapted for it. Let all without exception come, for Jesus Christ has called all.

Yet let not those come who are without a heart, for they are excused. There must be a heart before there can be love. But who is without a heart? Oh, come then, give this heart to God, and learn here how to make that donation.

All who desire prayer may do so easily, enabled by those ordinary graces and gifts of the Holy Spirit which are common to all men. Prayer is the sovereign good. It is the means of delivering us from every vice, and obtaining every virtue. It is by prayer alone that we are brought into God's presence and maintained in it without interruption.

You must learn, then, a kind of prayer that may be exercised at all times, a kind that does not obstruct outward employments, and may be practiced equally by princes, kings, prelates, priests and magistrates, soldiers and children, tradesmen, laborers, women, and sick persons. It is the prayer not of the head but of the heart. It is not a prayer of the understanding alone, but the prayer of the heart. Nothing can interrupt this prayer but disordered affections; and when once we have enjoyed God and the sweetness of his love, we shall find it impossible to relish anything but himself.

Nothing is so easily obtained as the possession and enjoyment of God. He is more present to us than we are to ourselves. He is more desirous of giving himself to us than we are to possess him. We need only to know how to seek him, and the way is easier and more natural to us than breathing.

Listen! You who think yourselves to be so dull and fit for nothing! By prayer you may live on God himself with less difficulty or interruption than you live in the vital air. Wouldn't it seem then to be highly sinful to neglect prayer?

*   *   *

When by an act of lively faith you are placed in the presence of God, read some truth in which there is substance. Pause gently at that point, not to employ the reason, but merely to fix the mind. Observe that the principal exercise should always be the presence of God.

Then let that lively faith in God which is immediately present in our innermost souls, produce an eager sinking into ourselves, restraining all our senses from wandering abroad. This serves to extricate us in the first place from numerous distractions, and to remove us far from external objects. It brings us near to God, who is to be found only in our innermost center, which is the Holy of Holies where he dwells. He has even promised to come and make his abode with him that does his will.[2] St. Augustine blames himself for the time he lost in prayer in not having sought God from the first in this manner of prayer.

When we are thus fully entered into ourselves, and warmly penetrated throughout with a lively sense of the divine Presence; when the senses are all recollected and withdrawn from the circumference to the center, and the soul is sweetly and silently employed on the truths we have read, we must allow them sweetly to repose, and (as it were) swallow what they have tasted.

Just as a person may enjoy the flavor of the finest foods in chewing them, yet receive no nourishment if he does not stop chewing and swallow; so when our affections are kindled, if we try to keep stirring them up, we extinguish the flame and the soul is deprived of its nourishment. Therefore we should swallow the blessed food we have received in a repose of love, full of respect and confidence. This will advance the soul more in a short time than some other method will in years.

A direct contest with our dissipated senses only serves to irritate and augment them. Therefore when we seek to contemplate the divine Presence, we should be careful to recall our senses by sinking within, under a view by faith of a present God, and simply recollecting ourselves. Thus we wage, without seeming to, a successful, though indirect war on our senses.

Beginners should be cautioned against wandering from truth to truth and from subject to subject. The right way to penetrate every divine truth and enjoy its full relish is to imprint it on the heart, and dwell upon it while its savor continues. Such recollection is difficult in the beginning; but God, whose one will toward his creatures is to communicate himself, imparts abundant grace and an experimental enjoyment of his Presence which makes it much easier.

*   *   *

Conversion is nothing more than turning from the creature in order to return to God.

It is not enough (however good and essential it is to salvation) when conversion consists simply in turning from sin to grace. To be complete it should take place from outside inwardly.

Once the soul is turned toward God, it finds a wonderful facility in continuing steadfast in its conversion; and the longer it remains thus converted, the nearer it approaches and the more firmly it adheres to God. And the nearer it draws to him, the further is it removed from the "creature" which is so contrary to him. It becomes so effectively established in conversion that the state becomes habitual and, so to speak, natural.

We are not to suppose that this change is effected by the soul's violent exertion of its own powers. The soul is not capable of, nor should it attempt, any other cooperation with divine grace except seek-

ing to withdraw itself from external objects and turning inward. After
that it has nothing further to do than to continue firm in its adherence
to God.

God has an attractive power which draws the soul more and more
strongly to himself; and in attracting, he purifies. This kind of introversion is very easy, and advances the soul naturally and without effort because God is our center. The center always exerts a powerful attraction,
and the more spiritual and exalted it is, the more violent and irresistible
are its attractions.

But besides the attracting virtue of the center, there is in every
creature a strong tendency to reunion with its center, which is vigorous
and active in proportion to the spirituality and perfection of the subject.

As soon as anything is turned toward its center, it is precipitated
toward it with extreme rapidity, unless it be held back by some invin-
cible obstacle. A stone held in the hand is no sooner disengaged than it
falls by its own weight to the earth as to its center. So also water and
fire, when unobstructed, flow inevitably toward their center.

Now, when the soul by its efforts to recollect itself is brought into
the influence of the central tendency, it falls gradually, without any
force other than the weight of love, into its proper center. The more
passive and tranquil it remains, and the freer from self-motion, the
more rapidly it advances, because the energy of the central attractive
virtue is unobstructed and has full liberty for action.

All our care therefore should be directed toward acquiring the
greatest degree of inward recollection. Nor should we be discouraged by
the difficulties we encounter in this exercise, which will soon be recompensed on the part of God. Abundant supplies of grace will render it
perfectly easy, provided we are faithful in withdrawing our hearts from
outward distractions and occupations, and returning to our center with
affections full of tenderness and serenity.

When at any time the passions are turbulent, a gentle retreat inward to a present God easily deadens them. Any other way of opposing
irritates rather than appeases them.

*   *   *

The soul that is faithful in the exercise of love and adherence to
God, as above described, is astonished to feel him gradually taking possession of its whole being. It now enjoys a continual sense of that presence which has become, as it were, natural to it. This as well as prayer
becomes a matter of habit. The soul feels an unusual serenity gradually
diffusing itself over all its faculties.

Silence now constitutes its whole prayer, while God communicates an infused love which is the beginning of ineffable blessedness.

We must urge it as a matter of the highest importance, to cease from self-action and self-exertion, so that God himself may act alone. He says by the mouth of his prophet David, "Be still and know that I am God."[3] But the creature is so infatuated with love and so attached to its own working that it does not believe that it works at all unless it can feel, know and distinguish all its operations.

It isn't aware that its inability minutely to observe the manner of its motion is occasioned by the swiftness of its progress; and that the operations of God, abounding more and more, absorb those of the creature. In the same way the stars shine brightly before the sun rises, but gradually vanish as the light advances, and become invisible—not from lack of light in themselves, but from the excess of it in the sun.

The case is similar here. There is a strong and universal light which absorbs all the little distinct lights of the soul. They grow faint and disappear under its powerful influence, and self-activity is now no longer distinguishable.

Those who accuse this prayer of inactivity greatly err. It is a charge that can only arise from inexperience. Oh! If they would only make some effort toward the attainment of it, they would soon become full of light and knowledge in relation to it. This appearance of inaction is indeed not the consequence of sterility, but of abundance. The fact will be clearly perceived by the experienced soul, who will recognize that the silence is full and powerful by reason of plenty.

There are two kinds of people that keep silence: the one because they have nothing to say, the other because they have too much. The latter is the case in this state. Silence is occasioned by excess and not by defect.

To be drowned and to die of thirst are deaths widely different; yet water may be said to be the cause of both. Abundance destroys in one case and dearth in the other. So here the fullness of grace stills the activity of self, and therefore it is of the utmost importance to remain as silent as possible.

The infant hanging at its mother's breast is a lively illustration of our subject. It begins to draw the milk by moving its little lips, but when its nourishment flows abundantly, it is content to swallow without effort. By any other course it would only hurt itself, spill the milk, and be obliged to quit the breast.

We must act in like manner in the beginning of prayer by moving the lips of the affections. But as soon as the milk of divine grace flows freely, we have nothing to do but in stillness sweetly to imbibe it; and when it ceases to flow, again stir up the affections as the infant moves its lips. Whoever acts otherwise cannot make the best use of this grace, which is bestowed to allure the soul into the repose of love, and not to force it into the multiplicity of self.

But what becomes of the baby that thus gently and without exertion drinks in the milk? The more peacefully it feeds, the better it thrives. What becomes of it? It drops asleep on its mother's bosom. So the soul that is tranquil and peaceful in prayer sinks into a slumber wherein all its powers are at rest. You see that in this process the soul is led naturally, without trouble, effort, art or study.

The interior is not a stronghold to be taken by storm and violence, but a kingdom of peace which is to be gained only by love. God demands nothing extraordinary nor too difficult; on the contrary, he is greatly pleased by a simple and childlike conduct.

The most sublime attainments in religion are those which are easiest reached. The most necessary ordinances are the least difficult. It is thus also in natural things: if you would reach the sea, embark on a river and you will be conveyed to it imperceptibly and without exertion. Would you go to God? Follow this sweet and simple path, and you will arrive at the desired object with an ease and expedition that will amaze you.

Oh, that you would once make the trial! How soon would you find that all I have said is too little, and that your own experience will carry you infinitely beyond it. What is it you fear? Why do you not instantly cast yourself into the arms of Love, who only extended them on the cross that he might embrace you?

What risk do you run in depending solely on God and abandoning yourself wholly to him? He will not deceive you, unless by bestowing an abundance beyond your highest hopes. But those who expect everything to come from themselves may hear the rebuke of God by his prophet Isaiah: "You have wearied yourselves in the multiplicity of your ways, and have not said, Let us rest in peace."[4]

*　　*　　*

The soul advanced thus far has no need of any preparation other than its quietude. Now the presence of God during the day, which is the great effect or rather continuation of prayer, begins to be infused, and almost without intermission. The soul certainly enjoys transcendent blessedness, and finds that God is more intimately present to it than it is to itself.

The only way to find him is by introversion. No sooner do the physical eyes close, than the soul is wrapped in prayer. It is amazed at so great a blessing, and enjoys an internal conversation which external matters cannot interrupt. Let it then remain faithful in this state; and beware of choosing or seeking any other disposition whatever than this simple rest, as a preparation either to confession or communion, to action or prayer; for its sole business is to allow itself to be filled with this divine effusion.

*　　*　　*

Some persons, when they hear of the prayer of silence, falsely imagine that the soul remains stupid, dead and inactive. But it unquestionably acts more nobly and more extensively than it had ever done before; for God himself is its mover, and it now acts by the agency of his Spirit. St. Paul would have us "led by the Spirit of God."[5] It is not meant that we should cease from action, but that we should act through the internal agency of his grace.

This activity of the soul is attended with the utmost tranquility. When it acts of itself, the act is forced and constrained, and therefore it is more easily distinguished. But when the action is under the influence of the Spirit of grace, it is so free, so easy and so natural that it almost seems as if we did not act at all. "He brought me forth into a large place; he delivered me, because he delighted in me."[6]

When a wheel rolls slowly we can easily perceive its spokes, but when its motion is rapid, we can distinguish nothing. So when the soul rests in God it has an activity noble and elevated, yet altogether peaceful; and the more peaceful it is, the swifter is its course, because it is given up to that Spirit by whom it is moved and directed.

Instead of encouraging sloth, then, we promote the highest activity by inculcating a total dependence on the Spirit of God as our moving principle; for it is in him and by him alone that we live and move and have our being.[7]

God originally formed us in his own image and likeness. He breathed into us the Spirit of his Word, that breath of Life[8] which he gave us at our creation. The image of God in us consisted of our participation in that Life, which is *one,* simple, pure, intimate, and always fruitful.

Because the devil has broken and deformed the divine image in the soul by sin, it is absolutely necessary for the soul's renovation to have the agency of that same Word whose Spirit was inbreathed at our creation. But no image can be repaired by its own efforts; it must remain passive for that purpose under the hand of the workman. Our activity therefore should consist in placing ourselves in a state of susceptibility to divine impressions, and pliability to all the operations of the Eternal Word.

If the easel is unsteady, the painter is unable to produce a correct picture upon it. Likewise every movement of self produces erroneous lineaments. It interrupts the work and defeats the design of this adorable Painter. We must then remain in peace, and move only when he moves us. Jesus Christ has life in himself,[9] and he must give life to every living thing. All other beings have only a borrowed life, but the Word has life in himself; and since it is his nature to communicate, he desires to bestow it upon man.

We should therefore make room for the influx of this life, which can only be done by the ejection and loss of the old, Adamic life and the suppression of the activity of self. St. Paul says, "If any man be in Christ, he is a new creation. Old things are passed away; behold, all things have become new."[10] But this state can be accomplished only by dying to ourselves and to all our own activity, that the activity of God may be substituted in its place.

Instead of prohibiting activity, therefore, we recommend it; but in absolute dependence on the Spirit of God, so that his activity may take the place of our own. This can only be effected by the consent of the creature; and this concurrence can only be yielded by moderating our own action, so that the activity of God may, little by little, be wholly substituted for it.

Jesus Christ exemplified this in the Gospel. Martha did what was right; but because she did it in her own spirit, Christ rebuked her.[11] The spirit of man is restless and turbulent, for which reason he does little, though he seems to do a great deal. What was it Mary chose? Repose, tranquility and peace. She had apparently ceased to act, that the Spirit of Christ might act in her. She had ceased to live, that Christ might be her life.

This shows how necessary it is to renounce ourselves and all our activity to follow Christ, for we cannot follow him if we are not animated by his Spirit. Now, in order that this Spirit may gain admittance, it is necessary that our own should be expelled: "He who unites himself with the Lord," says St. Paul, "is one with him in Spirit."[12]

Into this way, then, which is the divine motion and the Spirit of Jesus Christ, we must necessarily enter. To be Christ's, we must be filled with his Spirit and emptied of our own. "As many as are led by the Spirit of God, they are the sons of God."[13]

When the soul yields itself to the influence of this blessed Spirit, it perceives the witness of its divine sonship, and it feels also, with superadded joy, that it has received not the spirit of bondage, but the liberty of the children of God.[14] It finds that it acts freely and sweetly, though with vigor.

The Spirit of divine action is so necessary in all things that St. Paul bases that necessity on our ignorance as to what we should pray for. "The Spirit," he says, "helps us in our weakness. We do not know what we ought to pray, but the Spirit himself intercedes for us with groans that words cannot express."[15] This is plain enough. If we don't know what we stand in need of, or how to pray as we ought for those things which are necessary, and if the Spirit which is in us and to which we resign ourselves must ask for us, should we not permit him to give vent to his unutterable groanings on our behalf?

The Spirit is the Spirit of the Word, which is always heard, as he says himself: "I knew that you always hear me."[16] If we admit this Spirit to pray and intercede for us, we also shall always be heard. And why? Because the Spirit demands only what is conformable to the will of God.

Why, then, should we be burdened with superfluous cares, and weary ourselves in the multiplicity of our ways, without ever saying, "Let us rest ourselves and be at peace"? God himself invites us to cast all our care upon him. "Why spend money," he says, "on what is not bread; and your labor on what does not satisfy? Listen, listen to me, and eat what is good, and your soul will delight in the richest of fare."[17]

Oh! If we only knew the blessing of just listening to God, and how greatly the soul is strengthened thereby!

*   *   *

Until conversion is perfected, many reiterated acts are necessary; for with some it is progressive, though with others it is instantaneous. My act should consist in a continual turning to God, an exertion of every faculty and power of the soul purely for him. To give the heart to God is to have the whole energy of the soul ever centering in him, that we may be rendered conformable to his will. We must therefore continue to be invariably turned to God from the time we first direct ourselves to him.

The soul is unstable and easily distracted; but this evil will be counteracted if, when we perceive that we are wandering, we instantly replace ourselves in God by a pure act of return to him. As many reiterated acts form a habit, the soul contracts the habit of conversion; and that act which was before interrupted and distinct now becomes habitual. We err therefore in supposing that we must not form acts; we form them continually. But let them be conformable to the degree of our spiritual advancement.

Every state has its commencement, its progress, and its consummation, and it is an unhappy error to stop in the beginning. There is no art that does not have its own progress. At first we labor with toil, but at the end we reap the fruit of our industry.

When the vessel is in port, the mariners are obliged to exert all their strength in order to clear the harbor and put out to sea. But once at sea, they can steer the ship as easily as they wish. In the same way, while the soul remains in sin, much effort is required to free it. The cables which hold it must be loosed. Then by strong and vigorous effort it gathers itself inward, pushes off gradually from the old port of Self, and leaving it behind, proceeds to the interior haven so much desired.

Once the vessel is clear of the ways, it leaves the shore behind and heads out to sea. The farther it departs from land, the less effort is required to make it move. After awhile it gently gets under sail, and proceeds swiftly on its course. The oars, which now have become useless, are laid aside.

And how is the pilot now employed? He is content to spread the sails and hold the rudder.

To spread the sails is to lay ourselves before God in a prayer of simple openness to be moved by his Spirit. To hold the rudder is to restrain our heart from wandering from the true course, recalling it gently and guiding it steadily by the dictates of the Spirit of God, who gradually gains possession of the heart, just as the breeze fills the sails by degrees and so propels the ship.

While the winds are fair, the pilot and the sailors rest from their labors. What progress they make, and without the least fatigue! They go farther in one hour, while resting and leaving the vessel to the wind, than they did in a much longer time by all their former efforts. If they were now to attempt to use the oars, they would not only wear themselves out—they would actually retard the ship's movement by their useless exertions.

This is our proper course, interiorly speaking. A short time will advance us by the divine impulse farther than many reiterated acts of self-exertion. Whoever tries this path will find it the easiest in the world.

If the wind becomes contrary and blows up a storm, we must cast anchor to hold the ship. This anchor is simply trust in God and hope in his goodness, while waiting patiently the calming of the tempest and the return of a favorable gale.

*   *   *

If all who labored for the conversion of others sought to reach them *by the heart*, introducing them immediately to prayer and the interior life, numberless permanent conversions would ensue. On the other hand, few and transient fruit must result from labor which is confined to outward matters, such as burdening the disciple with a thousand rules for outward exercises, instead of leading the soul to Christ by the occupation of the heart in him.

What if ministers were diligent to instruct their church members in this way! Then the shepherds watching their flocks would have the spirit of the early Christians. The farmer at the plow would keep a dialogue of prayer going with his God. The hand-worker, while he became physically exhausted at work, would be renewed with inward strength. Much wrongdoing would disappear, and the congregation would become spiritually minded.

Once the heart is gained, how easily is all the rest corrected! That is why God above all other things requires the heart. By this means alone we may extirpate the terrible vices that are found in many sections of society—drunkenness, blasphemy, lewdness, fighting and crime. Jesus Christ would reign everywhere in peace, and the face of the church would be renewed throughout.

The decay of internal piety is unquestionably the source of the various errors and cults that have appeared in the world. Errors take possession of no soul except the one that is deficient in faith and prayer. If, instead of engaging our wandering brothers in constant disputations, we would but teach them simply to *believe*, and diligently to *pray*, we should lead them sweetly to God.

Oh, how inexpressibly great is the loss sustained by mankind from the neglect of the interior life! And what an account will those have to render who are entrusted with the care of souls, and have not discovered and communicated to their flock this hidden treasure!

Some excuse themselves by saying that there is danger in this way, or that simple persons are incapable of comprehending the things of the Spirit. But the Scriptures affirm the opposite. What danger can there be in walking in the only true way, which is Jesus Christ, giving ourselves up to him, fixing our eye continually on him, placing all our confidence in his grace, and tending with all the strength of our soul to his purest love?

The "simple" ones, so far from being incapable of this fulfillment, are by their docility, innocence, and humility, peculiarly qualified for its attainment. As they are not accustomed to reasoning, they are less tenacious of their own opinions. Even from their lack of learning they submit more freely to the teachings of the divine Spirit; while others, who are cramped and blinded by self-sufficiency, offer much greater resistance to the operations of grace.

We are told in Scripture, "The entrance of your words gives light; it gives understanding to the simple."[18] Let spiritual fathers be careful how they prevent their little ones from coming to Christ. He himself said to his Apostles that they should let the children come to him.[19]

Man frequently applies a remedy to the outward body when the disease lies at the heart. The reason that we are so unsuccessful at reforming mankind is that we begin with external matters. All our labors in this field simply produce fruit that will not endure. But if the key of the interior be first given, the exterior would be naturally and easily reformed.

Now this is very easy. To teach man to seek God in his heart; to thank him; to return to him whenever he finds he has wandered from him; and to do and suffer all things with a single eye to please him, is leading the soul to the source of all grace, and causing it to find there everything necessary for sanctification.

I therefore implore all of you that have the care of souls to see at once that they are established in this way, which is Jesus Christ. Indeed, it is he himself who charges you, by all the blood he has shed for those entrusted to you. "Speak to the heart of Jerusalem!"[20] O, dispensers of his grace, preachers of his Word, ministers of his sacraments: establish his Kingdom! And in order that it may indeed be established, make him ruler over the heart!

Just as it is the heart alone that can oppose his sovereignty, so it is by the subjection of the heart that his sovereignty is most highly honored. "Give glory to the holiness of God, and he shall become your sanctification."[21] Compose catechisms expressly to teach prayer, not by reasoning nor by method, for the simple are incapable of that; but to teach the prayer of the heart, not of the understanding; the prayer of God's Spirit, not of man's invention.

The pity of it is that by directing people to pray in elaborate forms, and being curiously critical about it, you create their chief obstacles. The children have been led astray from the best of fathers by your attempting to teach them too refined a language. Go, then, you poor children, to your Heavenly Father. Speak to him in your natural language; though it may be crude and barbarous, it is not so to him.

A father is better pleased with an address which love and respect have made confused (because he sees that it proceeds from the heart) than he is with a dry and barren harangue, be it ever so elaborate. The simple and undisguised emotions of love are infinitely more expressive than all language and all reasoning.

Men have desired to love Love by formal rules, and have thus lost much of that love. Oh, how unnecessary it is to teach an art of loving! The language of love is foreign to one who does not love, but perfectly natural to one who does. There is no better way to learn how to love God than to love him. The most ignorant often become the most perfect because they proceed with more cordiality and simplicity.

The Spirit of God does not need our arrangements. When it pleases him, he turns shepherds into prophets. So far from excluding any from the temple of prayer, he throws the gates wide open so that all may enter; and wisdom is directed to cry aloud in the highways, "Let all who are simple come in here!"[22] And does not Jesus Christ himself thank his Father for having "hidden these things from the wise and learned, and revealed them to little children"?[23]

*   *   *

Prayer, according to St. John, is an incense whose smoke ascends to God.[24] It is the effusion of the heart in the presence of God: "I have poured out my soul before the Lord," said the mother of Samuel.[25] Prayer is a certain warmth of love, melting, dissolving, and sublimating the soul, and causing it to ascend to God. As the soul is melted, odors rise from it; and these sweet exhalations proceed from the consuming fire of love within.

This is illustrated in the Song of Songs: "While the king was at his table, my perfume spread its fragrance."[26] The table is the center of the soul, and when God is there, and we know how to dwell near, and abide with him, the sacred Presence gradually dissolves the hardness of the soul; and as it melts, fragrance issues forth.

Thus does the soul ascend to God by giving up self to the destroying and annihilating power of divine love. This is a state of sacrifice essential to the Christian religion, in which the soul suffers itself to be destroyed and annihilated, that it may pay homage to the sovereignty of God. By the destruction of self we acknowledge the supreme existence of God. We must cease to exist in self in order that the Spirit of the Eternal Word may exist in us. It is by the giving up of our own life that we give place to his coming; and in dying to ourselves, he himself lives in us.

We must surrender our whole being to Christ Jesus, and cease to live any longer in ourselves, that he may become our life.[27] But how is it we pass into God? In no way but by leaving and forsaking ourselves, that we may be lost in him. This can be effected only by annihilation, which is the true prayer of adoration. It is the prayer of truth. It is worshiping "in spirit and in truth."[28] "In spirit" because we enter into the purity of that Spirit who prays within us. "In truth" because we are thereby placed in the truth of the all of God, and the nothing of the "creature."

Ah! did we but know the virtues and the blessings which the soul derives from this prayer, we should not be willing to do anything else. It is the pearl of great price, the hidden treasure,[29] and it is the full performance of the purest evangelical precepts.

Jesus Christ assures us that the Kingdom of God is within us,[30] and this is true in two senses: first, when God becomes so fully Master and Lord in us that nothing resists his dominion, then our interior is his kingdom. Again, when we possess God, who is the Supreme Good, we possess his Kingdom also, wherein is fullness of joy, and where we attain the end of our creation.

Thus it is said, "To serve God is to reign." The end of our creation, indeed, is to enjoy God, even in this life. But, alas! who thinks of it?

Notes

1. 1 Thessalonians 5:17, Mark 13:33, 37.
2. John 14:23.
3. Psalm 46:10.
4. Isaiah 57:10 (Vulgate). [See also John 5:39, 40—Ed.]
5. Romans 8:14.
6. Psalm 18:19.
7. Acts 17:28.
8. Genesis 2:7.
9. John 5:26.
10. 2 Corinthians 5:17.
11. Luke 10:41, 42.
12. 1 Corinthians 6:17.
13. Romans 8:14.
14. Romans 8:21.
15. Romans 8:26.
16. John 11:42.
17. Isaiah 55:2.
18. Psalm 119:130.
19. Matthew 19:14.
20. Isaiah 40:2 (Vulgate).
21. Isaiah 8:13, 14.

22. Proverbs 9:4.
23. Matthew 11:25.
24. Revelation 8:3, 4.
25. 1 Samuel 1:15.
26. Song of Solomon 1:12.
27. Cf. Colossians 3:3, 4.
28. John 4:23.
29. Matthew 13:45, 46.
30. Luke 17:21.

Excerpt from *A Short and Very Easy Method of Prayer* published by George W. McCalla, Philadelphia, 1925. The text may have been taken from an English translation by D. Macfayden, issued in London, 1902.

The outstanding name in German evangelical Christianity in the century after Martin Luther is Philip Jacob Spener (1635–1705), himself a devout Lutheran and the founder of German Pietism. What Wesley did for Britain, Spener did for Germany. Without leaving the state church to which he was consistently loyal, Spener introduced a Bible-oriented reformation whose effects are still felt throughout Lutheranism.

Born and reared in a Christian home in Alsace, Spener studied theology at Strasbourg. In later visits around the continent, he sat under teachers who (unlike many German pastors of that day) taught repentance and regeneration. After receiving a doctorate in theology, Spener became senior pastor in Frankfurt am Main, where he introduced the custom of gathering people in his home for Bible reading, prayer and discussion. This practice initiated what became the Pietist movement.

As Spener conceived it, Pietism was not an emotional reaction to the sterility of the established church. It was rather a carefully-reasoned program of reform intended to cultivate a less formal, more spiritual Christian life among both clergy and laity.

In his best-known work, the Pia Desideria (essential piety), first published in 1675, Spener reenforced his proposals with frequent references to Luther, whom he revered and emulated.

Spener upbraided the clergy for their spiritual laxity. Their plight, he held, could be traced to their training in the German universities under theological professors who were known less for spirituality than for disputation. The great need of ministerial candidates, he declared, was not intellectual knowledge (though Spener did not disparage this) but the new birth. Christianity, he insisted, was life, not knowledge. His emphasis on conversion provoked a prompt response from the academics, so that Spener and his followers were soon accused of heresy.

From Frankfurt Spener accepted a call to Dresden, where opposition increased. In 1691 the elector of Brandenburg invited Spener to Berlin. Here, until his death in 1705, he served as pastor of St. Nicholas Church (today a landmark in downtown West Berlin).

Pietism, as Spener preached it, revitalized much of the German Lutheran church, and in turn created a remarkable missionary movement. While Pietism was not without its weaknesses, its major strengths included evangelistic concern, compassion for the needy, the avoidance of controversy, development of the spiritual life, and the primacy of the Bible and Bible study.

13

From Pia Desideria
by Philip Jacob Spener

When you see a tree whose leaves are sickly, you know something is faulty with the roots. In the same way when you see people who are without good breeding, you conclude that no doubt their priests are lacking in holiness.[1]

I am happy to recognize the holiness of our godly calling [as preachers], and I know that God has caused many to remain in our order who take the work of the Lord zealously. Nor am I inclined to go to extremes and throw out the baby with the bath. However, the all-seeing Knower of hearts can see how sad is my soul as I often reflect on this matter and now write these lines: I cannot say other than that we preachers in our station need reformation as much as any station ever needed it.

When God planned a reformation, as in the Old Testament, he usually began it with the religious leaders. I do not count myself apart from those in our position who lack the strong reputation we should have before God and the church. More and more I recognize how weak I am, and I am prepared to be corrected by my brethren. Nothing, in fact, grieves me more than this: that I can hardly see how, in the face of such frightful corruption, someone like myself can possibly recover a good conscience.

Not only are men to be found here and there in our profession who are guilty of open scandals; but beyond appearances, there are few who really understand and practice true Christianity. As men judge, they may seem to be blameless; yet their lives reflect a worldly spirit marked by the lust of the flesh, the lust of the eye, and haughty behavior. Quite evidently they have never been inclined to take even the first practical principle of Christianity seriously, that is, the denial of self.

One sees how they seek promotions, change from parish to parish, and engage themselves in all sorts of routine work. Many, of whom one would like in Christian love to think better, are stuck deep in the old birth and do not actually show the essential characteristics of the new birth. As Paul complained, "They all seek their own interests, not those of Jesus Christ."[2]

Where such conduct is recognized, it causes great scandal. But when people get the idea that what they see in their preachers is in fact genuine Christianity, and their wrong conduct ought not be held against them, that is even greater scandal, inasmuch as the conduct is not recognized for what it is. The lives of many such preachers and the absence in them of the fruits of faith indicate that they are themselves weak in faith. What they take to be faith and the ground of their teaching is by no means the illumination, witness and sealing of the Holy Spirit, but rather, human imagination.

I will not conclude that therefore no good has been accomplished through such persons and their work, or that true faith and a true conversion may not have been brought about in somebody through them, for the Word receives its godly power not from the one who proclaims it, but from and of itself. But we cannot assume that those who preach to us are therefore loving, reborn children of God.

We find many preachers regard as unimportant what the Apostle mentioned to the Ephesians, namely, that "in Jesus there is righteous conduct."[3] As a result, the usual concept of how to be saved is not in keeping with the divine statement. If the preacher himself does not know this, how will he bring his hearers to know what is necessary?

I am alarmed and ashamed to realize that the teaching of an earnest, inner godliness is so unfamiliar and strange to some people that those who eagerly pursue such godliness are considered suspect as secret Papists or Quakers. What greater evidence of calamity and corruption can there be than that of seeking occasion for suspicion and evil report in things that are properly worthy of praise? Here the words, "If the foundations are destroyed, what can the righteous do?"[4] are apt and fitting.

There are many who think that so long as we are not attacked by opponents of a false religion, and are enjoying outward peace, the church is in a blessed position. They do not see the dangerous wounds at all; how, then, can they bind them up or heal them?

How poignantly the worthy and respected Dr. Nicholas Selnecker bewailed the current situation: "One finds an increasing stream of books that are full of quarreling, disputing, reproaching and reviling, and full of wrangling affairs which serve no purpose except that of scholastic fighting. On the other hand, where can one find or buy good books of instruction and comfort which set out the Word of God simply and honestly, and present pure doctrine correctly? If we reject books that contain unnecessary belligerence and disputation, vindictiveness, personal ambition and slander, we will surely find only a few books written in our time."[5]

The former Coburg superintendent Master Dinckel agreed with this lament and observed the damage that results: "The true teaching of faith, hope and love is relegated to second place, and the way is again paved for a *theologia spinosa* (that is, a spiny, thorny teaching) which scratches and irritates hearts and souls."[6]

When men's minds are stuffed with that kind of theology, it becomes exceedingly difficult to grasp and find pleasure in the real simplicity of Christ and his teaching. Such theology, while it preserves the foundation of faith as found in the Scriptures, adds to it so much wood, hay and stubble of human skepticism that the gold of truth can no longer be seen. This happens because men's taste becomes accustomed to the greater charm of reason, and after awhile the simplicity of Christ and his teaching seems tasteless.

Knowledge without love "puffs up."[7] It leaves man in his own love of self; indeed, it increasingly fosters and strengthens such love. Then appear subtleties unknown to the Scriptures, and it is evident those who introduce them desire to exhibit their wisdom and their superiority over others, to have a great name, and to profit from it in the world. Moreover, these subtleties are such that they stimulate a thirst for honor and other impulses which are unseemly to a true Christian, rather than a true fear of God.

When people are practiced in such subtleties they begin to introduce them at once into the church of Christ, even if they know little or nothing of what the church needs, since they hold the church in low esteem. They can hardly be restrained from taking to market what gives them the most pleasure, and they generally concentrate on something not very edifying to readers in search of salvation. What they really succeed in doing is to give hearers of ready minds a fair knowledge of religious controversies.

How, then, can one do anything but repeat the appeal of St. Paul? "My speech and my message were not in plausible words of wisdom," he said, "but in demonstration of the Spirit and power, that your faith might not rest in the wisdom of men but in the power of God."[8] Indeed, if the brilliant Apostle came among us today, he would probably understand but a little of what our airy geniuses sometimes say in holy places.

The Apostle Paul derived his knowledge not from human skill but from the enlightening of the Spirit, alternatives as far removed from each other as Heaven is from earth. Just as human skills can grasp but little of divine illumination, so souls filled with such illumination cannot comfortably stoop to the powerless phantasms of human ingenuity.

Long ago our beloved Savior gave us the identifying mark: "By this all men will know that you are my disciples, if you have love one for another."[9] Love is the distinguishing mark, not merely a pretended love that is hugged to one's heart in meaningless embrace, but a love that shows itself openly. First John teaches us, "Let us not love in word or speech but in deed and in truth."[10] If we judge by this mark of love, how difficult it will be to find, among the great mass of nominal Christians, even a small number of real and true disciples of Christ! The Word of the Lord does not deceive, however; it remains true now and in eternity.

How many there are who live such an openly unchristian life that they cannot deny breaking the law at every point, who have no intention of living otherwise in the future, and yet who, in spite of all this, appear to be firmly convinced they will be saved!

Ask such people on what they base their expectations, and you will discover (as they themselves confess) that their confidence rests on their belief in Christ and their trust in him. This foundation, they believe, cannot fail, and they will surely be saved by such faith. What they have is a fleshly illusion of faith (for godly faith will not come without the Holy Spirit, and will not stay in the face of hearty and assertive sin). To ascribe salvation to such a figment of the mind is the devil's fraud, as terrible an error as ever has been or can be.

How differently our dear Luther speaks of faith! In his preface to the Epistle to the Romans he writes: "Faith is not a human notion or a dream as some take it to be. Faith is a divine work in us, which changes us and causes us to be born anew. Faith kills the old Adam and makes us altogether different men in heart, in spirit, in mind, in all our energies. It brings with it the Holy Spirit. Oh, it is a living, creative, active, mighty thing, this faith! So it is impossible for it to fail to produce good works steadily. It does not ask whether there is good to do, but before the question is raised, it has already done it, and goes on doing it. Faith is not that human notion and dream that some hold for faith. Because they see that no betterment of life and no good works follow it, even though they hear and say much about faith, they fall into error and say, 'Faith is not enough; one must do works in order to be pious and be saved.' This is the reason why, when they hear the Gospel, they go ahead and by their own efforts fashion an idea in their hearts which says, 'I believe,' and they hold this for true faith. But it is a fiction, a human-based concept that never reaches the depths of the heart, and so nothing comes of it and no betterment follows it."[11]

You hear the Word of God. Well and good. But it is not enough that your ear hears it. Do you let it pierce your inner heart and let the heavenly food be digested so that you receive its vital power, or does it go in one ear and out the other? Can the words of the Lord in Luke 11:28 apply to you, "Blessed are those who hear the Word of God and keep it"? If not, then the work of hearing will not save you but will rather increase your damnation, because you have not made better use of the grace you have received. How many there are who cannot truly say that they have allowed God's Word to bear fruit in them, and who nonetheless think that they have served God and obeyed him so well that he must save them!

The more sincerely people love God and the more they want to see growth in hallowing his Name, in extending his Kingdom, and in doing his will, the more it pains them to see such abominations. The Jews who dwell among us are first of all scandalized by this. It strengthens their unbelief. How, they ask, can we believe that Christ is the true God when we do not follow his commands? Our Jesus, they believe, must have been a wicked man, to judge him and his teachings by our lives. Besides the Jews, we offend all sorts of heretics as well.

Some people raise the objection that we should not expose the failings and disgraces of our church, lest our opponents become aware of them. Instead they should be kept secret. But I answer that we do not expose the church's weakness before the world that the world might gloat. It is out of fervent love and zeal for God's honor that we bewail whatever is against him, and we demand that people concern themselves with it. It is love that causes me to uncover dangerous wounds in order to show them to those who can heal them. Moreover, we are not revealing anything that is not already generally known.

Surely God has promised his church here on earth a better state than this. Church history testifies to the fact that as a rule the early Christians were known for their godly lives, a condition that distinguished them from other people.

Tertullian wrote, "What insignia do we bear, if not the basic wisdom which teaches us not to adore the frivolous works of the human mind; the temperance, by which we abstain from that which is not ours; the chastity, which we do not pollute even with the eye; the mercy and compassion which prompts us to help the needy; the truth itself, which causes us not to offend; and the liberty for which we would gladly die? Whoever would understand what makes Christians will need these signs to help him."[12]

How well things stood then! Indeed, it was wonderful when beloved old Ignatius could say in his letter to the Ephesians, "Those who are Christians are known not only by what they say but also by what they practice."[13] And Justin records in his *Apology* that some souls were converted through the uprightness and justice of the Christians in their dealings with men.[14] And Origen boasts, "The teaching of Jesus can produce a wonder-working spirit of meekness and a complete change of character, a friendliness and graciousness and conciliatory spirit in people. These are those who accept the preaching of God and Christ and judgment as from the heart, and do not pretend to go along for the sake of the things of this life and human desires."[15]

The early Christians were careful to examine and probe the lives of those who wished to join them, and refused to admit people to the church until they saw that they would live worthy lives after the calling to which they were called. Justin declared, "Whoever is not living as he was taught, that is a clear sign that he is no Christian." In his well-known letter to Emperor Trajan, Pliny himself confessed that although he tortured some to get at the truth, he could not discover that they were guilty of any crime except following a religion forbidden by the Romans.[16]

One can only be deeply moved to read the extraordinary examples of glorious virtues demonstrated by various individual Christians. How ardent was the love among them when they not only called one another by the affectionate terms of "brother" and "sister," but also lived in such brotherly fellowship that they would die for one another if necessary.

By comparison, the state of the present-day Christian church puts us to shame, with its hot-and-cold stance. But it also demonstrates that what we are seeking is not as impossible to realize as many imagine. It is our own fault that we are lagging so far behind, for the same Holy Spirit who once effected all things in the early Christians is the same Holy Spirit whom God has bestowed on us. This selfsame Spirit is neither less able nor less active today to accomplish in us the work of holiness. If this blessing does not take place, the only reason for its lack must be that we hinder rather than encourage the Holy Spirit's work.

I gladly acknowledge my shortcomings. I do not presume to have special insight beyond that given to other ministers of God into ways of helping cure this common evil. Daily I find in myself defects. For that reason I wish from the bottom of my heart that more gifted men, men furnished with more light, understanding and experience than I, would take up this matter. Let them ponder it in the fear of the Lord, present to the whole evangelical Christian church their findings, and be mindful also of ways and means, through the grace of God, to implement such salutary suggestions as they may have discovered.

Thought should be given as to how to bring the Word of God more richly among us. We know that by nature we have no good in us. Any change must be brought about by God. The Word of God is the most powerful means to this end, since faith must be kindled through the Gospel. The more richly God's Word dwells among us, the more we shall bring about faith and its fruits.

It is certain that the diligent handling of God's Word (which consists not only of hearing preachments, but also of reading, meditating and conversing with other believers) must be the chief means for bettering anything.[17] God's Word alone is the seed from which all that is good in us must grow. If we can bring the people to find their joy by eagerly and zealously searching in the Book of Life, then their spiritual life will be wonderfully strengthened and they will become altogether different individuals.

People must get it into their heads that to have knowledge of the Christian faith is not enough, for Christianity consists also of practical outworking. Our dear Savior repeatedly enjoined love as the real mark of his disciples. In his old age the beloved John (according to the witness of Jerome in his letter to the Galatians) repeatedly and almost exclusively emphasized to his disciples, "Children, love one another!"[18]

His disciples and others who heard him finally became so annoyed that they asked him why he was always telling them the same thing. His answer was, "Because it is the Lord's command, and that is all that is necessary." Indeed, love is the fullness of life for the man who has faith and who through his faith is saved; for him love is the fulfilment of the laws of God.

If we can then awaken a zealous love among our Christians, first toward one another and then toward all men (according to 2 Peter 1:7), and can put this love into action, then all that we long for will come into being; for love is the sum of the commandments. People must not only be told this constantly, and have the excellencies of love for neighbor impressed upon their sight, but they must also practice such love.

Christians cannot afford to overlook any opportunity to serve a neighbor in love; but even while doing so, they must search their hearts to see whether they are acting truly in love, or for some other reason. If they are wronged, they should pay special attention to see that they refrain from all vengefulness. Indeed, they should earnestly seek opportunities to do good to their enemies; otherwise the old Adam will take vengeance instead of being tamed. If they do this, love will be planted even more deeply in their hearts.

We need to pay special attention to the way we engage in religious controversies with unbelievers or holders of false beliefs. We owe it to them, first, to pray that the fundamentally good God will give them the same light that he has given to us by his grace; that he will lead them into the clear truth; that he will give them opportunity to prepare their hearts; that he will thwart their dangerous errors; and that he will use what true knowledge of salvation in Christ they have to save them as brands from the burning.

We need to set these people a good example and take great pains not to offend them in any way, for offending them would give a bad impression of our true teaching and would make their conversion harder. To this should be added the expression of heartfelt love toward all unbelievers and heretics. We should indeed make it plain that we take no pleasure in the practice and propagation of their views; yet in other things pertaining to human life we should show that we look upon them as our neighbors, just as Christ showed the Samaritan to be the neighbor of the Jew (Luke 10:29-37).

We recognize them as our brethren by the right of common creation and the love of God that he extends to all, if not by the new birth. We therefore love them from our hearts, according to the commandment, as we love ourselves. To insult such people because of their religion of heresy or unbelief is to work up a zeal of the flesh, one that will only hinder their conversion. The best approach to false religion is not to weaken or cut off the love we owe to others.

It is evident therefore that disputation can neither maintain the truth among ourselves nor bring it successfully to unbelievers. What is necessary is the holy love of God. If only we Evangelicals would make it our goal to bring to God the fruits of his truth in heartfelt love, and thereby conduct ourselves in a way worthy of his calling! This would show itself in obvious and unsullied love of our neighbors, including those who are heretics.

Without doubt God would then begin to let us grow in our knowledge of the truth, and we would have the joy of seeing others whose error we now lament join us by conversion to the faith. If it is not viciously obstructed by those who declare it or by those who hear it, the Word of God has the power to convert men's hearts. A holy lifestyle does much to bring about conversion, as Peter teaches (1 Peter 3:1, 2).

Preachers bear the greatest responsibility in all these matters concerning the reformation of the church. And since their shortcomings do correspondingly great damage, it is highly important that only men who, above all, are themselves true Christians, and have the godly wisdom to guide others carefully on the way of the Lord, occupy the office of preacher. And it is therefore also important, even vital, for the reforming of the church that only such persons be called to the ministry who may be suitable; and that nothing but God's glory be kept in mind during the whole process of calling.

If such suitable persons are to be called to preach, they must be trained in our schools and universities. The students need to be instructed constantly that holy living is no less important than diligent study; indeed, study without piety is worthless. The person who grows in learning but declines in morality is decreasing rather than increasing in stature. This principle applies even more in the spiritual realm, and since theology is a practical discipline, everything must be geared to the practical working out of faith and life.

I cannot keep from quoting the beloved and godly theologian, Dr. John Gerhard: "Whoever is destitute in his love of Christ, and neglects the study of piety, will surely not receive the knowledge of the fullness of Christ or the more abundant gift of the Holy Spirit. To get a true, living, practical, saving understanding of divine things it is not sufficient to read and ponder the Scriptures. It is important also that the love of Christ be included, and that one does not sin against his conscience and thereby obstruct the Holy Spirit, but rather engage in an earnest study of godliness."[19]

Certainly theological students ought to realize early in their years of study, and build on the ground that they must die to the world and must live as persons who will be examples to their flock. Such living is not merely an ornament but a very necessary achievement. While without it they may indeed be students of what may be called a philosophy of holy things, they are not students of theology, instructed and kept in the light of the Holy Spirit alone.

Many indeed contend that while it would be fine if a theological student lived a good life, it is not all that necessary, providing he studies hard and becomes a learned man. Whether he lets himself be ruled by a worldly spirit and joins others in doing what they do in the world of pleasure is of secondary consideration, they say.

There is enough time, they add, to change the theologue's lifestyle when he becomes a preacher—as if this were always possible. A love of the world, once established, usually stays with people all their lives. In this case it spreads a bad reputation and does great harm. When they first begin to study theology, these precautions should be told to and inculcated in students. I would hope the benefits of this counsel would be seen throughout their years of study, and would bear fruit the rest of their lives.

One would especially hope that the professors who have these students entrusted to them would give attention to their lives as well as their studies, and would speak to them often as the need arises. They should note especially those students who, while outstanding in their studies, are also outstanding in shocking habits, drunkenness, ostentation, and bragging about their studies and other achievements. To sum up, these students show that they live after the world and not after Christ.

The professors should deal with such students so that they perceive that they are looked down upon by their preceptors because of their behavior, and that their outstanding abilities and excellent studies are not in and of themselves helpful. Rather the students are seen as persons who will do harm in proportion to their gifts.

On the other hand, professors should openly and specifically indicate how dear such students as lead godly lives are to their teachers, even if they are behind the others academically. It is certain that a young man who loves God with all his heart, even though blessed with limited talents, will be more useful to God's people despite his deficiency in studies, than a vain and worldly fool with two doctor's degrees who is full of skills but has not been taught by God.

Without someone to lead him truly by the hand, a beginning student cannot know what he needs and does not need in these matters. Lack of guidance will result in what the sainted Dr. Christopher Scheibler once described: "If someone devotes all his time to studying controversial matters, this will be the result: Either he will become a clumsy and inept preacher, no matter how learned he might be in such things; or he must start his theological studies all over again from a different perspective, simply becoming a beginner. Everyday experience is the proof of this."[20]

Above all it is important to contain controversies and reduce unnecessary arguments rather than increase them. All theology should be brought back again to apostolic simplicity. Professors can help greatly by adjusting all their studies and writings accordingly, and also by determinedly hindering and showing their displeasure repeatedly at the lustful ingenuity of misguided intellects.

Our religion is not exactly suffering from a dearth of sermons. The danger is not that there is a lack of preaching, but that much is lacking in the sermons. Such is the opinion of many godly persons. Preachers stuff their preaching with material that makes them seem to be learned men. (The hearers understand nothing of it.) They quote foreign languages, which nobody understands in the whole church. They work hard to have a proper introduction to the sermon, and a skillful outline, and good transitions, but are less concerned as to whether the material is developed by God's grace so that the hearers might be helped in their life and death needs.

This should not be. The pulpit is not the place for men to show off their artistry. It is the place to preach the Word of God simply but powerfully. Preaching is God's method to save people, and everything ought to work toward that goal.

All our Christianity is tested by the inner man or the new man, whose distinguishing mark is faith and its outworking in the fruits of love; and all preaching should be centered on that fact. The blessings of God which are directed toward the inner man should be presented in such a way that faith, and thus the inner man, may be increasingly strengthened. At the same time works should be set in motion so that people become accustomed to stress what is inward (the love of God and one's neighbor) and conduct themselves accordingly.

It is not enough to hear the Word only with our outward ear; we must also let it pierce our heart so that we hear the Holy Spirit speaking. Thus with stirred-up zeal and living trust we may feel the power of the Word and know the sealing of the Spirit. It is not enough to be baptized. Our inner man who has put on Christ our Mediator must keep him and bear witness to him in the outward life. It is not enough to receive the holy Supper of the Lord outwardly; the inner man as well must be truly fed with that blessed food. It is not enough that we pray outwardly only with the mouth; true prayer, the best prayer, takes place in the inner man, and either breaks out verbally or remains hidden in the soul. God will find it however and come upon it. It is not enough to worship God in an outward temple of brick and stone; the inner man best worships God in his own temple, whether or not he is in a temple building.

Since this is what constitutes the real power of Christianity, it would be only fair if sermons were preached to the people along such lines. Certainly if it were to happen, people would be built up a great deal more than they now are.

Finally, I call fervently on the God of all excellence and Giver of all good things. He has allowed much good seed of his Word to be scattered, and has powerfully blessed the grains that fell into godly hearts and bore fruit (for which eternal thanks be to him). May many teachers be refreshed and begin to preach with simplicity and power the kernel and heart of Christianity; and may many with devout and simple hearts be built up in the Holy Scriptures, and return to God their fruits of thanksgiving.

May this message also be a means for further reforming our church's wretched condition, which we so deeply deplore. May everything be to the glory of our great God himself and to the forwarding of his Kingdom for the sake of and according to the pleasure of Jesus Christ. Amen.

Notes

1. From John Chrysostom, *Homilies on the Gospel of St. Matthew*, 38.
2. Philippians 2:21.
3. Ephesians 4:21.
4. Psalm 11:3.
5. Selnecker (1530–1592) published a work on the Psalms at Nurnberg in 1869.
6. Dinckel (1545–1601) published an edition of Luther's *Little Book of Prayers*.
7. 1 Corinthians 8:1.
8. 1 Corinthians 2:4, 5.
9. John 13:35.
10. 1 John 3:18.
11. *Works of Martin Luther*, English translation, Holman, Philadelphia, 6, pp. 451, 452.
12. Tertullian, *Ad Nationes*, I, iv.
13. Ignatius, *Epistle to the Ephesians* (longer version), xiv.
14. Justin Martyr, *Second Apology*.
15. Origen, *Against Celsus*, I, xiii.
16. Pliny the Younger, *Epistolae*, x, 96.
17. Psalm 1:2.
18. Jerome, *Commentary on the Epistle to the Galatians*, III, 6.
19. *Harmonium Evangelistarum*, Frankfurt, 1652, II, 2, p. 1333.
20. *Manuale ad theologiam practicam*, Frankfurt, 1630.

Excerpt prepared from the original German of the 1676 edition published in Frankfurt, with special help from the English text translated and edited by Theodore G. Tappert, published as *Pia Desideria* by Fortress Press, Philadelphia, 1967.

The civil war that divided England in the mid-seventeenth century found some of the people represented in this volume on opposite sides. Jeremy Taylor (1613–1667) was a royalist. He served as chaplain to Charles I and ministered to his troops. During the days of Oliver Cromwell's Protectorate he went to prison. Nevertheless Taylor was known in his day as a symbol of toleration, and today he is admired as one of Britain's most celebrated preachers of the Gospel.

Taylor was born in Cambridge, educated at the university there, and at age twenty was ordained a priest of the Church of England. His preaching in London soon attracted notice and royal favor. After spending some time in prison when the cause of King Charles collapsed, Taylor sought protection in Wales until the return of Charles II in 1660. He was then appointed to a bishopric in Ireland and became vice-chancellor of the University of Dublin.

Of Taylor's many writings, Holy Living and Holy Dying are considered the most famous. Because of its emphasis on a well-ordered piety, and a preference for temperance and moderation in all things, Holy Living has been called a "characteristic expression of Anglican spirituality."

Taylor's prose has classic beauty, but more than beauty is here. He undertook to expound what he called "the whole duty of man," a theme whose breadth cannot be fully appreciated from just the brief extract we have chosen. Yet anyone who reads this discussion of faith, hope and love will surely be enlightened concerning God's ways with men. Taylor's rich imagery, powerful exposition, and lucid expression make him unique. He seems to balance the eloquence of Cicero with the spirited vigor of the Apostle Paul.

14

From The Rules and Exercises of Holy Living *by Jeremy Taylor*

Religion, in a large sense, signifies the whole duty of man, comprehending in it justice, love, and sobriety. All these being commanded by God, they become part of that honor and worship which we are bound to pay to him. Thus the word is used in James, "Pure religion and undefiled before God is this, to visit the fatherless and widows in their affliction, and to keep himself unspotted from the world."[1]

But in a more restrained sense, it is taken from that part of duty which particularly relates to God in our worshipings and adoration of him, in confessing his excellencies, loving his Person, admiring his goodness, believing his Word, and doing all that which may in a proper and direct manner do him honor. It contains the duties of the first five commandments only; and so it is called godliness, and is by Paul distinguished from justice and sobriety. In this sense I am now to explicate the parts of it.

I call the internal actions of religion those in which the soul only is employed, and ministers to God in the special actions of faith, hope and love. Faith believes the revelations of God; hope expects his promises; and love loves his excellencies and mercies.

Faith gives us understanding of God; hope gives up the passions and affections to Heaven and heavenly things; and love gives the will to the service of God. Faith is opposed to infidelity, hope to despair, love to enmity and hostility. These three sanctify the whole man and make our duty to God and obedience to his commandments to be chosen, reasonable and delightful, and therefore to be entire, persevering and universal.

The acts and offices of faith are to believe everything which God has revealed to us. Once we are convinced that God has spoken it, we are to make no farther inquiry, but humbly to submit, ever remembering that there are some things which our understanding cannot fathom, nor search out their depth.

We are to believe nothing concerning God but what is honorable and excellent. Faith is the parent of charity, and whatever faith entertains must be apt to produce love to God. But he that believes God to be cruel or unmerciful, or a rejoicer in damnation, or he that speaks one thing and privately means another, thinks evil thoughts concerning God. Our faith concerning God must be just as he himself has revealed concerning his own excellencies.

We are to give up ourselves wholly to Christ in heart and desire, to become disciples of his doctrine by choice as well as conviction. We are to take in greedily all that God has taught us, believing it infinitely and loving to believe it. For this is an act of love, or rather, an act of faith leaning upon love.

We are to believe all God's promises, being convinced that whatever is promised in Scripture shall, on God's part, be as surely performed as if we had it in possession. This act makes us rely upon God with the same confidence as we did on our parents when we were children. Then we had no doubt that we should have whatever we needed, if it were in their power.

We are to believe also the conditions of the promise, or that part of the revelation which concerns our duty. Many are apt to believe in the remission of sins, but without the condition of repentance or the fruits of holy life. That is to believe otherwise than God intended. For the covenant of the Gospel is the great object of faith, and it supposes our duty to answer his grace that God will be our God, so long as we are his people. The other is not faith, but flattery.

We are to profess publicly the doctrine of Jesus Christ, openly owning whatever he has revealed and commanded, not being ashamed of the Word of God, or of any practices enjoined by it. We are to do this without complying with any man's interest, nor regarding favor, nor being moved with good words, nor fearing disgrace or loss or inconvenience or death itself.

We are to pray without doubting, without weariness, without faintness, entertaining no jealousies or suspicions of God, but being confident of God's hearing us and of his returns to us. Whatever the manner or the instance be, we are to expect that if we do our duty, God will be gracious and merciful.

These acts of faith are in several degrees in the servants of Jesus. Some have it but as a grain of mustard seed.[2] Some grow up to a plant. Some have the fullness of faith. But the least faith should be a persuasion so strong as to make us undertake the doing of all that duty which Christ built upon the foundation of believing.

Here are the signs of true faith:

1. An earnest and vehement prayer. It is impossible that we should heartily believe the things of God and the glories of the Gospel, and not most importunately desire them. Everything is desired according to our belief in its excellency and possibility.

2. To do nothing for vain-glory, but wholly for the interests of religion and for these things which we believe. We are to value not at all the rumors of men, but rather the praise of God, to whom by faith we have given up all our intellectual faculties.

3. To be content with God for our judge, our patron, our Lord, and our friend; desiring God to be all in all to us, just as we, in our understanding and affections, are wholly his.

4. To be a stranger on the earth in our affections. To have all our thoughts and principal desires fixed upon the matters of faith, the things of Heaven. If a man were adopted heir to Caesar, he would (if he believed it real and effective) wholly be at court in his father's eye. His desires would outrun his swiftest speed. All his thoughts would spend themselves in creating ideas and images of his future condition.

Now, God has made us heirs of his Kingdom and coheirs with Jesus.[3] If we believed this, we would think and study accordingly. But he who rejoices in gain, and whose heart dwells in the world, and is espoused to a fair estate, and esteems disgrace or poverty in a good cause to be intolerable: this man either has no inheritance in Heaven, or believes none; and therefore believes not that he is adopted to be the son of God, the heir of eternal glory.

5. James' sign is the best: "Show me your faith by your works."[4] Faith makes the merchant diligent and venturous. Ferdinand of Aragon believed the story told him by Columbus, and therefore he furnished him with ships, and got the West Indies by his faith. But Henry VII of England believed him not, and therefore trusted him not with shipping, and lost all the purchase of that faith.

It is told by Christ, "He that forgives, shall be forgiven."[5] If we believe this, it is certain we shall forgive our enemies; for we all need and desire to be forgiven. No man can possibly despise or refuse to desire such excellent glories as are revealed to them that are servants of Christ; and yet we do nothing that is commanded us as a condition to obtain them.

No man could work a day's labor without faith; but because he believes that he shall have his wages at the day's or week's end, he does his duty. He that believes money gotten with danger is better than poverty with safety, will venture for it in unknown lands or seas; and so will he that believes it better to get to Heaven with labor, than to go to Hell with pleasure.

6. He that believes does not make haste, but waits patiently till the times of refreshment come, and dares trust God for the morrow. He is no more solicitous for the next year than he is for that which is past. If you dare trust to God when the case, to human reason, seems impossible, and trust to God then also out of choice—not because you have nothing else to trust to, but because he is the only support of a just confidence—then you give a good testimony of your faith.

7. True faith is confident. It will venture all the world upon the strength of its persuasion. Will you lay your life on it, your estate, your reputation, that the doctrine of Jesus Christ is true in every article? Then you have true faith. But he that fears men more than God, believes men more than he believes in God.

8. Faith, if it be true, living, and justifying, cannot be separated from a good life. It works miracles, makes a drunkard become sober, a lascivious person become chaste, a covetous man become liberal. It overcomes the world, works righteousness, and makes us diligently to do, and cheerfully to suffer, whatever God has placed in our way to Heaven.

The means and instruments to obtain faith are, first, a humble, willing, and docile mind, and a desire to be instructed in the way of God. Persuasion enters like a sunbeam, gently, and without violence. But open the window, and draw the curtain, and the Sun of righteousness will enliven your darkness.[6]

Then remove all prejudices and love to everything that may be contradicted by faith. Prayer, which is instrumental to everything, has a peculiar promise here. True faith is full of ingenuity and hearty simplicity. It is free from suspicion, wise and confident, trusting upon generals, without watching and prying into unnecessary or indiscernible particulars. No man carries his bed into his field to watch how his corn grows. He believes upon the general order of Providence and nature, and at harvest he finds himself not deceived.

Faith differs from hope. Faith relies only upon one proposition, that is, the truth of the Word of God. But that I shall enter into Heaven is the object of my hope, not of my faith.

The acts of hope are to rely upon God with a confident expectation of his promises, and to esteem that every promise of God is a magazine of grace and relief which we can need in that instance for which the promise is made. Every degree of hope is a degree of confidence.

It is an act of hope to esteem all the danger of an action, and the possibilities of miscarriage, to be no defect on God's part, but either a mercy on his part, or a fault on ours.

It is an act of hope to rejoice in the midst of a misfortune or seeming sadness, knowing that this may work for good. It is a direct act of hope to look through the cloud and look for a beam of the light from God. This is called in Scripture "rejoicing in tribulation,"[7] when the God of hope fills us with all joy in believing. Every degree of hope brings a degree of joy.

It is an act of hope to desire, to pray, and to long for the great object of our hope, the mighty prize of our high calling; and to desire the other things of this life as they are promised and made necessary and useful to us, in order to see God's glory and the great end of souls.

Hope and fasting are said to be the two wings of prayer. Fasting is but as the wing of a bird; but hope is like the wing of an angel, soaring up to Heaven, and bearing our prayers to the throne of grace. Without hope it is impossible to pray, but hope makes our prayers reasonable and passionate, for it relies upon God's promise.

Let your hope be well-founded, relying upon just confidences, that is, upon God according to his revelations and promises. Rely not in temporal things upon uncertain prophecies and astrology, not upon our own wit or industry, not upon gold or friends, not upon armies and princes. A hope that is easy and credulous is an arm of flesh, an ill supporter.

Let your hope be without vanity or garishness of spirit. Let your hope be of things possible, safe and useful. Let your hope be patient, without tediousness of spirit or hastiness of prefixing time. Make no limits or prescriptions to God, but let your prayers and endeavors go on. The men of Bethulia[8] resolved to wait upon God five days longer, but deliverance stayed seven days, and yet came at last. Take not every accident for an argument of despair, but go on still in hoping, and begin again to work.

God has obliged himself by promise, that we shall have the good of everything we desire; for even losses and denial shall work for the good of them that fear God. If we will trust the truth of God for performance of the general, we may well trust his wisdom to choose for us the particular. But the extraordinaries of God are apt to supply the defect of all natural and human possibilities.

God gave extraordinary virtue to a jawbone, to kill a multitude; to 300 men to destroy a great army; to Jonathan and his armor-bearer to rout a whole garrison.[9] He has given excellent sufferance and vigor to the sufferers, arming them with strange courage and glorious patience. Thus he lays no more upon us than we are able to bear.[10]

His Providence is extra-regular, and produces strange things beyond common rules. He led Israel through a sea and made a rock pour forth waters,[11] and the heavens to give them bread and flesh. He caused whole armies to be destroyed with fantastic noises, and the fortune of all France to be recovered and entirely revolved, by the arms and conduct of a girl, against the torrent of the English fortune and chivalry. Such a God can do what he pleases, and still retain the same affections to his people. It is impossible for that man to despair who remembers that his helper is omnipotent, and can do what he please.

If your case be brought to the last extremity, so that you are at the pit's brink, yet then despair not. At least put it off a little longer. Remember that whatever final accident takes away all hope from you, if you stay a little longer and bear it sweetly, it will take away all despair too.

Let no man despair of God's mercies to forgive him, since he is unable to read the scrolls of the eternal predestination. Despair belongs only to passionate fools or villains. "God hath placed truth and felicity in Heaven; curiosity and repentance upon earth; but misery and despair are the portions of Hell."

Gather together into your spirit and its treasure-house the memory of experience and the former senses of the Divine favors, so that from them you may argue from times past to the present, and enlarge to the future and to greater blessings. The conjectures and expectations of hope are a helmet against the scorchings of despair in temporal things, and an anchor of the soul sure and steadfast against the fluctuations of the spirit in matters of the soul. Secure the confident belief of the resurrection, and you cannot but hope for everything else which you may reasonably expect, or lawfully desire, upon the stock of the Divine mercies and promises.

Love is the greatest thing that God can give us: for himself is love. It is the greatest thing we can give to God, for it will also give ourselves, and carry with it all that is ours. The Apostle [Paul] calls it the bond of perfection. It is the old, and it is the new, and it is the great commandment, and it is all the commandments, for it is the fulfilling of the law.[12] It does the work of all other graces, without any instrument but its own immediate virtue.

Just as the love to sin makes a man sin against all his own reason, and the discourses of wisdom, and the advices of his friends, without temptation and without opportunity; so does the love of God. It makes a man chaste without the laborious arts of fasting and exterior disciplines, and temperate in the midst of feasts. It is active enough to choose itself without any intermedial appetites, and reaches at glory through the very heart of grace, without any other arms but those of love.

It is a grace that loves God for himself and our neighbors for God. The consideration of God's goodness and bounty, the experience of those excellent emanations from him, may be and most commonly are the first motive of our love. But when we are once entered and have tasted the goodness of God, we love the spring for its own excellency. We pass from passion to reason, from thanking to adoring, from sense to spirit, from considering ourselves to a union with God. This is the image of Heaven. It is beatitude in picture, or rather the infancy and beginnings of glory.

We need no incentives to move us to the love of God. We cannot love anything for any reason, real or imaginary, but the excellence is infinitely more eminent in God. Two things create love, perfection and usefulness. On our part we answer with admiration and desire; and both these are centered in love.

There is in God an infinite nature, immensity or vastness without extension or limit, immutability, eternity, omnipotence, omniscience, holiness, dominion, providence, bounty, mercy, justice, perfection in himself, and the end to which all things and actions must be directed, and will at last arrive.

Consider by contrast our distance from all these glories. Consider our smallness and limited nature, our nothing, our inconstancy, our age like a span, our weakness and ignorance, our poverty, our inadvertency and inconsideration, our disabilities and disaffections to do good, our harsh natures and unmerciful inclinations, our universal iniquity, our necessities and dependencies, not only on God, but even our need of the meanest of God's creatures, and our being obnoxious to the weakest and most contemptible.

As for desire, we may consider that in man is a torrent of pleasure for the voluptuous. He is the fountain of honor for the ambitious, an inexhaustible treasure for the covetous. Our vices are in love with fantastic pleasures and images of perfection which are truly and really to be found nowhere but in God.

Therefore our virtues have such proper objects that it is but reasonable they should all turn into love. It is certain that this love will turn all into virtue. In the scrutinies for righteousness and judgment, when it is inquired whether such a person be a good man or no, the meaning is not, "What does he believe?" or "What does he hope?" but what he loves.

Love does all things which may please the beloved person. It performs all his commandments, and this is one of the greatest instances and arguments of our love that God requires of us. This is love, "that we keep his commandments."[13] Love is obedient.

Love gives away all things, so that one may advance the interest of the beloved person. It relieves all that he would have relieved. Love is pliant, and liberal, and communicative. It suffers all things that are imposed by its beloved, or that can happen for his sake, or that intervene in his service, and suffers them cheerfully, sweetly, willingly. It expects that God should turn all such things into good, and make them instruments of felicity. "Love hopes all things, endures all things."[14] Love is patient and content with anything, so it be together with its beloved.

Love is also impatient of anything that may displease the beloved person, hating all sin as the enemy of its friend. For love contracts all the same relations, and marries the same friendships and the same hatreds; and all affection to a sin is perfectly inconsistent with the love of God.

Love is not divided between God and God's enemy. We must love God with all our heart; that is, give him a whole and undivided affection, having love for nothing else but such things which he allows, and which he commands, or loves himself.

Love endeavors to be present to converse with, to enjoy, to be united with its object. Love is always talking of him, reciting his praises, telling his stories, repeating his words, imitating his gestures, transcribing his copy in every thing. Every degree of union and every degree of likeness is a degree of love. It can endure anything but the displeasure and the absence of its beloved.

We are not to use God as men use perfumes, with which they are delighted when they have them, but can very well do without them. True love is restless till it enjoys God in such instances in which it wants him. It is like hunger and thirst; it must be fed or it cannot be answered. Nothing can supply the presence, or make recompense for the

absence of God, or of the effects of his favor and the light of his countenance.

True love looks upon the beloved person and observes his countenance, and how he approves or disapproves, and accordingly looks sad
or cheerful. He does not murmur at those changes which God chooses
to make in his family. He loves to learn where God is the teacher, but is
content to be ignorant or silent, where God is not pleased to open himself.

We must be careful to let our love for God be prudent and without illusion; that is, that it expresses itself in instances which God has
chosen. Love turns into doting when religion turns into superstition.
We cannot love God too much, but we may proclaim that love in in-
decent manners.

Let our love be firm, constant and inseparable, not coming and
returning like the tide, but descending like a never-failing river, running into the sea till it be turned into the vastness and immensity of a
blessed eternity. And a consideration of the divine excellencies and
mercies will produce in us love to God who is invisible, and yet not distant from us. We feel him in his blessings, he dwells in our hearts by
faith, we feed on him in the sacrament, and are made all one with him
in the incarnation and glorification of Jesus.

Here are helps to increase our love to God by way of exercise:

1. Cut off all earthly and sensual loves, for they pollute and un-
hallow the pure and spiritual love. Inordinate affection to the things of
this world is a perfect enemy to the love of God. It is a great shame to
take any part of our affection from the eternal God to bestow it upon his
creature in defiance of the Creator, or to give it to the devil, our open
enemy, in disparagement of God himself.

2. Lay fetters and restraints upon the imagination. Our fancy,
being an imperfect and higher faculty, is usually pleased with the entertainment of shadows and gauds. The things of the world fill the mind
with beauties and fantastic imagery which are amiable to the affections
and elective powers. Persons of fancy have always the most violent
loves. If we be careful with what representations we fill our fancy, we
may the sooner rectify our love.

3. Remove solicitude for worldly cares. If our passions be filled
with one object, and it is ignoble, they cannot attend another, more
excellent object. We contract friendships with those with whom we converse. Our very country is dear to us, for our being in it. The neighbors
of the same village, and those who buy and sell with us, have seized
upon portions of our love. Therefore if we dwell in the world, we shall

also grow in love with them. All our love or all our hatred, all our hopes or all our fears, which the eternal God would willingly secure to himself and esteem among his treasures and precious things, shall be spent upon trifles and vanities.

4. Secure your inclinations and aptnesses for God. It will be a hard thing for a man to do such a personal violence to his first desires as to choose whatsoever he has no mind to. A man will many times satisfy the importunity and daily solicitations of his first longings. Nothing can secure our loves to God but stopping the natural fountains.

5. Converse with God by frequent prayer, by ejaculations and communions and an assiduous daily devotion. Desire that your desires may be right. Discover to him all your wants. Complain to him of all your affronts. Do as Hezekiah did, lay your misfortunes and your ill news before him.[15] Spread them before the Lord. Call to him for health, run to him for counsel, beg of him for pardon. It is as natural to love him, to whom we make such addresses, and of whom we have such dependences, as it is for children to love their parents.

6. Consider the immensity and vastness of the Divine love to us, expressed in all the emanations of his Providence, in his creation and in his conservation of us. For it is not my prince, or my patron, or my friend, that supports me or relieves my needs, but God. He made the corn that my friend sends me. He created the grapes and supported him who has as many dependences and as many necessities and as perfect disabilities as myself. God, indeed, made him the instrument of his Providence to me, as he has made his own love or his own cattle to him: with this difference, that God, by his ministration to me, intends to do him a favor and a reward, which to natural instruments he does not.

Consider his Divine love in giving his Son, in forgiving our sins, in adopting us to glory, and ten thousand times ten thousand little accidents and instances, happening in the doing of every one of these. It is not possible but that for such great love we should give love again. For God, we should give man. For felicity, we should part with our misery. So great is the love of the holy Jesus, God incarnate, that he would leave all his triumphant glories and die once more for man, if it were necessary for procuring happiness to him.

In the use of these instruments, love will grow in several knots and steps, like the sugar cane of India, according to a thousand varieties in the persons loving. It will be great or less, in several persons, each according to his growth in Christianity.

There are but two states of love, and those are labor of love, and zeal of love. The first is duty, the second is perfection. The least love that is, must be obedient, pure, simple and communicative. It must exclude all affection to sin and all inordinate affection to the world, and must be expressive, according to our power, in the instances of duty, and must be love for love's sake.

Of this love, martyrdom is the highest instance: that is, a readiness of mind to suffer any evil, than to do any. Of this our blessed Savior affirmed that no man had greater love.[16] This is the highest point of duty, the greatest love, that God requires of man. And yet he that is the most imperfect must have this love also in preparation of mind, and must differ from another in nothing except in the degrees of promptness and alacrity.

In this sense, he that loves God truly (though with but a beginning and tender love), yet he loves God with all his heart, that is, with that degree of love which is the highest point of duty and of God's charge upon us. He that loves God with all his heart may yet increase with the increase of God, just as there are degrees of love to God among the saints, and yet each of them love him with all their powers and capacities.

The greater state of love is the zeal of love, which runs out into excrescences and suckers, like a fruitful and pleasant tree, or bursting into gums, and producing fruits, not of a monstrous, but of an extraordinary and heroical greatness. Zeal is not a direct duty. Nowhere is it commanded for itself. Therefore it is only acceptable when it advances the love of God and our neighbors, whose circumstance it is.

That zeal is only safe, only acceptable, which increases love directly. Because love to our neighbor and obedience to God are the two great portions of love, we must never account our zeal to be good except as it advances both of these, if it be in a matter that relates to both. Paul's zeal was expressed in preaching without any offerings or stipend, in traveling, in spending and being spent for his flock, in suffering, in willing to be accursed for love of the people of God and his countrymen. Let our zeal be as great as his was, just so it be in affection to others, and not in anger against them. In the former there is no danger, in the second there is no safety.

Love is as communicative as fire, as busy and as active, and it has four twin daughters, extremely like each other. Their names are (1) Mercy, (2) Beneficence, or Well-doing, (3) Liberality and (4) Alms, which is commonly called Charity.

The first, or eldest, is seated in the affection; for mercy without alms is acceptable when the person is disabled to express outwardly what he heartily desires. But alms without mercy are like prayers without devotion, or religion without humility. Beneficence, or Well-doing, is a promptness and nobleness of mind, making us do offices of courtesy and humanity to all sorts of persons in their need, or out of their need.

Liberality is a disposition of mind opposite to covetousness, and consists in the despite and neglect of money upon just occasions, and relates to our friends, children, kindred, servants and other relatives. But Alms is a relieving of the poor and needy.

The first and the last only are duties of Christianity. The second and third are circumstances and adjuncts of these duties; for liberality increases the degree of alms, making our gift greater, and beneficence extends it to more persons and orders of men, spreading it wider.

Mercy and alms are the body and soul of that charity which we must pay to our neighbor's need, and it is a precept which God therefore enjoined to the world. The motives to this duty are such as Holy Scripture has propounded to us by way of consideration and proposition of its excellences and consequent reward.[17]

If you have no money, yet you must have mercy, and are bound to pity the poor and pray for them. If you do what you are able, be it little or great, corporal or spiritual, the charity of alms or the charity of prayers, a cup of wine or a cup of water; if it be but love to the brethren, or a desire to help all or any of Christ's poor, it shall be acceptable according to what a man has, and not according to what he has not. For love is all this, and all the other commandments; and it will express itself where it can; and where it cannot, yet it is love still.

Notes

1. James 1:27.
2. Mark 4:31.
3. Romans 8:17.
4. Cf. James 2:18.
5. Cf. Matthew 6:14.
6. Malachi 4:2.
7. Cf. Romans 12:12.
8. Cf. Judith 7:30ff. (Apocrypha).
9. Judges 15:15ff., Judges 7:7ff., 1 Samuel 14:6ff.
10. Cf. 1 Corinthians 10:13.
11. Cf. Numbers 20:8ff.
12. Colossians 3:14, Romans 13:10.
13. 1 John 5:3.
14. 1 Corinthians 13:7.
15. 2 Kings 19:14.
16. Cf. John 15:13.
17. Cf. Matthew 25:34–40.

Passage from *The Rules and Exercises of Holy Living, Together with Prayers Containing the Whole Duty of a Christian, and the Parts of Devotion Fitted to All Occasions, and Furnished for All Necessities* published before 1900 by William L. Allison, New York. The excerpts are from sections 1, 2, 3 and 4 of chapter 4.